For information regarding permission, write to:
Roxanne.modafferi@gmail.com
Roxanne Modafferi

6980 W. Warm Springs Rd #190
Las Vegas, NV 89113

This book was originally published in paperback by Burning Horse Media in 2013.
ISBN - 13: 978-0-578-15406-0
ISBN – 10: 0578154064

Printed in the USA
First Burning Horse Media paperback printing, October 2013

Memoirs of a Happy Warrior was written in full by Roxanne Modafferi

Front and back covers designed by Sue Buenger
www.suebueart.com

Front cover photo Roxanne Modafferi is courtesy of Matthew Kaplowitz from **www.thefightnerd.com**

Back cover photo of Roxanne Modafferi is courtesy of Dave Mandel from www.sherdog.com

Memoirs of a Happy Warrior

Roxanne Modafferi

Memoirs of a Happy Warrior is an autobiographical account of professional mixed martial arts fighter Roxanne Modafferi. The book takes place over the course of two yearswhen Roxanne decided to move from the United States to Japan for her junior year of college. After settling in with her host family and figuring out how become more Japanese, Roxanne immediately continued her martial arts training. From there, she embarked on her professional MMA career and never looked back. Roxanne toppled several tough opponents and eventually pulled off the remarkable feat of capturing the IFC middleweight championship.

Memoirs of a Happy Warrior takes you, the reader, on her journey of becoming lost in Tokyo and its surrounding cities, figuring out how to use the country's public transportation, living in the Mecca of anime and the birthplace of some of the most respected martial arts in the world. It wasn't always easy for Roxanne, though, as she often found herself struggling to communicate with those around her as well as suffering a nasty injury during one of the most crucial times of her early MMA career.

Still, Roxanne persevered and tackled some of the toughest women in Japanese MMA and held her own against them all. *Memoirs of a Happy Warrior* describes what it was like for someone who never, ever wanted to hurt anybody to be able to find the inner strength to inflict punishment onto her opponent and have her hand raised in victory over and over. Training and fighting is not an easy career to pursue, but Roxanne Modafferi not only embraced the challenges; she conquered them to become a legitimate world champion. Over the years, she would continue to fight and eventually landed a coveted spot on the 18th season of the wildly popular UFC-based reality TV series *The Ultimate Fighter*.

Forward

"Roxanne Modafferi is the bravest fighter I know, with the purest soul, and I know thousands. Her unique 20-year journey in martial arts from the earliest days of WMMA to its ferocious peaks today has taught me invaluable, incalculable lessons in what it is to be a warrior, and a human being. Now you can learn them, too."

Kirik Jenness, official records keeper for mixed martial arts.

Chapter 1 - The Arrival: Meet the Host Family

"When in Japan, do as the Japanese do."

August 31, 2003

The taxicab driver turned around in his seat and said, "I'm sorry, I can't find your house."

I opened my eyes and lifted my head off the doily-covered seat back.

"What?" I asked.

I thought I didn't have to pay attention anymore after turning myself over to the little old man, who sped us down the mysterious back streets of Musashi Koganei City. After all, he seemed so professional sitting in his spotless black suit, his taxi decorated with almost limousine-like quality. As soon as he had finished straining himself getting my mammoth suitcases into his trunk, he'd whipped out his wrinkled map and pinpointed our destination. Or so I thought.

"Mana, did he just say he doesn't know how to get to the house?" I asked the slender Japanese girl sitting next to me.

"Just a minute," she said. She leaned forward and conversed with the driver, using Japanese vocabulary that went over my head. If I'd been tense, I would have cried, but jetlag and physical exhaustion made me feel like I was in another universe, not to mention all the short Japanese people walking around everywhere. Mana would handle it. She was my guide, after all.

I rolled the windows down a little lower and I leaned back again. The cool fingers of the night breeze brushed my face and neck.

The International Christian University (ICU) was one of the Ivy League colleges in Japan, famous for being difficult to get into, and turning out students who could speak English. It reportedly had the highest percentage of foreign students out of all the schools in Japan. When it came time to choose a school to do my junior year exchange at, I'd picked it off a list of choices, not really knowing it from the next school listed. Fate must have been guiding my hand, for it led me down an adventurous road to not only a wonderful education, but to a successful fighting career and securing a job after college.

ICU had arranged for a student to pick me up at the airport and drop me off at my host family's house. I couldn't have gotten anyone better than Mana Ogawa. The cute 19-year old's big round smile greeted me as I trudged through the international flight doors, exhausted, with a massive amount of luggage in tow. At one point I'd been proud of the amount I managed to cram into the big black suitcase without going over the 60-pound weight limit. Not anymore.

After our introductions, it was the first thing she mentioned.

"That's a lot of luggage," she had commented with a laugh, taking over dragging one of my two huge black suitcases.

"Yeah, well I am moving here for a year!" I rationalized. "I want to be prepared!"

"Oh!" She laughed again. Her eyes disappeared in her face because she smiled so widely. That smile never faltered, even after three hours of navigating through the hectic Tokyo rush hour.

On the long train ride from Narita International Airport to Musashi Koganei, she spoke broken English to me, and I spoke broken Japanese right back to her. We passed fields of crops with rice and other vegetables, traditional looking houses, manufacturing plants, commercial buildings, and other things I couldn't recognize.

Up until then, I had virtually no Japanese speaking practice in the US other than what I did to study for dreaded speaking tests. My heart raced every time I produced a sentence. "I'm speaking Japanese, I'm speaking Japanese!" cycled through my head like a cheer. It was my dream to be fluent in two languages. Before I'd studied Japanese, it seemed almost incomprehensible to me that two sets of words unrelated to each other could make sense and function in someone's mind.

"Don't worry about speaking practice now," said Martin Holman sensei, my Japanese teacher at the University of Massachusetts (UMass). As third year students, my class had been complaining about not practicing enough in class. I remember the tall man sitting on the desk in the front, wearing his usual brown suit and tie, swinging his legs. His round face broke into a knowing smile when he teased, which always frustrated the dickens out of us.

"When you're in Japan, you'll get more speaking practice in a week than you can get here in a year," he said, and just kept on with the grammar lessons. He was right. I spoke "Tarzan-Japanese," as Holman sensei liked to say. "Yes, me want go on train. This way right? How much me pay ticket?"

When you're speaking a foreign language, often you can tell the second the words leave your mouth if you've said it right or not. "That didn't sound quite right," something inside says. It's very discouraging to muff it up, but you develop a kind of tolerance for failure. You have to, or else you won't want to say anything at all. Courage is what makes or breaks a Japanese student - if you speak and put your feelings on the line to be crushed again and again by failure and frustration, you will eventually learn and get stronger. If not, nothing happens at all, and the student turns into someone who's studied for four years, but can't get a job because his or her skills aren't good enough. I was determined to not be this type of student.

After rolling passing the rice fields, we arrived in Shinjuku Ward. The title of "the biggest train station in Japan" goes to Tokyo Station, but Shinjuku has the most people pass through it on a given work day, earning it the unofficial title of "the busiest train station in Japan."

We used the elevator a few times to get from the platform to the other gates of the station, but at one point had to use the stairs. My total luggage count was as follows: two sixty-pound suitcases, a shoulder-strapped gym bag stuffed to the gills with my Brazilian jiu jitsu (BJJ) uniform (gi) and kickboxing pads, my laptop bag, and finally a twenty-pound LL Bean book bag. I know the weight because I plopped it down on my bathroom scale before I left. I felt like an ant, carrying a burden multiple times my body weight.

After what felt like weeks, we stumbled out of what I hoped were the last set of gates. A McDonald's greeted me directly ahead, sitting next to what looked like a pharmacy. Lines of taxis waited for fares along the sides of the roads and in a little parking lot right in front of us.

"Is this really it?" I gasped, glancing to my right at Mana. I set down the huge suitcase whose handle had been digging into my palm for the past three hours.

"Yes, this is it!" Mana said, whipping a small notepad out of her pocket. She took one last glance at its pages. Cute Disney characters danced along the sides. "This is Musashi Koganei!"

I grinned. We were almost to my host family's house. I was starving.

"Oh, thank you," I said. Sweat stained my T-shirt, but the warm breeze of late summer managed to dry the rivulets that ran down my face. Mana wore a cute outfit typical of a nineteen-year-old girl, with random lace fringing the bottom of a tight-fitting top of some multi-color combination. The short skirt had either pockets or stitches, making it impossible to remember the exact features.

"So what do we do now?" I asked Mana.

"Take a taxi!" she replied, pointing to the nearest one.

I'd been impressed with the soft cushions and professional address of the driver. Rather than of sliding into the back of a New York cab with peeling plastic seats and a plastic window separating the driver and customers, I reclined in the lap of luxury. "Where shall I take you today?" greeted us from the driver, rather than, "Where ya goin'?" Mana told him.

The small automobile darted through small, extremely narrow alleyways. Stark white concrete walls surrounded all the houses. I closed my eyes.

That was when, ten minutes later, the driver stopped his car and turned off the fare counter. Abashed, he twisted around and told Mana that he didn't know how to get to the address on the paper.

Now, if you get into a taxi in a major city in the US and say, "I want to go to 101 Nowhere Street in the Confusingville section of town," the guy will most assuredly say, "Yep! No problem!" and motor you right there. My stomach rumbled impatiently as I sat in the cab, listening to Mana and the driver discuss the problem. The address was something resembling "1-23-45 Naka-cho."

"We're in this ward, now," Mana explained. I hadn't the slightest idea what the numbers meant, so I peeked out the window to see if I could spot any street signs. A metal plaque with numbers hung off a lamppost. Unfortunately, they had no resemblance to our goal. We ended up calling my host mother on Mana's cell phone.

"She's coming to get us!" Mana announced, hanging up her phone. "Let's just wait."

My first sight of Sadako was of her short stocky frame running down the narrow road towards our cab. Dashing was more like it. She ran as if being chased by a pack of rabid dogs.

"That must be her. Why doesn't she just walk?" I wondered. I guessed it was considered impolite to walk if you know someone is waiting. I've seen my share of businessmen and women in suits and skirts sprinting down hallways and streets. Plus, store clerks dash through store isles to find something a customer wanted. Also, if there was an express train about to leave the station, everyone, from kindergarten children to 60-year-old grandparents, made a dash to avoid waiting the extra ten minutes or so. This may also be why people stay so thin, other than genetics.

The coffee shop where the taxi decided to idle turned out to be right across from her house. The driver maneuvered carefully down a paved path so narrow that branches of coniferous trees swatted at his side-view mirror. Hard white concrete walls loomed over us on the other side.

"Ah, good evening!" Sadako burst out as we got out of the car to meet her.

"Hi, I'm Roxanne..." I said, trying to bow.

"Ah! Nice to meet you! Nice to meet you! I'm so sorry!" she said to me, and then turned to the driver. "I'm so sorry!" she repeated.

I had just enough time to wonder why she was apologizing when the driver started apologizing as well. I wondered if I should, too. Sadako then told the driver to pull into the extremely narrow driveway that turned out to be a road. We stood off to the side as he deftly maneuvered closer to the house, which was apparently right around the corner. There were a few minutes of silence as we waited. Despite my determination to speak a lot, I was scared. I knew she would ask me stuff I wouldn't understand, and then there would be awkwardness.

Too bad.

"The trip must have been long and horrible, right?!" she said in Japanese.

Mana grunted an affirmative, "Um!" and nodded.

"Oh yes, long, horrible, very long, well actually no, it was okay," I said back in Japanese. Or I think that's what I said.

Sadako smiled. "The house is that way," she said, and we followed where the taxi had gone. "You have a lot of nimotsu, right?"

I blinked and tried not to panic at the unknown word that had popped up. "Nimotsu?" I hated to do it, but I glanced at Mana and mouthed, "What's nimotsu?"

"Luggage," she replied, grinning.

"Ah ha! Hai, lots of nimotsu." My host mother's eyes almost shot out straight out of her skull when she saw my suitcases.

"Whoa, you have so much!" she said at least five times as we lugged my belongings inside. At the door, we met the first of the family - the dog. She called it Ho-chan. Chan is a suffix like Mr. or Miss, but is used mainly for children or pets. Therefore, I thought the golden Labrador's name was "Ho" and that they added the chan afterward to cutify the name. That would have been a pretty strange name had it been real, which I thought it was for several months, until I found out that its real name is "Fortune." The Japanese pronunciation of the letter F is different, making it sound just like the letter H; Ho-chan.

Before arriving, I had thought long and hard about how to address my host mother. After studying about the varying degrees of politeness in the language, I worried that it would be too formal to call her by her last name. On the other hand, I didn't want to call her Okaasan like the other exchange students, which means "mother." I had my own mother I loved very much, and it wasn't

12

her. I therefore called her Sadako-san, which was somewhere in the middle.

Sadako-san invited Mana to stay for a sushi dinner, which disappeared in a blur of chopstick action. Some time during the meal, I think Sadako-san commented on my skill at using chopsticks. I was so distracted by the delicious eel and raw squid that I don't remember my response. I complimented her on her sushi-making skills, but she responded with a laugh that she had bought it at the store. Then we then found out that it was only a ten to twelve minute walk to the house from the station. It'd taken us over half an hour by taxi. Mana and I exchanged glances and laughed out loud. The dog cocked its head at us, its puzzled expression mirrored in the face of my host mother.

Sadako-san stood about five-foot five. Fluffy brown hair highlighted red framed her round face. It stuck out from under the white bucket hat which she liked to wear when outside. Her eyes were always laughing at everything, even when her head shook in disgust or disapproval. She liked to repeat herself when she felt strongly about an issue, but impressed me as logical, flexible, and fun to talk with. That is, it was fun once I could figure out what she was saying in Japanese.

Sadako-san showed us around the house.

The bathroom was a closet-like compartment that a football player couldn't have squeezed his shoulders into. It was composed of a small window over a toilet with a queer electronic seat, and that was it. There was so little space between the door and the toilet that I couldn't bend over to pull down my pants. A control panel stuck off to one side with buttons, which caused the toilet to perform various functions. A person could heat the seat, make water spurt out of the bowl, cause air to shoot up at you, and other things I didn't understand and wasn't sure I wanted to.

Once you finished, you had to leave the toilet room and go around the corner to get to the other washroom to use the sink. Once in there, the translucent sliding glass door screeched a greeting at me as it slid stiffly along its warped wooden runners. It stuck often, making a loud bang when a person tried to open it quickly and failed.

The sink and mirror stood immediately to the left, and I had to open another obnoxious glass door to access the tub area. What I saw confused me. A green colored Japanese bathtub was built right into the floor. It was approximately four feet long, and if filled, deep enough for the water to come up to my neck if I sat. The floor next to the tub was tiled, and a step down from the carpeted sink area. A showerhead stuck out over the tiles at the height of my thighs.

"Um, how do I use this?" I asked.

"Ah, here, this is Japanese style," Mana said. "You stand here next to the tub, uh, wash, and then sit in the hot tub! You can sit for long time!"

"I see, great," I said, nodding. Soaking sounded too boring. The setup of the bathroom seemed unnatural. I felt like I was instructed to use an American shower without a curtain so that the water would fall out all over the bathroom floor.

The height of the showerhead baffled me as well. It aimed at my legs rather than torso. The Japanese sit on a short stool while washing themselves, but since this house had none I had no choice but to shower on my knees.

"What's upstairs?" I asked.

"Oh, that's everyone's bedroom," she answered casually, not inviting me to look. "You sleep in the tatami room." She led me around a corner into a tidy square room with a wooden smell.

"I get my own room?" I said incredulous, yet grateful. I'd been hoping I'd get my own room, but wouldn't have been surprised to share. Tokyo homes were tiny and expensive.

"Yes," Sadako-san replied. "And I sleep in this room next to you. Or sometimes I fall asleep on the sofa in the dining room. Hahaha!" she laughed. I blinked. No mention was made of her husband, whom I had yet to meet. I didn't ask.

"Are you staying for dinner?" My host mother turned to Mana.

"Oh, I have to get back soon..." she said.

"Oh please?" I put in, anxiously. I didn't feel ready to let go of my English lifeline. What if my host mother actually tried talking to me in Japanese?

14

"Okay," She agreed, much to my delight.

Indeed, my nervousness at making a good impression impacted my speaking ability. Sadako-san spoke absolutely no English at all. That was the idea of a host family, after all. Sadako-san told Mana and I about the rest of the family. I ended up going to bed early and didn't get to meet them.

My host brother, Mitsunori, was a 30-year-old dentist who loved K-1 kickboxing, horseracing, and curry-rice. He looked just like Sadako, but male and constantly sleepy. He was the most tech-savvy out of everyone in the family, and we sometimes ended up chatted about fighting.

My host sister, Takae, worked at a bakery full time. She liked watching sumo and playing the piano. There was an old one in a spare room between the kitchen and my room. She also had Sadako's round face, but was slightly taller. I hardly spoke to her, as our schedules were completely opposite, but sometimes passed her as she bustled around in the kitchen in the morning.

Tetsuo, my host father, was a skinny 70-year old retired businessman who had gone to school at the prestigious University of Kyoto. According to Sadako-san, he retired from a good company. Well, I assumed it was good, since they all seemed to live comfortably.

The house had cable and satellite connections, along with high-speed internet broadband, which Mitsunori-san used religiously. Some people read the paper at breakfast. Every morning, however, Mitsunori would clomp downstairs in his nightclothes with laptop tucked under his arm. After plugging it into the broadband box on the shelf behind the table, he would surf the web while munching down a light "American" breakfast of toast and broccoli. Broccoli?

Sadako-san and I would watch the morning news.

"Ah!" Sadako-san suddenly exclaimed. "And this is Nobi-chan! Right, Nobi-chan? You're so cute, Nobi-chan! Look at who we have here! A new Nei-chan, big sister!"

The elderly woman reached down and picked up the "host cat," which turned out to be my arch nemesis of the household. That ugly Persian feline decided I was her best friend after I pet her once. Her white puffy fur rivaled the clouds in their softness and lightness. The face, however, looked like the squashed mug of a bulldog or a pug. Due to her inhibited nasal capacity, she sniffed and snorted constantly, making me nauseous just listening to her. She had a crush on Fortune, and constantly went over to the big dog to say hello. The large excitable Labrador couldn't get enough of sniffing her rear end. He also pawed and nudged her until she started mewing loudly in protest and indignation, but strangely didn't move away. This continued until Sadako-san scolded the animals and shooed the cat away. Then the cat went back, which always stimulated the dog. The incessant cycle drove me crazy.

Finally, Mana left. I chatted with Sadako for a bit longer and then went to bed. I tried lying down on the thin futon she gave me, but it wasn't thick enough. My back injury from a Judo competition five years back bothered me.

"Sorry, do you happen to have another one?" I asked, embarrassed.

"Uh sure, here, pile this up, I guess," Sadako-san said, sticking her head back in the closet. She dug around and pulled out four thick Japanese comforters. I ended up piling them on top of each other, raising myself a foot off the floor. It looked silly, but it proved adequate. Soon jetlag took control and whisked my consciousness away.

September 1

I woke up at 3:30am and then again at 5:30 in time to hear my host mother get up to walk the dog. I decided to go with her. The two-year-old Fortune couldn't handle the excitement of a second person present, and jerked my host mother back and forth like a fish on a line. Later that morning, Sadako-san took me into town to get a bank account and register as a foreign resident with the city. For lunch I enjoyed a scrumptious Japanese home-cooked meal.

"You must love to cook," I said, sucking down yakisoba.

"I went to culinary school for two years," she said proudly. When I asked about work, she shook her head and laughed.

"I take care of the house and raised the kid!" she said.

I nodded. "I see! You never wanted to work?"

"Nope!" she said, and made some other comment in Japanese I couldn't quite catch. She then told me stories about how she made her children commute an hour to get to the best schools in Tokyo.

"The schools around Koganei are okay," she said, starting to wash up. "Just average."

At first I felt sorry imagining little Takae, trekking to the train station every day to join the intimidating mass of businessmen and woman heading to work. This was normal, and remains a normal custom.

The Japanese society emphasizes success in school so strongly that it causes the Japanese parents to put maybe ridiculous amounts of pressure on their children. Particularly enthusiastic Japanese mothers are called kyoiku mama, or "education mothers." Many times they are housewives or women who quit work to dedicate themselves fully towards ensuring that their children could have an edge in the cutthroat competition of Japan's educational system. They find tutors and juku to get their child extra support in areas the child is weakest in. A juku is a nighttime cram school to help one prepare for high school and college entrance exams. Japanese students must pass tests to get into high school, unlike in the United States where you automatically go. In fact, getting into a good high school is almost more important than what college you get into.

I don't know how far Sadako-san went, but she didn't strike me as an extreme sort of woman; dedicated, but not unreasonable. Maybe her kids were just really smart, but both Takae and Mitsunori got into decent high schools and colleges. Mitsunori went to a University and then dental school.

Later that day she showed me the way to ICU so I could begin to memorize the route.

"Here, ride this bike," she said, dragging a rickety clunker out from behind the car in the garage. "It used to be mine before I got this one. I always lend it to my exchange students."

"Okay....wait!"

"Try and remember, okay?" she called back to me, already out the gate. "No, Fortune! Get back inside!" She scolded the dog, and then took off down the street. I desperately peddled after her.

"Make sure you remember!" she called back over her shoulder.

I desperately wanted to remember. Unfortunately, Sadako-san used the most zigzagging path she could think of. I attempted to make mental notes as she lead me through the neighborhood.

More importantly, we were driving on the wrong side of the road! Cars ride on the left. Cyclists ride on both sides, although Sadako-san tried to stick to the left side, European style. In fact, the more I rode in Japan, the more I realized that cyclists went wherever they wanted. If there were sidewalks, and often times there weren't, cyclists rode right beside the pedestrians. If a pedestrian was in the way, riders chimed their bells. At the sound, people calmly got out of the way for them. If I was chimed at, it startled the bejesus out of me and I practically leaped out of my sneakers.

"Why can't they chime at me a good ten feet away instead of right when they're about to run me over?" I often thought. "Oh well."

I tried this chiming method in Boston when I went home for a visit and promptly got yelled at by the Bostonians. They quite rudely told me to get off the sidewalk and bike on the street. There was no way I was biking on the streets in Boston; I actually enjoyed living.

The narrow streets in Japan left almost no room for bicyclists. I wondered what other road rules I was ignorant of, but one could only worry about so many things. Like not colliding with the little old lady pushing a grocery cart in my path!

Sadako-san swerved and deftly avoided her.

I had to screech to a stop because a car was coming, nearly crashing into a light post. My confidence in my ability to squeeze

18

between the post and concrete wall was close to zero. The breaks on my old bike screeched and the old lady jumped.

"Sumimasen! Sorry!" I called.

The woman kept on teetering along without really acknowledging me.

I worried about the rickety contraption Sadako-san lent me. I hit a pothole and I heard a crunch. Looking down, I took in the bent metal wheel guard, rusted gears and crooked handlebars. The left brake wasn't quite as tight as it should have been.

Sadako-san's peddling figure sped farther away. I pumped the pedals harder to catch up with her. I hadn't biked since I was a kid and on any other occasion it would have been kind of fun.

"Okay, there's a red sign that says 'fire hydrant' on this corner," I thought to myself, but then I saw five more.

"Okay, there's a Japanese-looking house with a crooked tree with needles growing over the wall," I noted, but as we went, almost every other house had those attributes.

The Japanese love potted plants. They hang potted plants on hooks outside their houses and do their best to foster the nature around them. My host family had a tiny back yard about the size of a college dorm room with a flower garden, several shrubs and short trees. They kept a singed metal trashcan for burning garbage that couldn't be recycled.

Sadako-san took me through a gravel path onto the deserted campus. A high school complete with a soccer and baseball field nestled itself right on the edge of the ICU campus. With so many foreigners going to ICU, the kids never gave me a second glance when I biked past their sports practices or kicked a stray soccer ball back to them.

Sadako-san and I easily spotted the church, which would host the welcoming ceremony. Its impressive white steeple stood tall above the trees. With not much else to do, we went home again. I wonder if my host mother realized that taking me a different way home did not improve my chances of finding ICU the next day.

I liked the location of the University, which snuggled itself in Mitaka, a suburban city on the outskirts of Tokyo City in the humungous Tokyo prefecture. By using the word suburb, I mean

19

"can't see skyscrapers." Outskirts simply means that you can hop on a train or bus and in fifteen minutes be swept off your feet in a sea of pedestrians downtown.

I had chosen to live with a host family in the suburbs rather than live on campus dormitories with other gaijin, or foreigners. Sadako-san's house was fifteen minutes from the school by bike. Compared to all other schools in Japan, ICU was known for having the highest number of foreigners on campus. It offered a wide variety of classes in English in addition to those for native Japanese. Being an English-orientated school, all Japanese students were required to take English classes, and before they graduated, had to take a certain number of classes taught by native English speakers about any topic. I often had fourth year students sitting in my linguistics classes, or economics class. I got excited reading descriptions about their international relations, global economics, and high-level Japanese classes. I had my schedule planned out way ahead of time, but ended up changing everything around once I discovered that three of the classes I wanted were only offered in Japanese. Although I hoped to achieve that level of fluency someday, I knew those classes were far beyond my current skill level.

"I'll definitely become fluent!" I told my clenched fist as I scurried down the hall to request a change in classes. It wasn't the first time I sung that chant to myself, and it wouldn't be the last.

Chapter 2 - Meeting Cayte and Finding Cross Point
September 2

The second day after I arrived was college orientation and I had to find my way to school by myself. I took a few wrong turns because the roads all looked alike, but eventually made it. I thank Mickey Mouse for this. On top of a pedestal attached to a gate, one family placed a foot-tall statue of Disney's favorite mouse. Dressed in his purple magician's cloak and hat, he merrily gestured towards the turn I had to take.

I parked my bike and followed lines of new students walking by themselves or with parents across the campus. I became good at following others' examples during my stay in Japan. All the students gathered at the chapel.

Sitting down, I chose to introduce myself to the girl sitting next to me.

"My name's Catherine, but call me Cayte," she said.

This outspoken, enthusiastic girl was completely blind in her right eye and almost blind in her left. She and her guide dog Yogi came from Cornell University in Ithaca, New York, and enjoyed a dorm room on campus rather than host family. She triple majored in Japanese, Linguistics, and Political Science, and held an outstanding GPA. Her accomplishments continued to baffle me the more I learned about her.

"How do you study?" I asked.

"My computer talks to me," she laughed.

"Huh?"

"I scan pages of books onto my computer, and then this program reads it back to me. I'll show ya later."

The monotonous electronic voice amused me to no end. We liked typing in nonsense words and hear the computer struggle to say them. If we input a string of consonants together like "gggrrhht" it sounded like the computer was choking on a frog. Cayte had come on the ICU summer program in June, so she offered to show me the ropes after orientation.

When the speeches ended, they let us out onto the big grassy lawn like puppies allowed to run free. The ICU campus was beautiful, especially in the warm autumn sun. It's widely recognized as being the nicest campus in Tokyo. Tall deciduous trees forest the grounds, which was medium-small by American University standards, but enormous by Japanese standards. Sakura trees bloomed everywhere during springtime, along with well-kept flowering bushes and shrubbery. Students liked eating lunch on two grassy mounts called *baka yama* (stupid mountain) and *aho yama* (idiot mountain), in front of the honkan, or main hall. Unlike my home University of Massachusetts, Amherst, where you have to hike fifteen minutes across campus to get to classes, almost every single class took place in the four-story honkan.

"Today, I wanna check out a jiu jitsu club in a place called Kichijoji," I said to Cayte after orientation. "Do you know how to get there?"

"Kichijoji?" she laughed. "That's one of the most popular places ICU students hang out! I'll go with ya."

"Wow, that's great! Are you sure you don't mind?"

"Nah! You are me three months ago," she said, tugging on Yogi's leash. The big golden lab stopped sniffing at a grass clump and obediently led her forward.

We walked ten minutes to a bus stop right outside the ICU main gate and paid two dollars to ride. I had my face glued to the window half the time, checking out the lay of the land. It wasn't quite suburban but it wasn't quite urban, either. One second we would pass a leafy park with bike paths, and the next second a mass of stores and business buildings would pop up on the other side of the street. It was Tokyo.

Fifteen minutes later, the bus pulled onto a particularly narrow yet lively street. I drew back from the window as the corner of a building loomed too close to the bus. The driver maneuvered his bus into the street with expert care, just barely missing the pedestrians who seemed to pay it no mind. They darted here and there in its path. Cayte and I stepped off into a pool of hustle and bustle. An arcade jingled at me from straight ahead. A group of five schoolgirls almost bumped into me from the right, and

22

everywhere I looked, small restaurants and stores had their doors flung wide open. It was Kichijoji.

Kichijoji, the word itself meaning something like "lucky shrine," soon became my favorite city in Japan. The moment I stepped off the bus, I was swept up in the current of people flowing over the sidewalks.

My host mother called Kichijoji "a city for young people." I could see why. Every other building had a restaurant in it, cheap and expensive ones, both traditional and western. Wide, partially roofed streets called "The Sunroads" cut the city down the center. Arcades dotted the street corners. Shops for socks, shoes, funny costumes, household items and bathroom supplies ran side by side. Colorful vertical signs written in English combined with Japanese characters hung from the sides of multi-storied buildings, so those walking on the sidewalks could know the stores each building contained. The shops on ground level overflowed onto the street with their tables of wears, trying to attract customers.

"So do you know where this place is?" I asked, foolishly turning my hand-drawn map this way and that. Cayte led me around as if she'd memorized every square inch of the city. I'd never have guessed she was partially blind. The train station sat on the corner of a large four-way traffic intersection that ran under a train overpass. When the pedestrian walk light turned green, a little melody began playing from some unidentifiable location. It was cute the first fifty times I heard it, but it tended to get stuck in my head. I'd hate to be one of the traffic directors or construction workers I saw milling around who had no choice but to listen to the same twenty notes all day long.

Cayte and Yogi were a spectacle because no one was used to Seeing Eye dogs. Dogs in Japan are regarded as the cutest thing created in the Universe. According to some unspoken law, every Japanese person who saw one was required to fall to their hands and knees, fondle the dog gently, and say about one hundred times how adorable and wonderful the animal was. This behavior distracted Yogi and was not appreciated by Cayte, who depended on the dog to be her eyes. She constantly told the people not to touch the dog because he was "working." Ninety-nine percent of the people disobeyed her, even though they understood.

"Maybe they don't understand," I suggested to Cayte, after she sharply yanked Yogi away from a cooing teenage girl.

"No, they definitely understand because I looked up the right way to ask them to stay the hell away from my dog," Cayte grumbled. "Yogi's more obedient than the average Japanese!"

We located Cross Point Kichijoji Dojo below a Chinese restaurant. The building was sandwiched in between all the other buildings down a side street, where ever-entertaining business signs glowed after dark. I never did find out if the building across the street was a house for prostitutes, but I suspected some related activities went on. A man in a suit always stood outside asking passers-by, "How about it, sir?" while gesturing to the interior. In the second story window, they had placed a billboard of two almost-naked Caucasian girls, smiling down at the street.

I found out about Cross Point from *Nikuraba's Japanese MMA Online* Bible, which listed MMA, BKK, and Muay Thai dojos. The Kichijoji branch was an affiliate of Paraestra Tokyo, which was run by Yuki Nakai. Muay Thai world number two Rambar taught Muay Thai twice a week, and a former All-Japan kickboxing champ Genki Yamaguchi taught five times a week.

Excitement bubbled in my stomach as I pulled open the heavy metal door. Nobody appeared to be there. Disconcerted, I took off my shoes and put them in a shoe rack standing outside the door. Cayte and Yogi popped their heads inside as I slowly entered. Then I noticed the one peaceful looking man, tall and heavyset for Japanese, sitting behind a tall counter. The counter was so tall and the chair so short, that I almost didn't notice him. I told him in my poor Japanese that I was interested in joining. He handed me a schedule and started explaining times and classes. I understood nothing except the words for the days of the week. I looked to Cayte who looked like she caught it, and she translated for me.

"The kickboxing class starts at 6:30, and then there's the jiu jitsu class," she explained. It was 3:30.

24

"I think I'll go home now, and then come back to watch. I want to observe now so I can decide if I want to join."

After we bussed back to ICU, we exchanged phone numbers and went our separate ways, promising to meet tomorrow at the language placement tests. I hopped on my bike and hightailed it home. I would have made it home in twelve minutes had I not gotten lost when I tried to enter the neighborhood. I knew this would happen, and I had to ask directions from a random person on the street. Luckily, I saw my host mother standing outside talking to a neighbor. I told her, in Japanese of course, about my new friend and orientation. She seemed happy for me.

"I even went to Kichijoji, but I have to go back tonight to watch the jiu jitsu class."

"What's jiu jitsu?" she asked me, cocking her head.

"Uh, it's like judo," I said.

"Ah, you do judo?!" she exclaimed.

"Well, I used to do judo, but now I do Brazilian jiu jitsu."

"She does judo!" Sadako-san repeated to her neighbor, in case she hadn't quite understood.

I smiled patiently. "Yes, well, I used to do judo, but now..."

My host mother continued, "You're busy, aren't you! You must be exhausted!"

Even though jetlag and the effort of biking dragged down my eyelids, I denied it. I just wanted to drink water and lay down, but my host brother, Mitsunori, was sitting at the table using his laptop computer. It was the first time I met him and had to introduce myself. He started asking me questions about my laptop. I noticed a long blue cable stretching from a little blinking box on the mantle into his computer, so I asked him if I could also hook mine up to his broadband. We tried it. It wouldn't work at first, but after fiddling with settings, a week later it mysteriously started working.

Five minutes later saw me lying on the floor in my new room, trying to catch a few moments rest. The world was almost spinning above me. I closed my eyes. Peace. And then....

"Bring me along," said my jiu jitsu gi to my prone figure.

"No," I answered it. "If I bring you, I'll want to train. I need to observe first."

"Bring me," it tried coaxing, but I firmly said no.

I finally remembered the way back to ICU, and caught the bus the way Cayte showed me. My heart thumping, I tugged open the door and surreptitiously slipped inside. The slapping sound of bare legs hitting heavy bags and handheld pads assaulted my ears, along with the shouting of the instructor. The familiar humidity of many sweating bodies hung in the air. The beginner's kickboxing class was in full swing.

I turned to the man behind the desk who'd been there that afternoon. He nodded and pointed to a bench in a corner. I nearly tripped over five gym bags getting there.

The training area itself wasn't very large. The mats were of decent quality foam that looked like puzzle piece squares stuck together. The walls were lined with thin mats as tall as one's shoulders to make the environment safer for sparring. Four heavy bags hung in the corner across the gym, and behind the bags stood a creaky shelf screwed into the wall that held the gym's Thai pads, gloves, and shin guards. Every time somebody strong went to town on the bags, the shelf shook and rained down equipment. Near the door was a front desk, and next to that was a waist-high freezer-refrigerator combination with some tiny ice packs and beverages for sale. Facing the desk was a bathroom built into the wall. One had to walk a few feet across the gym floor to get to the shower room and then a third room called the changing room. Cubbies were built into one corner of the training area, and two black benches stood in front of them for those who wanted to watch.

The instructor guided the class through various dodge and counter techniques, but it wasn't anything I hadn't seen before. I thought of Sityodtong, my Muay Thai gym back home in Boston. Kru Mark DellaGrotte played Thai music running in the background as he pushed us through one drill after another. Hearing his crisp voice with its Boston accent shouting at the class made me want to train until the point of exhaustion just to have him notice me.

Genki Yamaguchi, who we all called Genki-san, had that same authoritative voice that rose above the grunts and smacks to guide the class through the exercises. He was still no Mark. Plus it was the beginner's class, so of course he wouldn't show hardcore competition-style moves.

Around ten people showed up to the Brazilian jiu jitsu class, and Brazilian style, three of them showed up late, after warm-ups were completed. I wasn't impressed how they warmed up slowly and chatted while doing them. The instructor was the heavy-set man I'd first talked to when I first entered the club that afternoon. He carried the rank of purple belt, which is very good but still far below black belt level. The technique he showed was good but didn't strike me as cool as the stuff I learned back at New England Brazilian Jiu jitsu in Everett, now an associate of the Brazilian Top Team. I knew I was being hypercritical and every club has its slow days. I decided to give the club a chance and participate the next day.

My eyelids drooped lower and lower until I nearly nodded off in front of the class. It wasn't the class itself, I knew, for everyone had started sparring and I watched with interest.

"Sleepy?" asked Genki.

"Ah, yes, I'm sorry. I'm still ...how do you say it? I just arrived yesterday."

"Yesterday?!" he exclaimed. "Really? So you feel 'jisa-bo-ke'," he said, and thus I learned the word for "jetlagged." It literally means "time-stupid." Although I wanted to watch the Shooto class scheduled after BJJ, I knew I wouldn't make it until nine. The friendliness of the people left me with a lasting good impression. Also, training partners and instructors of high caliber and status are naturally very important to make a good training environment. Two additional purple belts joined the class. According to a woman from the kickboxing class who I chatted with, one of them was a Shooto champion. Shooto is a combination of kickboxing stand up techniques, followed by takedowns, wrestling, and submission grappling. One thing that separates it from general MMA is the lack of strikes while on the ground.

Unfortunately, the financial reality caught me with my hands down. The registration fee was about 150 dollars, plus I had to pay for the current month and one month in advance. I definitely wanted to make sure I liked the club before I joined. I found the bus stop and nearly missed the ICU stop, which I reached at 10pm. I hopped on my bike and made my way through the dark deserted campus towards the side gate. I suddenly realized that the light on the front of my bike was broken. I shrugged it off as no big deal until I peddled always out of range of the lights that illuminated the dorms and athletic fields. As pitch blackness fell around me, I couldn't see a damn thing. My bike jolted as I ran over tree roots and cracked twigs.

I slowed my bike to a crawl, debating whether to get off and walk. I was breaking three of Mother's rules. One, don't drive if you can't see where you're going. Two, don't go strange places alone. Three, don't go into dark, unknown places at night or you could get assaulted.

The irony was not lost on me that I was a fighter biking home from a kickboxing class. I bet a gang of Japanese mafia is going to jump out of the bushes any minute! I worried but continued to ride blindly. An excruciating minute later, I emerged from the black hole into the well-lit gate area. I was in for another shock, and laughed out loud. The gate had been shut. I didn't know any other way out of ICU. The sturdy metal gate stood like jail bars a foot taller than me. I thought for a few minutes.

Dismounting, I lifted my bike over my head and over the fence. The bike was light by American bike standards, but it also could have been a whole lot lighter as I struggled to keep it from crashing to the ground. I held it over the bars with one arm, and stuck my other arm through the bars to lower it gently. Feeling very proud of myself, I hoisted myself over the gate and jumped. The cool wind dried the sweat on my grinning face as I peddled. Unfortunately for me, the darkness disguised my path, sending me down various twists and turns in the road. I took a wrong turn three or four times, but eventually made it. My host mother flipped out when I described my adventures to her.

"The train would have been so much faster!" she exclaimed. "I can't believe you did that! Wow, it must have been hard!" It was then I learned how to take the train.

Chapter 3 - Muay Thai and Brazilian Jiu jitsu in Kichijoji
Wednesday, September 3

My host mother's voice permeated the construction-strength earplugs I wore when I slept, once again awakening me at 5:30am the next morning.

"Wait! Wait! What are you doing? Hey!" she scolded the dog. The animal's nails clacked on the pavement. From the way it jumped and skittered around, I knew Sadako-san was chasing it with the leash in hand. A cool breeze drifted in through the open windows, bringing relief from the hot stickiness of the previous day. I sat up on my futon made of blankets. Through the screen door, I could see a sparse blanket of new weeds on the backyard dirt, proof of midnight rain showers.

The only reason I went to ICU that day was to take the Japanese language placement tests. After completing them, I took my time and enjoyed the scenery. I biked around the woodsy parts of campus near the dorms before going to Japanese class. The insects, which hung from leaves and flew around under the canopy of deciduous trees, differed greatly from those back home. And the crows were huge. If I was a cat and I saw those birds, I would run away. They even grew bigger than the cute little dogs that the Japanese love to pamper. The jet-black birds hopped around, calling out in their eerie human-like voices. The University of Massachusetts in Amherst was the home bushes full of squirrels, both gray and black, so I suppose every campus has its favorite species of animal.

The air thinned and cooled as I left roads surrounded by concrete walls. The temperature must have been at least 45 degrees on the road, which ran by a park. Gazebos overlooked a manmade rain overflow canal that ran parallel the street.

I witnessed a curious thing when I entered my neighborhood. A woman rode by with a good-sized dog in the basket tied onto the back of her bike. It was sitting there casually with its tongue hanging out, peaceful as if it went for rides all the time. I also saw a mother with one kid in a child's seat behind her, plus another one in the basket (not a child seat – an actual basket) attached over the front wheel. The basket wasn't made for the kid, who was about four, but rather it seemed like the kind of thing you would carry around a supermarket. I cringed to think what would happen if the mother lost her balance and crashed the bike.

I passed many older people who walked their dogs by tying the leash to their handlebars and riding through the park.

When I got home, I asked my host mother about this.

"Isn't that kind of dangerous?" I said. "I mean, if the dog decides to bolt, wouldn't the rider be flung off the bike?"

"Yes, absolutely." She agreed with me wholeheartedly. "As a matter of fact," she continued, "I did it."

"You do it, too?" I asked.

She shook her head and waved her arms. "I tried it with Fortune, but you know Fortune. I broke my teeth. See these?" She pointed at her face. "They aren't my real teeth."

My jaw dropped.

"And my finger! It got bent like this!"

I cringed and averted my eyes as she began twisting her fingers every which way.

"What's wrong, are you scared to look," she asked. "Look! Now I can't bend my finger like this!" She did something, but I wasn't watching.

"Oh, that's horrible...I'm so sorry," I muttered towards the wall.

She suddenly chuckled. "I'm making hotto keiki for lunch. Are you hungry?"

"Yeah! But what are hotto keiki?"

"Hotto keiki are hotto keiki," she said. "Look!"

Taking a hold of my elbow, she tugged me into the kitchen and showed me a bag of pancake mix.

"Oh, oh, 'hotcakes,'" I supplied. "Great! My favorite food ever!" I exclaimed. Nobody can beat my mom's special wholegrain recipe, though.

Once she set a pile of flapjacks down in front of me, I asked for the syrup.

"Oh, Japanese people don't put much syrup on their pancakes. Want butter?"

"Oh? Oh. No, thanks," I said, extremely crestfallen. What? No syrup? "Do you have jam?"

Peanut butter and jam managed to do the trick, but that very afternoon I made my first solo trip to a grocery store. A tiny bottle of fake syrupy stuff cost the equivalent of three dollars.

"Now I see why she's using butter," I thought.

Later that afternoon, Sadako-san showed me the way to the Musashi Koganei train Station.

"So you wanna go to Kichijoji?" she said. "It's easy!"

The system confused me, though. I confronted a large machine with maps labeled in kanji - Chinese characters - that I didn't recognize yet. My host mother bypassed the ticket machine and bought me a ticket from the fellow at the window by the gate. She tried to tell me that I should take the train on track number 3. Then she changed her mind and told me to go to track number 2. Changing her mind again, she repeated track number 3.

Frustrated, I finally blurted out, "Okay, I got it!" and walked through the gates. This was a lie, of course. I had no idea where to go.

"Bye bye! Have fun!" Sadako-san waved at me. I smiled, waved back, and climbed the stairs to a track. As soon as I was out of sight, I looked for some help. I approached a nice young lady and asked which way to Kichijoji. She pointed to track two with a smile that might have meant, "Awe, a foreigner struggling to speak my language! How cute!"

Later, I came to understand that there are two tracks I could take. I just had to be careful because one train turned into an express at some point, so therefore wouldn't stop where I wanted it.

No one is too good for the train. Businessmen, mothers, school kids, and regular looking people sat or stood patiently waiting. They listened to earphones connected by thin wires into CD or MP3 players tucked away in the folds of their clothing. Busy fingers punched text messages to friends on cell phones. I saw no foreigners at all that day, although in the following days I would see a few.

32

In Kichijoji station, the usual river of people swept me up and buoyed out the main gates. I walked in the wrong direction for a good ten minutes, before stopping a young couple on the street for directions. Based off a map I'd sketched they pointed me in the right direction. Then, they asked me where I was going.

In the United States, if I said, "I do jiu jitsu," they'd say, "What's that? Is that karate? Hiyaaaa!" and make a funny pose. If I said, "I do kickboxing" they might say, "Oh, so you mean you kick butt? Don't hurt me."

Therefore, I tried out a vague Japanese response I'd learned the other day. *Eeh, sore wa chotto,* which loosely translates to, "Um, that's, well, kind of." The man looked at me funny. I wondered why. My Japanese teacher told me that it was okay to be vague. In fact, he said that everyone was vague all of the time, so I expected people to accept my vagueness. It didn't seem to be working out...

I continued, "Well there's a club near a sushi place..."

He probably thought, "What is with this weird foreign girl?" In fact, in Japan training kickboxing or jiu jitsu wasn't unusual at all, and if I had told him the truth, he would have smiled and gone on his way.

Once I found it, I got to watch the end of the beginner's kickboxing class again. I told Genki-san, who was sitting behind the desk that day, that I wanted to sign up for class. At first, he discouraged me from taking the Muay Thai class and I couldn't figure out why. I thought it was my poor Japanese. After a few minutes of stressful incomprehension, he suggested that I try this class called "kick-diet," which he described as "a good class for women." A cardio-kickboxing for women would not help my MMA training, however, so I told him I'd pass on that.

"But why can't I take the Muay Thai class?"

"You can," he said.

"Then what's the problem?"

Genki-san looked hard at the table, his frowning in concentration as he tried to think of the English.

"Ehh, errrr, more...experience...fighter...." he got out.

"Do you mean that it's more difficult?" I asked in Japanese.

"Yes, yes," he replied, his face breaking into a relieved smile.

"Oh, excellent!" I said.

He looked confused.

"I'll try it! I've been doing Muay Thai for two years, so it's okay."

He gave up trying to persuade me, and just showed me the changing room.

Rambar, the instructor, spoke an impossible mixture of Thai, English, and Japanese. I had to speak to Genki-san who spoke some Thai, and have him translate. That was amusing but frustrating at the same time. I eventually came to communicate with him in simple un-conjugated Japanese with a few English words thrown in. He had a great sense of humor, and liked talking to me about Hawaii, the only place in the U.S. he'd been to. I came to like him a lot.

Although I had trained kickboxing for over two years, I didn't consider myself very good at it. I also hadn't done it in a few weeks at that point, so my technique looked terrible. All my moves felt off and everybody treated me like a beginner. Rambar wouldn't let me hold pads for my partner, although granted my partner was a tall 200 lb Australian. Rambar told me to sit out a few exercises, which was irritating.

As I had feared, the Japanese guys didn't want to come near me. I kept telling myself that it was only my first day so nobody knew what I was capable of. Once I trained for a while, they would feel more comfortable sparring with me and actually try and land a punch. When I sparred one heavy-set man, his punches stayed a foot from my face, and when I stopped attacking, he didn't attack back. Because of this, I was off balance when he did throw something, so he hit me easily.

"Oh great," I thought, "That just reaffirms his belief that I suck."

During a head tie drill, my partner reached out to grab my head but didn't come into physical contact. This defeats the purpose of the drill, which involves pulling on the back of the head,

34

and jerking them around to controlling their movements. I didn't want to make anyone uncomfortable so I didn't force the issue.

Seeing this, Rambar came over and yelled, "What are you doing?! Go go go!" The man reluctantly began to do the drill correctly with me.

At that point, I just wanted to grapple. I always want to grapple, but the desire was particularly strong during that class. I guessed Rambar was a good NHB fighter, but to this day I am uncertain if he's had any fights other than Thai boxing. He definitely had skill, though, for in the middle of class when he told us to shadow box, he turned around and jumped on a BJJ purple belt who had been innocently sitting off to the side. They engaged and did some pretty cool jiu jitsu techniques.

Practically drooling to test myself against him on the ground, I asked him if he wanted to fight NHB. He said "not today," and told me to fight the purple belt instead. The young, muscular Japanese man was sitting on the side taping his wrists with athletic tape. Naoya Uematsu was his name- a champion in Shooto, the oldest and most famous mixed martial arts organization in Japan.

The Thai boxing class lasted for two hours. For the last portion, we did hands-only sparring and then incorporated kicks. I was getting my rhythm back, and practiced my movement so I wouldn't stay flat-footed. I sparred with this handsome New Zealand man, Jason, who spoke English. He was more ready to throw attacks, and I had a good session. I was able to practice real slips and ducks because he was aiming for my face instead of the air above it. His skill level was far above mine, but he knew how to step up the pace without totally overwhelming me.

After sparing, the class ended and everybody began their own training. Some packed up and went home. Others did weight training over in the far corner where a small rack of dumbbells stood. A few kicked the heavy bags.

Rambar kept hounding me to fight the Uematsu-san, who was chatting with Genki-san. I couldn't sense if he really wanted to fight or not, since Rambar was the one volunteering him. After some confusion, Uematsu-san grinned and waved me over.

That match was the highlight of my night. Even though he was holding back, his technique was superb. I seemed to fall into leg locks, arm locks, or anything that crossed his mind. He tapped me at will, making me vow to myself to work hard so I could do the same thing some day. It was because of him that I finally decided to join the dojo a few days later, hoping I would become the leg-lock queen if I trained under him long enough.

After we stopped fighting, I happily began fixing my hair, when Genki came out from behind the desk and commented on my shirt. It was a Jason Morris Judo Camp shirt, and because all the instructors knew him immediately. I knew my old instructor Morris was known internationally, but what I didn't realize was that he lost to a Japanese fighter in the Olympics in 1992. Actually, he lost to Hidehiko Yoshida who went on to fight MMA in Pride. It's a small world.

"Ah, Jason Morris?" he exclaimed. "Judo, huh? He's amazing! You used to train with him!"

Rambar snuck up on me and started squeezing my arm muscle while I was talking to Uematsu. He said something in Thai to Genki, who said something back. Uematsu asked me if I wanted to compete, and I said yes. I asked him if he ever heard of "Smackgirl," a woman-only MMA fighting organization in Japan.

Uematsu pointed to a woman sitting in the corner and said a whole lot of something I couldn't understand. I gathered that she fought in Smackgirl, but it seemed too good to be true! I went over and introduced myself. Her name was Jet Izumi, and did indeed fight in Smackgirl several times.

The two instructors asked my weight- 135 lbs, or about 61.5 kilos. Genki looked something up on the computer behind the counter, and returned with a few girls' names.

"There are some girls your weight, so it'll be okay," he said.

"Be okay?" I repeated, uncertainly.

"Yes! That means you can do it!"
Uematsu asked me if I wanted to join the gym.

"You'd have to pay for the current month, a month in advance, and a one time joining fee," he explained slowly, while I jotted down notes on a memo pad. I calculated the yen to dollars, and it totaled a little over three hundred. They didn't take cash, but tapped into every member's bank account every month. I agreed.

Business settled, I stepped out the door and shouted "Otsukare sama desu," as everyone is supposed to do when leaving the dojo. It means, "Good work."

I'd just finished tying my shoelaces when a middle-aged man and a slightly younger woman came out a door across from the dojo door. The man started talking to me, saying something about working hard and doing a good job. I figured that maybe they had been watching class, but somehow it didn't seem right. The woman said something, which I totally didn't understand, so I just smiled and finished tying my sneakers.

They went up the narrow stairway slowly. I followed close behind, seeing as that was the only way to get back to the street. The man advanced one slow step at a time, and eventually looked back. Then he burst out laughing and kept going. Anxious to get home, I picked up my pace and passed them at the top of the stairs. The woman turned to me and held out her hand expectantly. I shook it, very confused. She seemed very happy, but I had no idea who she was.

The man said something about taking a shower and something about water, so I thought, "He's telling me to go take a shower? Maybe it's not appropriate to go out onto the streets after a workout not having showered." My shirt and hair were soaked with sweat.

Confused that a stranger would say something like that to me, I smiled and said, "Is that so?" and quickly hurried away. Later, I realized that the dojo was right next to a bar. Maybe they weren't even talking to me at all. The man and woman were probably a tipsy couple trying to stagger home. Sore from class, I'm sure I staggered harder.

Thursday, September 4

Sadako-san helped me sign up for health insurance in town. I understood virtually none of what was being said between the official dressed in a sharp business suit and Sadako-san.

"Here, just fill this out," my host mother instructed. I complied, writing down my contact information on some forms, and came away with a green card.

"I'd like to walk around town a little by myself, if that's alright," I said.

"Sure, take your time. Go that way. And that way is the way home. Can you remember?"

"Yes!" I replied, more confidently than I felt.

"Good." My host mother strode off.

I found a grocery store first, or rather, a small room with tables of food open to the street. The store was 60% fresh fish. I openly gawked. Whole fish lay on ice with their glossy lidless eyes staring at the ceiling. Squid lay in a straight line, still wet and floppy. I found shrink-wrapped octopus stacked like we would find ground beef in American markets. Salmon roe and other fish eggs were put on white cardboard and wrapped up with see-through plastic, again in the same way meat would be. There was fruit I'd never seen before, including huge grape-like balls, but twice the size of normal grapes and five times as expensive. Everything was ridiculously expensive.

As soon as I entered any store or restaurant and as soon as the owners noticed me, they called out *irrashai* or *irrashaimase*, which means "welcome." They greet every customer who walks in this way. In the post office, there was a police officer whose job seemed to only be to stand by the door and say that to everyone who entered. My host mother said we needn't even respond. With all the greeting going on with me going in and out of stores, I noticed when I wasn't greeted.

In a cozy store that sold expensive teacups and other fine things, the owner was an old balding man. He sat on a stool, hunched over a table with a cash register and piles of papers. When I entered, he looked up at me said nothing, probably thinking, "This young female foreigner wouldn't purchase my pricey wears." He was correct. His attitude made me uncomfortable, so I looked around as respectfully as possible and quickly left.

After wandering around some more, I went home for dinner before training. My host mother welcomed me with Hokkaido fried fish, leftover teriyaki chicken, broccoli, asparagus and fried zucchini.

On Thursdays, Uematsu runs the BJJ class followed directly by a once-a-week Shooto class. I overestimated the travel time so I wouldn't be late, and ended up an hour early.

"Uematsu-san," I said to the fighter, who sat on the black bench near the storage cubbies, taping his wrists.

. "Can I sit off to the side and read while I wait?"

He shrugged, and said, "Of course!"

Hoping no one from the ongoing kick boxing class would step on me, I sat with my back against the refrigerator and took out my magazine.

"Can I sit here?" I asked him.

"Sure, there is fine, the bench is fine, and here is fine, too." He patted his lap and grinned. I chuckled, as did a few people around us. Some tension was dispelled and I liked him immediately. I pulled out the magazine I'd just bought, and bent over it intently. The English text "Let's Do MMA!" stood out across the top. Funny afro-topped, MMA glove-sporting stick figures danced on the cover.

A few minutes later, Uematsu peered over at me and my magazine. I noticed him trying to see, so I told him that I wanted to translate some of the technique pages for my instructor back home. He lowered himself off the bench a few feet away and leaned over on his side, indicating the page with step-by-step technique instructions.

"That...me!" he said in English. I looked at him in surprise. "What? Really?"

He grinned and jabbed his finger into my magazine.

"Me! Me!" he insisted.

I looked closely.

"Hey, it IS you!" I confirmed.

"And that, him!" He pointed to the purple belt who was standing by the door with a slight smile, regarding us.

Satoshi Kotani, co-owner of Cross Point Kichijoji, held the rank of black belt in judo. At the time, he wore a purple belt in Brazilian jiu jitsu, but has been since promoted to black by famous BJJ black belt Yuki Nakai, owner and founder of Paraestra. He was a strong, solid-looking man.

"No way." My mouth dropped open. I flipped through the pages, and true enough, Uematsu and Kotani had indeed done an instructional section. They had ten or more pages dedicated to technique and fight coverage.

"Sugoi! That's amazing!" I exclaimed. Uematsu laughed and went back to his seat.

Before class started, I met a white belt named Ando Tatsuya. He spoke English pretty well.

"Call me "Tatsu," the friendly man said. In his late 20's/early 30's, he was kind, enthusiastic, and made a big effort to help me out during my year in Japan. He spoke proudly about his one-year home stay in Colorado during his college years.

This BJJ class impressed me more than the first one I'd watched. The instructor of the day was Kotani.

After warm-ups, the first techniques he showed some judo throws. After drilling them, he let us ronduri, or "free spar." The overall skill level was average, although I didn't do much better since I hadn't practiced straight judo in over three years. After the judo technique, he showed newaza, or "ground technique." We drilled those moves and then free-sparred grappling. A big electric timer sitting on top of the refrigerator rang every five minutes, signaling a change in partners.

I met a delightful woman named Kazuyo Akikawa. Her friends called her Zuyo for short. Smiling and laughing almost constantly, she joked around and made me feel completely at home. A secretary for a bigwig in some office, Zuyo didn't strike me as the mild-mannered secretarial type. Her enthusiasm was mirrored in her light brown hair, which hung below her ears. Too short to pull back, but too long to be considered very short, it bounced around when we sparred. If she had something on her mind, she'd say it and say it well. Although I outweighed her by a good fifteen pounds, she put up a great fight. She was somewhere in her early thirties, but seemed to be the kind of person who'd never grow old.

BJJ class ended as soon as everyone finished sparring, and Shooto began. A few people from the BJJ class took off their gi tops and stuck around, and were joined by about eight others who came just for Shooto. I changed from my gi to shorts and T-shirt, the typical garb for that type of class. Uematsu didn't waste any time in warming us up, but went straight into a standup clinching technique. We practiced different ways to grip the arms, head and neck with a partner for a few minutes.

Throughout the entire class, my comprehension of the dialogue and explanations was about 30%, so I basically learned by watching and imitating. After technique, Uematsu called our attention to the middle of the room. He roughly grabbed a student by the shirt collar and tugged him into the center of the mat, proceeding to rapidly show a bunch of extremely cool techniques, which included a jumping heel hook, flying knee bar, flying arm bar, and variations of slams and suplexes. Then with a wave of his arm, he said something I didn't quite catch and the class started dispersing. Some people went to the edge of the mat and sat down, and some found partners and started sparring.

"So, what are we doing now?" I asked my partner, confused. "Which of those moves do we practice?"

"This... free fighting," he replied in English.

"Oh I see," I thought. "I guess that means free sparring time." He and I moved away from the wall and began to tussle for a head tie. Twenty seconds into it, I tried a jumping heel hook that Uematsu had just showed. I executed it perfectly by grabbing into his shoulder to support myself, entwining my legs with his from the side, and taking him over backwards.

"NO!" screamed Uematsu from across the room. I froze. The entire class froze and looked.

Tatsu hurried over to translate. "Those were the moves you weren't supposed to do!" he exclaimed in English.

Mortified, I fell to my knees and bowed repeatedly, saying, "Gomen nasai! I'm sorry! I'm sorry!" Then I turned to my partner and said sorry to him, too. Uematsu pretended to soccer-kick me, but then told me not to worry about it. My partner looked embarrassed that I was apologizing so much. I wasn't sure what to do in such a situation. Everyone just went back to sparring.

The rest of the class went well. Uematsu showed a rolling toehold, and then we sparred again. After class, the purple belt popped in a video tape into a small TV sitting next to the refrigerator. I got to watch Jet Izumi fight MMA in a Smackgirl event from earlier that year. My eyes wide, I watched her totally crush her opponent. I couldn't wait to train with her, and learn more from Uematsu.

Chapter 4 - Getting Settled In
Friday, September 5

Friday marked the end of my first week in Japan, and I felt like my life was picking up speed.

After class I met Cayte and we hopped the bus to a department store in Musashi Sakai, the next town over. Our goal: To get me a cell phone.

The store was set up much like Sears in the United States, and we soon found the electronics department. A friendly young man in a neat brown suit hurried over to the counter. He presented the payment plans, but I didn't understand his explanation. Cayte translated, and I chose a company called AU as my carrier. It would be the cheapest plan and would cost me about $25 dollars a month. She helped me fill out the registration form and the man asked us to choose which phone I wanted.

I touched my finger to my lip in thought, staring at a row of sample cell phones on the counter. Price tags hung above each one. I wanted to get the cheapest cell phone possible. The first rectangular cell phone on the left looked particularly zany with a zebra stripe decoration on the exterior plastic.

"Hey Cayte," I finally said. "Does that sign really say this phone costs one yen?"

"Yeah, it really does," she answered, bending over and closely inspecting the sign with her eye that could still see a little.

"And one yen is less than a penny, right?" I persisted.

"Right."

"Okay, I'll take that one," I said in Japanese to the salesman, indicating the zebra-phone.

The young man pointed to my choice and said "Ah, this one?" He picked it up, his face full of complete rejection and disappointment. Clasping his hands and bowing slightly, he said, "I'm very, very sorry, but this cell phone does not come with a digital camera built in. Is that all right?"

I looked at Cayte and burst out laughing. Here we were in Japan and this salesman was apologizing profusely, asking me if it was all right that my one-cent phone didn't have a camera. It was 2003, and cameras in cell phones had just come out. I remembered that one week before I left for Japan a friend came into my gym showing off his $400 dollar new cell phone. It had the latest technology that included a digital camera and internet browser. We all gathered around and literally "ooh-ed" and "aaah-ed" over the mind-blowing genius of those who could install a camera in a cell phone. I'd never considered the possibility I might own one. I wanted my digital camera separate because the pictures would be better quality, so I was quite delighted with my one-yen cell phone. The service plan was simple, surprisingly much cheaper than my $50 Verizon Wireless plan in the States.

The salesman swiped my credit card and told us to come back in forty-five minutes. We decided to kill two birds with one stone and shop for digital cameras. The dollar/yen exchange rate was roughly a dollar per hundred yen, so I could easily calculate the approximate price of things by hacking off the last two zeros. A camera costing 24,000 yen equaled a little less than $240. I found one I liked and Cayte and I struggled to ask the cameraman about batteries, warranties, video capabilities and usability. Eventually satisfied, we decided to buy it. Unfortunately, the cash register wouldn't take my credit card. After fifteen minutes of failed attempts and apologies, we left camera-less. When I spoke to my dad the next day, he said that he'd gotten a phone call from the credit card company alerting him that someone in a foreign country was trying to use the card, so they froze the account. It was a theft protection safeguard. My dad notified them of my status and got them to release the hold.

That evening I took a day off from training and also from talking to my host mother. I had nothing against her, but every moment seemed like a constant speaking test and I was feeling stressed. I reflected on how much Japanese I learned in the short period since I arrived. The results so far instilled me with confidence that I would some day achieve my goal of becoming fluent in Japanese as long as I practiced and did my best. However, that night I wanted a break. I excused myself from the table after dinner, and went to watch an episode of anime on my computer in

44

my room. My brain protested the further exposure to the Japanese language, so I put on some of my favorite music. It was Japanese rock music. Turning that off, I realized that I couldn't escape. This was the thing called cultural immersion.

Saturday, September 6
The Imperial Palace

On Saturday my host sister Takae took a day off from work at the bakery. She offered to take me sightseeing and I readily agreed. We studied maps of Tokyo and decided to go to the Imperial Palace in the center of Tokyo. It took us two hours by train.

Downtown Tokyo city reminded me of the business sections of major cities, rather than the fun shopping mall-like scene of Kichijoji. Amidst the tall bland skyscrapers, an actual castle stood surrounded by a moat and major roadways. Pine trees grew around the moat and Takae and I walked up a wide gravel walkway. We walked right up to the gates, but weren't allowed inside the Palace. It wasn't very interesting from the outside.

We then headed to the Meiji Jingu Shrine nearby in Akihabara District. At the entrance stood the tallest Tori shrine gate I've ever seen. A wooden sign stuck next to it said in English that it was one of the largest in Japan, standing about 40 feet tall, with a span of about 30 feet from post to post. The Tori poles must have been made out of giant tree trunks, but I could barely imagine trees being so thick. I stood in awe staring up at them for several minutes before passing through and starting down the wide gravel path. Families with nicely-dressed children strode by purposefully on a Saturday outing to pray. The air cooled as it passed through the leaves, bringing some relief to the heat of the late Tokyo summer.

A Shinto wedding happened to be going on as we came upon the main Shrine complex. The bride was dressed in a white kimono with a huge hairpiece that seemed to balance on the top of her head. The rest of the family followed behind the bride and the groom, who was dressed all in black. Typically people wear white to funerals and black to weddings, but elements of Western marriages may have crept into tradition. Both bride and groom walked together under the shadow of a huge traditional-looking umbrella held for them by helpers, followed by two Shinto Priests with very tall oval-triangle hats.

Takae and I gave the ceremony a respectful berth and went up a few steps into an offering area. Takae showed me how to toss a one-yen coin into a coin bin, bow, clap my hands together twice, bow again, and step away. The clanking of the coin on the metal change bin is supposed to summon the attention of the kami, ancestor-spirits who live all around us and in the shrine. People also claps their hands and rings the bell that is hung outside the shrine. People always say a prayer for good health and prosperity, or to honor an ancestor, or to help them with whatever problems they might be experiencing at the time.

An element of commercialism had seeped into such traditions in the form of a little store off to the side. I bought a little ceramic doll shaped like a Shinto Priest for myself for 800 yen, which is about eight dollars. It had a little bell inside it. The priests supposedly blessed them so they could bring the carrier good health, safe driving, and general good luck.

We left the Meiji shrine area and went to a city called Shinjuku next. There, Takae led me into this wonderful Japanese restaurant. Every waitress we passed said "Irrashaimase!" Instead of water and a basket of bread, a waiter brought ground up radish, tea, and wet cloths to wipe our hands on.

Pictures on the menu made my food selection easy to decide, and the waitress took our order with a wonderful electronic device. Pushing a button is much easier than scribbling down words on a notepad while a customer is asking you questions about the meals. The different contrasts of technology and tradition in Japan struck me in the face. Right across the street from a digital camera store, you can see a traditional Shinto shrine.

I ordered ebi-don, which is rice and fried shrimp patties on top of egg surrounded by onions. It was wonderful. A small serving of soba buckwheat noodles came as a side dish, served in this square box on what looked like a miniature tatami mat. I found

46

this very strange. Why not put it in a bowl? Next to the box was a little cup with a lid on it that had wasabi, radish, and greenish onions. Takae instructed me to take the cap off and put them in. Then, I was to dip the bland noodles in and eat them. I found I love Japanese food.

After we finished, we stopped at the Citibank and I was elated to discover that I could withdraw cash out of the ATM with my American Fleet card. Unfortunately, I found out that I was charged five dollars for the transaction, so I only withdraw once a month when I needed to pay the rent to my host mother.

I withdrew three hundred dollars to buy a digital camera, and Takae helped me look for one in Shinjuku. We shopped around in a few of the myriad electronic stores, and eventually found one for 24,499 yen (very roughly $315) Our adventures ended with that purchase, and we headed home to another one of Sadako's amazing meals.

Sunday, September 7

I discovered a wonderful place called The 100 Yen Store in Musashi Sakai, a neighboring town. It's equivalent to The Dollar Store in the States and had all sorts of cheap snacks, plastic containers, and bins, which I bought to hold my stuff. To finish off my shopping spree, I popped in the bakery next door and sampled a fried bread bun with curry inside, which the Japanese call "curry bread." It was strange but oddly tasty. I returned home to deposit my purchases at home, and then took the train to Kichijoji for Brazilian jiu jitsu.

My heart fell when I looked around the class and saw mostly white belts. I always try and train with blue belts and higher to provide myself with a better workout, although I have no problems with working with white belts now and then. I thought wistfully of BTT Boston where roughly seventy percent of the students were blue belts, with at least six purple belts who regularly attended, plus a few black belts. Despite my disappointment, I really enjoyed doing judo ronduri sparring at Cross Point. I've always regretted that I've had to stop practicing judo regularly due to a back injury that acts up if I'm thrown repetitively. Doing it now and then is okay, but it wouldn't be wise to join a dojo.

It felt strange to not be the smallest person in class. This enabled me to successfully execute moves and positions I normally couldn't pull off because stronger men back home used size and strength to resist. At the same time, sometimes I didn't know if I was doing the technique correctly, or if I did it because I was bigger than my partner was. I missed my training partners in Amherst and Boston deeply. I had something special there. Everyone has a comradery that's impossible to find anywhere else. All throughout class, all I could think about was my Brazilian friends in Boston. As I did a reversal sweep on a purple belt, I wondered if he was really trying to resist. I remembered when my black belt friend Cesar Santos swept my base, took my back and choked me out, chiding me afterwards with a smile. "Don't let me catch you with that!" I shed my first tears in Japan for them.

Homesickness began striking in waves. At one point, I was so overcome with emotion that I had to excuse myself from drills and collect myself in the changing room. I closed my eyes. Boston exploded into existence. The gray and red tatami mats. Faces broke into grins when I pushed open the glass door.

"You haven't left yet?" Mirel exclaimed, clasping my hand warmly.

"I'm leaving tomorrow," I answered.

"Wow! And yet you're here!" His smile was like that of a brother.

"Hey! Long time no see! I hear ya goin' to Japan!" Marcelo took my other hand. Everyone doing drills across the floor looked up, nodding, waving, smiling. They were all my brothers.

"Are ya gonna come back with a Japanese boyfriend now?"

"Good luck, Roxy!"

"Train hard, Roxy."

I wondered when I'd visit again.

"Have fun in Japan!" Mirel called to me as the glass door swung shut, cutting off the grunts and laughs of family training together. The welcoming smell of wet gi.

Pressed against the rack of used jiu jitsu gis and broken exercise equipment, I clenched my fists. This was nothing, only emotions. I vowed to plow ahead as fast as I could, to accomplish as much as I could. If I stopped and thought about things, I might get stuck in the dark, afraid and lonely.

"I'll never be alone. Never alone. Not now that I've discovered jiu jitsu, and entered the fight world."

That night I unloaded all my nostalgia on my mother over the phone. I felt fifty percent better. After some comforting advice, she added gently, "Well, you know you're not in Japan to do jiu jitsu." My response was, "Uh, well actually..."

Chapter 5 - Classes, Festivals, and the "Engrish" language
Monday, September 8

I especially enjoyed Genki Yamaguchi's kickboxing classes, which he held on Mondays. Individuals were expected to stretch and warm up a little bit on their own while waiting for class to start. After a brief warm-up, which involved shadow boxing and sometimes jogging, everyone found a partner, put on 16 oz boxing gloves and shin guards. Genki-san then proceeded to show techniques or combinations, which we took turns doing with our partner. We usually did three or four per class, which took half of the hour-long period. If there were an odd number of people and I was the only girl in the class, instead of asking me to sit out, Genki-san would be my partner, for which I was eternally grateful.

After combinations, one partner took off their gloves and strapped thick Thai pads to their arms. For the next five minutes, Genki-san would call out combinations of strikes. The person with the gloves would hit the pads their partner held for them. After the allotted time, the partners switched and Genki-san would call out the same combinations so both people could get an equal workout.

Finally, if there was still time, we would do light sparring. Another instructor and professional Shooto fighter, Tiger Ishi, also ran class this way. Depending on how many people there were that day, half the class would sit out and the other half would line up in two rows facing each other. After approximately three or four minutes, the line would rotate and you'd face someone new.

In terms of sparring intensity, it varied from person to person. Those who participated in competitions tended to go all out, while the average person who trained for fun tended to go lighter. They also shied away from hitting me, probably because of my gender.

I always want to spar as hard as possible, but it always proved difficult to get Japanese men to attack me. Even when I explained that I needed to prepare myself for competition someday, the majority still didn't step up the pace at all. I ended up bopping them on the forehead with my jab-cross combination, while their returning jabs flew a few feet over my head or off to the side. Having men change their fighting methods while fighting me has always been a pet peeve of mine, and turned into the most frustrating aspect of my training in Japan. I knew I wasn't so good at kickboxing, and I don't expect people to punch me as hard as they can, but they have to at least aim for my face, or I can't judge distance and fight effectively. It messes me up.

It was especially irritating when the women of the class didn't spar aggressively with me, either. One friendly-looking girl stopped trying to hit me after she socked me once in the face, probably figuring I didn't know what I was doing so she had better take it easy. This wasn't always the case, though. Women who trained were scarce, but one lady was better than I was and I had to remember to keep my hands up around her.

There were also a few men who I loved sparring with because they treated me like a serious competitor. One skinny man who always wore a black shirt went full force no matter what, and I got a lot of slipping and angling practice with him. I always made extra efforts to be in the same sparring group as him.

Tuesday September 9

It dodged to the right! It headed for my futon! I threw myself down, flung back the heavy blankets, and squish! Indignantly, I inspected my heel. Whatever kind of bug that was, it left a silvery mess on my skin. I trotted into the bathroom to wash it off. Upon completion, I inspected myself and found that two red bumps, which I assumed to be bug bites, had faded on my thigh, but two more popped up that morning on my hand. Cayte had said that if I slept on the floor rather than elevated bed, I was probably visited by the local fauna. I noticed other students had similar red bumps on various parts of their bodies. I accepted the itchiness as an inevitable part of being in Japan.

Acceptance lasted an entire morning. By lunchtime, I decided my middle name wasn't "mosquito bait," and something needed to be done. That afternoon, I walked into a drug store next to the Musashi Koganei train station.

"Irrashaimase," called out a motherly clerk with gray hair from behind the counter.

"Konnichiwa," I said, taking a deep breath. I should have looked up "bug repellant" before I left home.

"Excuse me," I began in my best Tarzan-Japanese. "But at night, bugs eat me! They eat me a lot. Do you have bug stuff?" She must have gotten the gist, because she nodded! Then she said something that went right over my head. I smiled vacantly. From my lack of nodding, she knew I didn't get it. When you get it, you always nod.

She came around the counter and showed me a rack with bug repellant. Cute cartoon images of cute little sad-faced, dying mosquitoes decorated the cans. I liked the picture on the can labeled "Mushi bye-bye," the mushi meaning, "insect." The woman recommended Mushi Yo-ke, whatever that meant. Another store clerk wanted to get in on the fun of helping the stupid foreigner, so he tried to explain more about the products. However, I didn't understand a word he said either. I stuck with the Mushi Yo-ke. Before I went to bed, I sprayed my limbs and neck. It worked very well and I hardly suffered from any more bites.

My Japanese class turned out to be stressful. The teacher, Hirata-sensei, spoke only in Japanese. This was a good thing. I would have been dissatisfied had she used a lot of English, because we wouldn't have learned as much. However, when she made announcements concerning assignments and grades, I couldn't always understand and had to turn to a classmate who translated for me. This became humiliating after a while since everyone else except me seemed to understand.

Grammatical explanations in English would have been helpful as well when we didn't understand what she was talking about. We started the first lesson with a confusing reading, which made me feel stupid for being clueless in an intermediate level class. Hirata-sensei talked about a cat in a garden, and then the cat was helping someone, but it had a narrow forehead. She posed a question to the class, and students started talking about "bull's eyes." How these things were related, I had no idea, and continued to be perplexed for several days. Then, suddenly the cat was carrying a koban and this was supposed to be significant. A koban is an oblong gold coin, which was the monetary unit of Japan a long time ago.

It makes partner work difficult when you have to say to your partner, "I'm sorry, I have no idea what we're talking about and what we're supposed to do now." After the third day I figured out that neko ni koban, which isn't even a complete sentence, means "Give a koban to a cat." Therefore, it became a saying meaning "what a waste!" because of course a cat can't use money. The Japanese use it as an idiom, so chapter one was merely about animal idioms. I resented this.

"Why do they gotta teach me some obscure idiom, when I'm struggling to talk my way out of a paper bag?" I thought, annoyed.

Added to the stress of Japanese class, I found out that I'd accidentally signed up for two classes taught only in Japanese. My Japanese was obviously not up to the challenge, and I had to quickly remake my entire schedule. "International Political Economics" became "Economic Growth of Japan," taught by a balding plump Japanese man with passable English.

My much-anticipated class about the United Nations became "Training for Intercultural Persuasion and Negotiation." Whatever that meant. I would find out later that the class was more an exploration of diversity and cultural communication than actual "persuasion." Not being able to take the UN course depressed me at first because I was considering someday working for the United Nations as a translator. It worked out in the end that not only did the persuasion class become one of my favorite classes of all time, but also another new friend named Katie was in it.

This class was unusual in that it began at 3:30 in the afternoon and ended at 7pm. The students and teachers at ICU called those types of class "go-ro-chi," because it took place during fifth, sixth, and seventh periods once a week. In Japanese, five is "go," six is "roku," and seven is "shichi," so they combined the words to make a new one. Gorochi slipped into the exchange student's English vocabulary in the way foreign loan words do. I had no problem with the lateness, because I didn't care for the particular Cross Point class on Wednesday night.

The next day was the anniversary of the Bombing of the World Trade Towers. I'd forgotten until I wrote the date down in my journal. No one in Japan said anything, but I quietly thought about my country and its trials and tribulations. I love America, although didn't always approve of President Bush or his politics.

Wednesday, September 10

When I walked into my gorochi class, "Training for Intercultural Persuasion," a medley of foreign faces greeted me. Out of approximately fifteen students, there were two Americans, a bunch of Japanese, a Korean, one from southern Asian country, and the rest from various European countries. My teacher himself was of a mixed Polish background, and right from the get-go he wanted to emphasize how important people's backgrounds were. Although I'm half Italian and half Lithuanian, he seemed to conveniently forget my Italian heritage and refer to me as "the Lithuanian" because Lithuania is closer to Poland. He said that it's one example of how it's important for negotiators and people in International Relations to fully understand people's biases.

It was rather tedious for both student and teacher to sit through such a long class. Studies show that student's attentions can be held for an hour at best. We did take fifteen minutes after two hours, but even so it was difficult. I had to bike home in the dark after it ended. Luckily the side gate wasn't locked, and I hurried home to a host mother feast. Over yakisoba, which are fried noodles with vegetables, Sadako-san told me about a matsuri, or "festival" which would take place in Kichijoji on Saturday. I arranged to meet Cayte and Mana and go check it out that weekend.

Saturday, September 13
Mikoshi Matsuri

"Nemaru?" I asked hesitantly.

"Nameru!" Mana corrected me with a laugh. I had been trying to remember the word for "lick" ever since Yogi first slobbered on me on the bus to Kichijoji.

The matsuri was supposed to start at 11 and run into the afternoon, so Mana, Cayte, her dog Yogi and I met at 11am in front of the church on ICU campus. From there we caught the bus. I felt bad asking Mana to come since she had to commute two hours from Yokohama, a large city south of Tokyo. However, she seemed excited to spend time with us, and told us not to worry about the distance.

The warm sunlight poured in through the windows and we chatted in a mixture of Japanese and English as the bus bumped along. An old lady in drab clothing boarded the bus a few stops later and sat down across from us. We could see her start when she noticed Cayte's huge golden lab lying in the middle of the aisle floor. There was no convenient place for him to be, so people had to step around. The lady exclaimed something I couldn't understand to another old lady sitting next to her, and then said, "Kowakatta!" which means, "I'm scared." The wrinkly old lady didn't look terribly frightened to me, and even poked Yogi's leg once with her cane. I pursed my lips to keep myself from laughing. Shortly after, the lady said loudly to Cayte, "Daijobu ka?" Are you okay? And then without waiting for a response, started a one-sided conversation with Mana. Mana looked uncomfortable and made polite listening noises while smiling.

"Everyone always asks me if I'm 'all right,'" Cayte whispered to me. "What do they expect me to say? No, I'm fine, I'm just blind!"

I didn't know what to say.

"I know Seeing Eye dogs are rare in Japan, but I still wish people would get a grip and stop flipping out over my dog," she grumbled.

We stood up to let some more old people sit down. After a few minutes of hanging onto the rings attached to the ceiling, I noticed that the girl standing next to me start fidgeting. Yogi had started to sniff people's bare ankles with his slobbery dog mouth. She was wearing high-heeled sandals that went with a stylishly short, sleeveless skirt. I decided to sacrifice my socks and go stand between her and Yogi. The girl gave me a grateful look. "Nameru," I repeated to myself. "Nameru."

The booming drumbeats of the matsuri turned our heads as soon as the bus spit us out onto the sidewalks. We followed our ears and soon saw the Mikoshi, a fancy portable shrine as big as a two-seat couch. The shrine looked like a little room with an elaborate roof sitting on top like a mushroom head. Dragon statues snaked up the four corners of the shrine. They ran up the roof and met at the top where a larger statue of a gold plated phoenix roosted, its wings and tail reflecting the sunlight. The shrine rested on a platform with two long poles built into either side and, in fact, reminded me of the Ark in Indiana Jones: Raiders of the Lost Ark.

A policeman on horseback rode in front of the procession and stopped traffic when necessary. Roughly ten or fifteen people dressed alike in checkered white and blue shirts and shorts hoisted the Mikoshi poles on their shoulders. They carried it through the streets surrounded by men, youths, women and children all dressed in the robe-like garments clapping, dancing, and chanting to celebrate the Shinto holiday. I admit; I wasn't entirely sure of the occasion for this one. The scene could have been lifted off the dirt paths of the capital from hundreds of years ago.

The people decided to take a break in front of a department store, so we went in search of more entertainment. A few blocks down, we ran into people in purple shirts playing drums and other percussion metal instruments. Another block down we found a group of people performing some kind of play or dance. A woman dressed in a traditional kimono was jumping around waving a fan. Two men pretending to be horses sat astride polls with a fake horse head on the end, like a toy a child would ride. They leaped and danced like real frolicking ponies.

Next, we hit Baskin Robbins Ice Cream shop. High prices confronted us, but the ice cream was delicious. I had two cones and paid about five dollars for them. We naturally progressed to shopping, and came upon this wonderful T-shirt store. I saw a shirt that read *Under God Dragon* and thought, "Maybe they have Engrish shirts here so I can give them as souvenirs to my friends back home!" Engrish is how we native English speakers make fun of the Japanese for the incorrect usage of English. For example, they might name a brand of gum "Delicious Yummy," or "Chewing Good Satisfaction."

The shirt right under "Under God Dragon" read: *Doragon Head: a new history of regend begin when these two dragons each other mix.*

I also found another shirt I bought for a friend that says the following long paragraph: *Everyday objects became devices to trigger confusion. These metaphorical tricksters keep mutating like viral atrocities. I work with a large format camerd and between the black hood, the camerd and subject there are demons of dreams. A visual pun, mnemonic devices, a story by the model perhaps will bring manifestations betond any one identity. I am just a tool of a bigger force. People, objects, and ideas come my way. I become a caretaker of sorts. I would like for people to say that I'm taking good care. It's based on some uncommon love I discovered with some deaths*

They lost me once they hit 'camerd.' Either that's the best example of Engrish ever, or my puny American mind isn't deep enough to understand the profound statement they were trying to make. I'd been looking through the shelves for shirts with Kanji on them, but couldn't find even one. Japanese wanted English letters, whether or not it made sense – not Kanji.

After running into a used English bookstore, we stopped to have a teriyaki burger at McDonalds. I was impressed in that although the meat patty was significantly smaller and thinner than those in the US and it seemed much less greasy. Even so, I never went back to McDonalds, deciding that if I had to have fast food, I could at least have it Japanese style. As Cayte, Mana and I ate and laughed together, I knew I was blessed to have found such good people so quickly. Our day ended at 4 o'clock. We'd seen all we wanted to see and were tired of exploring the nooks and crannies of Kichijoji.

I find the mikoshi matsuri to be the most endearing celebration because they occur right in the midst of the big city. The people keep the tradition and don't let the passing of time or the building of roads and skyscrapers deter them from their dance and parade. I'm sure every culture has parades like these that go way back in the history of the country. Maybe the Kichijoji mikoshi matsuri struck me so deeply because it was my first experience. It would not be my last.

Chapter 6 – Getting a Taste of Tokyo
September 14, Sunday morning

I spent the entire morning dutifully engrossed in my Japanese history assignment. Then, with scribbled directions in hand, I threw my gym bag over my shoulder and I set out in search of Gutsman Shooto Gym. I'd heard good things about the gym and wanted to see if they had more MMA sparring classes than Cross Point. Maybe I could go to both schools. On the way, I wolfed down a package of sushi at the conbini.

"It's nuts how I can get good quality sushi in a convenience store," I thought. "My host mother would probably disagree, though. Seems like the Japanese can taste the difference between the quality of sushi cut early that morning versus five minutes before hitting your plate. Oh no, what's that?"

A nutty chocolate cake had caught my eye in a bakery.

"Now, Roxy," I said sternly to myself, acutely conscious of my impending weight gain, "Cayte said it's impolite to eat while walking. Or while standing on the street. Or on the train. Or on the bus. Or anywhere in public, for that matter. Therefore, you must not buy that nut cake."

After buying the nut cake, I looked around for a place to eat it. Trying to be a good citizen, I stood behind a pole down a side street. Looking suspiciously around, I whispered, "Itadaki masu!" which means, "Ready to eat!"

In reality, a foreign girl lurking behind a pole would encourage more curious stares than chomping down on a dessert in plain view.

I took the Chu train line to Kichijoji, and transferred to the Inokashira line. My stop was Meidaimae station. I quickly learned how to recognize place names in Kanji. Couldn't write them from memory, but my Kanji recognition improved significantly over time. I also learned the pronunciation of each character because the train conductor always calls out over the loudspeaker, "We are now arriving in..."

"Finally," I thought, "Meidaimae! That took about 40 minutes."

Hopping off the train, I whipped out my directions. Convenience stores, drug stores, and little mom-and-pop shops lined the streets, but the area was mainly residential. In less than a minute, I found Gutsman Gym. It was practically in view of the station. I entered ten minutes before the striking class started. The nice Japanese man who greeted me reminded me of two of my former training partners back in Amherst; John Baccman and Rob Feiner. That meant he was pretty good-looking. Homesickness stabbed me like a knife, though kind of like a butter knife. I was too excited to be lonely.

The main instructor then came over and attempted conversation, but for some reason, we weren't very successful. I did manage to get information about the classes and schedules via the paper he handed me, but he spoke fast and kept using words I didn't know.

"I'm currently training at Cross Point in Kichijoji," I said, pretty sure my Japanese was dead on.

"What?" he said.

"Do you know Cross Point?"

"What?" he repeated.

"She said that she's training at Cross Point in Kichijoji," the John-Rob-looking guy filled in, using practically the exact wording I did. I sighed. Must have been my pronunciation.

"I do Brazilian jiu jitsu and Muay Thai there," I said.

"Blah blah blah! Feel free!" the main instructor said with a smile, gesturing towards people warming up.

"Oh, thank you!" I said. "I think I'll just watch."

He paused, then smiled, then went away to attend to something else.

I sat in a corner hugging my knees. The class was alright. I missed the Muay Thai gym Sityodtong back in Boston. The guys in the Gutsman class did basic movements first, like bouncing back and forth, on their toes, jabbing for a minute, then jab-cross combinations for a minute.

A young lady hurried in a few minutes late.

60

Let's see how they treat her, I thought, watching everyone's behavior intently.

As I feared, there were an odd number of people. When the men paired up to do drills and hold focus mitts for each other, the instructor told her to hit the heavy bag off to the side. He didn't give her any particular combinations to work on. She didn't seem to have any aim, or know what to do. She threw single kicks and single punches only. I felt bad for her, and feared that if I joined class, I'd share the same fate. She 'worked over' the heavy bag for at least one third of the class.

What are the grappling classes like, I wondered.

I had heard they were pretty good. I also wanted to find a gym that held MMA classes. Cross Point had one "Shooto" day on Thursday evenings, but people didn't do "MMA sparring." Everyone I talked to said that it was rare to find a dojo that held the mixed martial arts sessions. They either did stand-up like Muay Thai or kickboxing, or ground like BJJ or submission grappling.

I pondered these things while watching the class progress, and finally the students did light sparring. The class was decent enough that I'd enjoy training there, but at the same time I wasn't blown out of the water with dazzling new moves.

"Don't forget, Rox, you weren't so impressed when you saw Cross Point's first class," I reminded myself.

"Thanks so much for letting me watch. Maybe I'll come back and observe the grappling class next time!" I told the John-Rob-looking instructor after the class had ended.

"You're more than welcome!" the friendly Japanese man said with a smile.

I picked up my bag and headed to the door only to be faced with main owner again. He had in tow a man who could speak a little English, and we chatted some more.

In hindsight, now I know that it's very unusual for someone to train at two different dojos. In Japan, people have loyalty to one gym. At the time, I didn't know this.

"Well, could I train here, too? But could I possibly pay a reduced price? I can't afford to pay two gyms at once..."

"Oh, I'm sorry...that might be difficult... Why don't you try it?"

I blinked. "Try what?"

"Give it a try. Here are some gloves. Here, he will hold pads for you." He motioned towards the handsome instructor.

"Oh, I have to get going," I said, inching towards the door again.

"Nonsense, nonsense!" They all laughed at me and motioned at me again to don my gloves. I finally took off my glasses and faced the hot instructor.

"Okay, jab!" he called out. I squinted at the mitt and then jabbed. My glove made a loud "thwack," which echoed over the abandoned mat. All the students who were gathering their gear off to the side paused to watch us.

"Whoa! Sugoi! Amazing!" he shrieked. "Jab cross!"

I hit the mitt twice in succession.

"Sugoi sugoi!" he yelled, every time it connected.

It wasn't really that amazing. I knew for a fact that my aim wasn't that good, but he was compensating for me. Anyone's glove will make a loud smacking sound against the plastic front of the focus mitt.

He changed the combinations to jab cross, jab uppercut. The owner called out various combos, and the instructor complied. I felt like I was being tested. I hoped that somehow if I passed, they would let me have a discount.

After the owner was done calling out moves, I bowed to everyone and we put away our equipment.

Embarrassed, I jokingly asked, "So, now that I passed the test, can I have a discount?"

"Oh, difficult," came the response, this time accompanied with a laugh. I had yet to learn that people never made exceptions in Japan.

"Then that's the end of that," I thought. "Might as well not bother coming back to watch the grappling class. I'm sure it's a good, gym, but I already joined Cross Point."

Putting my glasses back on, feeling a little sweaty, I noticed everyone standing around watching me. I didn't know what to do with myself after that.

Promising to return to watch their grappling class, which was a lie, I excused myself and went to Cross Point. I never went back, although I'm sure they had much better classes than the one I observed. I've heard of some good fighters coming out of that dojo, making it to promotions like Shooto, Deep, Pancrase, etc.

It only took 20 minutes to get back to Kichijoji, and I threw myself into training. This was my home, and I didn't have to worry about choosing one or the other.

My excitement was short-lived when I tweaked my shoulder, forcing me to stop training early.

Damn my luck, I thought, trudging home. At 4:30 I pushed open the creaky wooden door, but before I could unpack, I was greeted by my host mother.

"I won at the horse race!" she announced.

I grinned. "Oh great! Congratulations!" I knew that during the season, she went to the racetracks quiet frequently.

"I got sushi!" she continued.

"YAY!" I cheered. A smile bloomed on her face, seeing my pleased reaction. We both loved sushi, and she bought the 'high quality' stuff after winning at the racetracks.

"Hey, Nei-san," my host mother said to me after dinner. She spoke loudly to be heard over the TV news. "Do you have plans tomorrow? It's a national holiday: Grandparent's Day. No school, right?"

"Actually, I was going to go to Asakusa with Cayte tomorrow," I replied.

"Did you promise?"

"Um...."

She said some things I didn't understand about skiing, the mountains, and their "se-kon-do ha-oos."

"Se...seko?" I tried to repeat.

"Hai, se-kon-do haoose."

I ran the Japanese through my brain filter a few more times. "Oh, second house? Like a summer house?"

With real estate prices being through the roof, how could a family have a house in Tokyo, and then a vacation house elsewhere?

"Yes, we have a second house in the mountains," my host mother insisted. "Will you come?"

"Uh, sure." Going to Asakusa with Cayte could wait.

"Okay, let's go! We'll wait for Mitsunori-san to come home."

"Wait, now? You want to go tonight?" My jaw dropped. It was almost eight o'clock Sunday night.

"Yes, yes! In an hour! We'll come back on Tuesday. What time is your first class?"

"Oh! Uh. It's, uh, at 10am. Okay. I'll call my friend back..."

"I'm sorry!" My host mother smiled and began to collect the dirty dishes. "I'm sorry!"

"It's okay. No problem!" I said, and went into the other room, thinking, "She certainly apologizes a lot. Maybe I should apologize back." Picking up my cell phone, I speed dialed Cayte's number.

"Hi Cayte? Yeah, my host family randomly wants to take me to their summer house tonight and just told me..."

I heard Cayte laugh on the other end of the line. "That's totally fine! Host families tend to do that."

"They do, huh?"

"Yeah. We'll go to Asakusa some other time! Have fun with your family!"

"Okay, thanks."

I packed my recharger and was just going through my clothes when my host mother stuck her head in my room. "It's cold, so pack pants and long sleeves!" she said. I nodded.

"Cold, huh?" I muttered out loud. We have different definitions of temperatures. Her "cool" was my "kind of warm and sticky."

I dutifully packed jeans, two long sleeve shirts, and my warm fleece soccer jacket. An hour later found me climbing into the back seat of her Volvo with Fortune. The dog sat tense and expectant on the seat beside me for all of five seconds before

64

fidgeting. The big golden lab tried to climb into the front, poking his head out the window, and climb on me.

"Get down," I ordered tiredly, buckling my seat belt. "I wish I could buckle you in, too." He laid his head on my lap.

"Cute, but um, no. Dog drool!" I pushed it off. Residual slobber discolored the thigh of my pants. "Ick."

With my host brother at the wheel, we pulled out of the driveway. He expertly navigated the back alleyways, deftly turning sharp corners and squeezing down paths almost the very width of the car.

"By the way, how long is the ride?" I called up front, arching my neck, trying to read the street signs as we turn onto the main road.

"About three hours."

"Oh," I said, surprised. We really were going to the mountains.

Driving in Japan is much different from driving in the States. It took half an hour for us to get to a highway. Tokyo is its own experience.

"This road is so narrow," I commented. "It's like they're not even made for cars at all!"

"I know!" Sadako called back to me. "Tokyo streets are so narrow!"

"What happens if we meet another car? Oh!" A pair of headlights nearly blinded us as another car came around the corner. The other driver quickly turned them down. Mitsunori-san brought the car to an abrupt stop, and put it in reverse. We backed up a few yards to a wide shoulder and let the other car pass.

"I see," I said.

I really enjoyed the car ride. Japanese drivers show politeness and patience by non-aggressive driving. I heard that some people speed, but I didn't notice anybody go zooming by us on the highway, as I would have in the States. The speed limits were lower, and I noticed that buses drove especially slower.

It was dark so I missed a lot of the scenery, but instead I was treated to a view of multicolored lights spanning out across the country. I kept my face plastered to the side window and watched

Tokyo fade away. As the car climbed a hill, I watched the magnificent skyscrapers sink lower and lower. Lights from smaller buildings and homes spread out as our raised highway took us past the suburbs. Not only yellows and reds lit up the night, but also blues and greens and all colors of the rainbow.

"What city are we passing by?" I asked. They said a name I didn't recognize.

My brain was drifting in and out of dreamland when the car crunched down a gravel driveway halted in front of a mass of nature. As soon as Sadako-san opened the back door, Fortune bounded out and went crashing unseen through the brush. Groggy, I blinked and looked around. A few neighboring houses were all but enclosed in woods. Twigs snapped to my left. A second later, leaves rustled to my right. I turned my face upwards. Through the trees, I saw red Mars, sitting serenely in the sky. Next to me, Mitomori-san lit a cigarette. Sadako-san walked down a stone path to turn the outside lights on.

"We're here! The second house!" Sadako-san called back to me. Fortune came pelting across my line of vision, suddenly illuminated by the floodlights, and just as quickly vanished.

Their "second house" turned out to be as big as their house in Koganei. Surrounded by nature, it had a modern flavor surrounded by a traditional air. Sadako-san informed me that they've owned it for twenty years, and kept it in amazing condition. Aside from dead bugs scattered everywhere, the tatami mats were practically dirt free and absolutely stainless. Things like linens and futons were neatly tucked away in closets. In fact, it seemed like every wall opened into a closet, and those that didn't were doors that slid sideways open and shut. I started to wonder how the house was supported if everything could slide.

There was only cold running water until Sadako-san went back outside to turn a knob. A wide family room with a wood burning stove connected the hall and the good-sized kitchen. After briefly showing me around, we got out the futons and went to bed.

Monday, September 15

Sadako-san brought out leftover sushi for breakfast.

"I'll never get tired of sushi," I commented, stuffing my face with the last tuna roll sushi. "I could eat this every day!"

After cleaning up after breakfast, my host mother went into her room and came out with a towel. She tossed it at me.

"We're going to an onsen now!" she announced. "You've never been to one before, right?"

I shook my head. I'd been warned about onsen, a Japanese hot spring. Everybody got naked and took a bath together. The pools were separated by gender, of course.

Sadako-san smiled at my less than enthusiastic reaction.

"You're embarrassed, right? Foreigners are always embarrassed to get naked with others, right?"

"Well..." That wasn't really the reason. Although I wasn't keen on walking around naked, it just sounded, well, kind of boring. I was determined to withhold judgment until after tried it.

Japanese hot springs are known all over the world as being relaxing, luxurious, and healing. It took us about ten minutes by car to arrive at the small, cozy wooden building.

"Will you be alright?" Sadako-san kept asking on the drive there, continually glancing over her shoulder at me in the back. "Will you be embarrassed?"

From her amused smile, I could tell she was looking forward to 'introducing' the bashful foreigner to traditional Japanese customs.

It wasn't so bad. Once you see no one else has a problem, you feel better about it. Cayte later joked that if a bunch of Americans ever went together, everyone would be too self-conscious and end up all going in with bathing suits.

We went into the back room and stripped off our clothes.

"Here, put them in this cubby," my host mother instructed. Our bare feet thudded on the wood tiles of the changing room. I followed her into the shower room, and our footfalls went 'slap slap' on the smooth tiles. Short knee-high stools stood lined up side by side in front of a wall that had shower heads attached to tubes.

"First you wash yourself," my elderly host mother explained, "Then get in the hot springs. Then get out, wash yourself, get in, get out, get in, like this," Sadako-san said, making the motions of washing her arms. "Your skin becomes tsuru tsuru." I blinked.

"It becomes what?"

"Tsuru tsuru!" she exclaimed, rubbing her bare arms vigorously, and then nearly shoved me towards a stool.

"Oh, okay." I dumbly washed myself, and then followed her outside to a pond held by rocks. The water came up to my waist. A fountain of mineral water spurted out of a cluster of rocks off to the side. We lowered ourselves in and sat on the rocky floor. The water came up to our necks. It was warm, but not too hot.

Sadako-san heaved a heavy sigh of contentment as she lowered herself into the steamy waters.

"This feels great, doesn't it?" she said, sinking in up to her neck and gliding around the pool.

"Oh, sure," I mumbled into the water. A bug that wasn't quite an ant crawled up the rock I was leaning against. I watched it intently. In the water floated little yellow particles of metal sulfides and gypsum that looked like ocean sponge fragments. They slid through my fingers when I tried to catch one. Finally catching one against the rock wall, I squished it. It smeared like mud in my palm.

"So, Nei-san," my host mother said, floating over to me. She bumped shoulders with me as she sat herself down on my rock shelf. "So now we stay in here, and then you get out and wash yourself over there again, and then you come back here. You do that a bunch of times and it really feels great."

"Yeah, you had said that before," I said, still unconvinced. It all sounded kind of stupid to me. "I think I'll stay here."

"But you'll become..." and said a word that didn't register in my vocabulary.

"I'll become....?"

"Your skin!"

"Oh, that's okay," I said, guessing it meant 'wrinkly.' "No problem," if it did indeed mean wrinkly. Didn't want to change into a mutant or something, due to over-sulfide exposure.

I felt a little guilty conveying such indifference to my host mother, who earnestly wanted to share this wonderful Japanese experience with me. In fact, besides the naked part, every other person I've met adored the onsen except me. *I guess I'm just a weirdo*, I thought.

There was another smaller pool indoors near the showers, but it was extremely hot, and I couldn't stand to get in. I figured it must be for onsen veterans who undoubtedly train three times a day. The goal? To bear the hot liquid and earn the title "I-can-stay-in-the-hottest-pool-the-longest" Champion of the World title belt. Or maybe it was for boiling lobsters to have for lunch after soaking. I couldn't think of another reason to have that pool that temperature.

Overall, I had a good time chatting with my host mother and learning new words. Tsuru tsuru meant "smooth" or "slippery." I felt overwhelmed with relief when she suggested leaving. I'd gotten bored near the end, and all I could think about was how much homework I had to do.

My family paid my onsen fee, for which I was very grateful. "We'll stop at an outdoor grocery on the way home," Sadako-san said, as we all piled into the car. However, when Mitsunori pulled over, instead of tables of cabbages and carrots, I found myself looking up at a huge field with dozens of satellite dishes lined up like crops to be harvested. And at the far end of the field...

"Um, is this the..."

"No, no, this is a side-stop," Sadako-san said. Mitsunori smiled. "It's the biggest 45mm radio dish in the world!"

"Wow, uh okay." How random.

To get closer to the main dish, we walked down a path that led through a field of one-story tall satellite dishes with their faces upturned to the sky. It gave me a strange futuristic feeling. I've certainly never seen anything like that in the United States. The smaller dishes were planted in neat, organized rows, as if a giant were growing a garden. The mother dish loomed in the distance.

My digital camera captured the moment, and when we went into a tiny museum, I picked up an English brochure. The museum was more like a picture gallery with photos of space exploration hanging on every wall. They also had a flight simulator, but the line was long and we didn't tarry.

The next stop was an open-air market with cabbage, apples, pears, eggplant, and other vegetables piled high on tables. I enjoyed the ride through the mountain countrysides and took lots of pictures of the cloud-hidden mountaintops. I could see how the sights inspired poets and travelers, and how religious personages felt in touch with their gods in a place like Japan.

We didn't do anything amazing after lunch except sleep, study, and take a nature walk. The plan had been to return early Tuesday morning, but Sadako-san changed her mind.

"We'll go back tonight," she announced abruptly as we sat around watching TV. "After the baseball finishes at 9pm!"

What a random day, I thought, as we packed up the car. Soon enough, we were speeding home towards Tokyo.

Friday, September 19

A beautiful Japanese woman walked into the Cross Point dojo. I looked up from chatting with Zuyo on the sidelines. The ice pack balanced on my aching shoulder slipped off, and I reached to retrieve it. On the mat, students clad in the thick white jiu jitsu gis had just started free sparring. Kotani wandered around supervising.

"That girl is a purple belt!" Zuyo exclaimed quite audibly. "Her name is Yukie."

Hearing her, the slender lady looked over and smiled shyly. Kindness radiated from her gentle oval face. Her fashionable style showed off her lovely slender figure. My jaw almost dropped.

"She's also a black belt in judo," Zuyo continued, nodding to Yukie, as she approached. "She's also Uematsu-san's girlfriend, you know," Zuyo added in a hushed whisper.

70

Blinking away my surprise, I politely stood. "Hello, I'm Roxanne," I introduced myself, shaking her hand and bowing my head.

"I'm Yukie," she replied. "Nice to meet you." Her almost shoulder-length brown hair fell forward when she nodded her head, and then fell back, neatly framing her face.

"You're training today?" I asked.

"Yes," she said.

"Oh, boy!" I thought. "I'll get to try my skills against a Japanese purple belt!"

I grinned, my shoulder ache almost forgotten. She went to change and I practically drooled while waiting for her to come out. Mostly men populated full-contact martial arts clubs around the world. I'd only trained with one other female purple belt named Thayse at the Brazilian Top Team Boston's school in Everett, near Boston. Women rely more on technique than strength, being smaller than their male counterparts who can often get away with using muscle to force a win.

Sliding my ice pack back in the freezer, I asked her if she wanted to spar a round. She pointed to my shoulder but I made light of it.

We had an excellent sparring match. I was impressed by her technique, and I didn't do too badly.

"Don't kid yourself, Roxy," I told myself. "You still have a ways to go before you reach purple belt. You had fifteen pounds on her, and plus, you didn't even give her a chance to warm up."

"Are you going to come often from now on?" I asked her during an interval between rounds.

"I'm afraid not," she replied. "I still have nagging injuries. And I'm also very busy with work and everything."

"What do you do?"

"I'm an elementary school teacher."

Fighting with Yukie had started my shoulder throbbing, so I reclaimed my seat on the side with the ice pack. Zuyo soon re-joined me. I loved talking to her. She understood my bad Japanese, and made a big effort to explain new words to me.

As we watched, the jiu jitsu class moved over to one side of the room, and a kickboxing class started warming up on the other. I wanted to join in, but didn't want to stress my shoulder. I turned to Luke, a bilingual second generation Japanese-American. He was drinking some water between rounds of sparring.

"What's the word for 'torture?'" I asked.

"Goumo," he replied. I immediately turned to Kotani-sensei and said "Miru dake wa goumo desu." This was my attempt to say, "Just watching is torture."

"Eeeeh?!" he exclaimed. Zuyo burst out laughing. Tatsu came over and said, "Goumo is pubic hair!"

"What?" I exclaimed. "Then what's 'torture?'"

"Goumon," Tatsu said.

"I said 'goumo!' I protested.

"No, no. With an 'n,'" he corrected, with a smile.

"Oooh! Hey, that's not fair!" I protested. The Japanese nasalize their "N's" and English speakers' ears often don't pick it up.

"Luke, I hate you!" I called to him.

"I said 'goumon!'" he insisted from across the room. The rest of the class hid smiles and chuckled to themselves. The dojo wasn't that big, so of course everyone could hear the exchange.

On the way home, I had a very Japanese-style experience of being crammed onto a rush hour train. Long lines of people waited in an orderly fashion on the platform. The train pulled up, and all of a sudden, all politeness was forgotten. People already in the train tried to place their buts in the seats of those who got up to disembark. Those on the platform pushed and shoved to get on.

That night, the train was especially crowded. As I stepped onto the train, or rather backed in, I believed that I was the last one who could possibly fit aboard that particular car. Apparently I was wrong. The girl behind me exclaimed Uso! or "No way!" and tried to cram herself in behind me. Well, in front of me. As if the next train wasn't coming in five minutes.

I tried to step forward to make more room. The entire mass of people started to fall forward as one. I tottered awkwardly diagonally. She and three friends squeezed in after me. The doors closed a little, opened again, and closed a little before finally

72

managing to close completely. I was leaning full force against the man in front of me, who was pressed against someone else. The girl behind me rested her chin on my shoulder, and the guy on my left had his elbow on my boob for two more stops. He wore nice cologne, though. I, on the other hand, most definitely stunk from working out.

The surprising thing was that I didn't really mind. It amused me, actually. Every human being has a sphere of personal space. If you step into that space, the person will unconsciously move out of it, by taking a step forward or to the side. I studied this in my University psychology class, and tested it out on unknowing acquaintances a few times. However, in places like crowded trains or in elevators, which forces people to get into close proximity, people do everything they can to pretend they don't notice. People avoid eye contact, stare at the floor counter screen in elevators, etc. I noticed that everyone on the train either looked at reading material, cell phones, or the advertisements hanging off the ceiling.

At one point the girl next to me wanted to get out. Unfortunately for her, the doors farthest away from us opened. I wondered how she would manage to get to the other side of the car since no one could move, but somehow she slithered through. I said ganbatte, or "good luck!" and she and her friends laughed. There was much smiling, bumping, and stepping on feet, but no one really said excuse me.

"There's a saying in Japan," my Japanese teacher, Hirata-sensei once said. "If a businessman said 'excuse me' to everyone he bumped into in the morning, he wouldn't get to work on time. It's not about being rude. There's simply no space."

Saturday, September 20
"Ikebukuro"

I collapsed on the tatami-mat floor of my bedroom Saturday afternoon wet, exhausted, and hungry.

"What the hell did I just buy?" I thought, letting my bags fall to either side of me. My host mother called out a greeting to me. I muttered something back.

Cayte introduced me to Candie, and we fast became friends. Candie, in turn, introduced me to Rachel. We four Americans made the hour and a half trip to the lively district of Tokyo called Ikebukuro. There stood Animate: largest anime store I've ever seen in my life. It hosted eight floors of anime goodness, which induced massive bouts of money spending. One floor was manga, Japanese comic books, for girls. The next floor was manga for boys. Then DVDs and music CDs, trading cards and toys, VHS tapes, clothes and accessories, and any kind of models, nick-knacks or do-dads you could imagine. I found myself picking up a box or a thing wrapped in plastic, murmuring to myself, "What is this? What does this do? Maybe I'll buy it because it has a picture of Goku on it," which is probably just what the manufacturers want us to think.

We emerged almost dizzily, and the girls started talking about dinner.

"I gotta get back," I said apologetically. "I have to train. There's a kickboxing class tonight."

Rachel gave me directions to the station, and told me which lines I needed to take. The train system wasn't that confusing, but changing lines can be complicated, especially when you're hungry. And your shoulder hurts. And you're soaking wet. The half an hour wait at the Musashi Sakai bus station frustrated me further, after which I was blessed with the experience of biking home in the rain. I mimicked the Japanese by holding an umbrella in one hand and the handlebars in the other.

"How do they not kill themselves on a daily basis," I asked myself, as my bike splashed through puddles. My precious anime merchandise bounced on my back as I flew through the dusk. I worried about it getting wet as the wind blew the rain under my umbrella.

I made it back in time for dinner.

"What? You just got back, and now you're going to kickboxing?" My host mother was incredulous.

74

"Yes, I have to train!" I said, wolfing down some sweetened potatoes and beef stew. Somehow I had enough energy for a fine night of kickboxing.

Chapter 7 – The Language Barrier
Sunday, September 21

I woke up in an excellent mood. I dreamt that I'd returned home to Boston for Christmas.

"Already?" I thought. "It feels like I barely spent any time in Tokyo at all! I need to go back!"

During the dream, I drove around the twisted Boston streets in my 2000 black Toyota Corolla. "Sure beats biking in the rain."

Shortly after this dream, I adopted a positive saying to help me look on the bright side of a bad situation: "At least I'm not peddling."

Slowly, I drifted back to the real world. My spine cracked as I sat bolt upright. The previous night at jiu-jitsu, I'd done everything I'd been aching to do. I boxed with a professional fighter and sparred MMA, doing reasonably well both times. I drove myself to make that extra effort that's so hard to achieve when you're bone tired. Lately, I'd been running up sets of stairs and biking a lot, always keeping my goals in mind - I wanted to fight professionally.

The incessant rain didn't stop me from biking to a video rental store on the way to the train station.

VHS tapes and DVDs of both American and Japanese movies lined the shelves from floor to ceiling. Passing into the anime section was like walking into heaven.

"This is like a dream!" I thought, perusing the aisles of anime. "Or rather, more like a nightmare!"

It was like Pandora's Box. Although I saw countless anime I longed to watch, none of them had English subtitles. "Why should they?" We were in Japan. I wanted to rent something, but not too difficult.

"Hmmm, what looks interesting?" I wondered, trying to judge the DVD by its cover. Then I saw it- scrawled in kanji with the English under it: *She, the Last Weapon*.

"Weird," I thought, and snagged the next Shaman King DVD. The fan-subbing group stopped at episode 30. "Maybe I can finally find out what happens to You-kun and Amidamaru!"

Paying roughly six dollars, I hurried home and popped the "She" tape in the VCR. To my disappointment, there was only one episode on the tape.

As I had feared, I didn't really understand *She, The Last Weapon*. Something about a high school boy and girl who had feelings for each other, and then suddenly their country was bombed for reasons that escaped me. Finally, the girl turned into something with metal wings, and the boy was surprised. Very surprised. I could see the surprise written all over his face. The camera zoomed in to get a closer view of his surprise. The end. It lasted all of 20 minutes.

"Uh-huh. Damn, only one episode? Okay, bad choice. Next."

Shaman King made a little more sense because I'd been watching that series for a year with subtitles, and knew how the characters spoke.

The rain rode in on a cold front. As I sat down to do some homework, I wrapped a blanket around my shoulders. My fingers clicked clacked against the keyboard of my laptop.

Tick tick. "Hmmm I feel a draft. Where? To my right."

The blanket fell from my shoulders as I went to investigate the source. To my right stood wall-length sliding glass doors near my bed. They were closed, but my heart sunk when I saw the crack. The word "crack" doesn't do it justice. It was a gap. The door was crooked or warped, making it impossible to close all the way. Wind whistled through a space about an inch wide. Visions filled my mind of turning into a Popsicle in my sleep.

"Nah, I'll be warm enough," I told himself, and went back to my homework. Little did I know that old Japanese houses had no indoor heating.

Monday, September 22

"Surely they must have it here," I thought as I entered the giant discount shop, Don Quixote. The reasoning behind the name escaped me as much as why the store logo is a little, stoned-looking blue penguin with a D written on his stomach.

I eventually located what appeared to be the electronics department. A myriad of colorful fascinating gadgets hung off hooks from shelves everywhere. An assortment of nonsensical T-shirts hung from walls and the ceiling, stealing my attention away from the matter at hand.

"I must not get distracted. I'm on a mission!"

A tall, skinny store clerk in his early 20's stood with his arms full of merchandize, stocking the shelves.

"Excuse me," I said in Japanese to the man.

"Yes?" the man said, shifting his attention to me. His face smiled. His eyes said, "Oh, no, a foreigner! I can't speak English..."

"I'm looking for something."

"Yes?"

"Well...I don't know how to say it in Japanese."

He looked at me expectantly. I sighed and launched into my best description: "It's small and when batteries are finished, you put them inside, and electricity goes in. Then you take the batteries out, and they're new again."

The man blinked. His smile froze on his lips.

"No?" I took a deep breath. "Uh, it's a small 'machine,'" I threw in the English word. "And you 'plug' it in." This seemed to throw him into a panic, and he looked around wildly, as if a co-worker would suddenly materialize and rescue him. I continued hurriedly, "And so anyway, you put 'batteries' inside. The electricity goes in, and they come out new! The batteries, that is."

The man shook his head. "There's nothing like that here," he said. His hands twitched, eager to return to their previous task.

All I wanted was a damn battery charger. I've been asking in every store that sold electronics and nobody seemed to know what I was talking about. In my mind, old batteries + machine + electricity = new batteries is a simple enough concept that might cause any person other than a five year old child to guess correctly.

Maybe I was conjugating "to go in" incorrectly. Maybe they didn't use "ba-te'ri" for "batteries." (They didn't, actually, they used denchi but I didn't realize it at the time.) Or maybe it was my gaijin foreign accent. Nevertheless, my numerous descriptions weren't good enough for three store clerks at three different stores, although the fourth one got the idea when I decided to add the "goes in old, comes out new!" part.

"Sorry, we don't have it," he informed me politely, yet firmly. Or maybe he just wanted me to leave and torture some other store clerk.

"I'm spending so much freaking money on batteries for my CD player," I lamented silently. "And why isn't this word in my dictionary? It has to exist!" I thought near tears, checking for the fifth time. In an electronically advanced country like Japan, it just had to.

The quest had become less about being an ecologically-friendly cheapskate, and more to a personal failure on my part to attain what I was looking for. I gave up looking after an entire afternoon of search.

Next item...a space heater.

"What?! Not in the season?" I repeated the words of a clerk, incredulous. "It sure is cold, though, isn't it!"

"Um, well..." The nice middle-aged man of Yamada Denki didn't seem to share my opinion. "That may be, but it's still not the season," he said matter-of-factly, not impressed that a foreigner could kind of speak Japanese. "But in another month or so, they should cost roughly two hundred dollars for a good one.

The next day at school, I ranted to Cayte about my futile searches. "What is their idea of cold?" I exclaimed.

"I dunno," Cayte had shrugged. "The Japanese are...different."

This became a very common explanation of things we found strange or disconcerting in Japan. And my new motto was born: accept it, handle it, and move on.

Tuesday, September 23

"That's one big hanging lantern thingy," I said out loud to myself, as I stood at the Kaminari Mon – Lightning Gate. After one hour, plus eight dollars worth of train tickets, I found myself in the city district called Asakusa.

Tourist shops lined the streets starting right in front of subway exit. I found myself accosted by the urge to buy everything I saw. It either looked delicious, culturally interesting, or screamed out "souvenir!"

From Kaminari mon, I walked approximately 250 meters down the Nakamise street to the huge temple Hozo mon. Shops jammed side-by-side attracted tourists with their colorful bobbles. It is said that the street retains the feeling of downtown Edo in the Meiji era (1867-1912). Such a condensed setup began when laborers, who were forced to clean the temple compound, were permitted to set up shops as compensation. The shops were merely little rooms about the size of a college dorm that sold anything you could ever want in a souvenir. I saw 50 varieties of key chains, statues, dolls, kimono, fake swords, real swords, shoes, chopsticks, kitchenware, snacks, mirrors, scrolls, and an infinite number of collectable figurines. Some of them had stickers that said, "Made in China," and a few of the T-shirts were made in the USA.

A Hayao Miyazaki specialty store hit me first. It sold merchandise from movies done by the famous director, such as *Princess Mononoke, Spirited Away,* and *Kiki's Delivery Service.* The urge to buy everything was like an unreachable itch in the back of my mind. My fingers twitched to constantly reach into my back pocket to pull out my wallet. I stopped in a store with traditional Japanese fans and hanging-scrolls. They also had little models and figurines of chickens.

"Excuse me," I ended up asking the plump little old shop owner. She finished wrapping another customer's goods and turned a bored-looking face in my direction. "Why are there so many chickens everywhere?"

She replied using some vocabulary I didn't understand, followed by "It's the year of the chicken."

80

"Oh!" I said. "The Chinese zodiac! Right?" She simply nodded.

Many shrines all around Japan had been burned down either by accident a few hundred years ago, or in World War II, but the cultural landmarks had been rebuilt. Halfway down the Nakamise, I spotted the top floors of the Five Story Pagoda, built on the edge of the compound. Originally constructed by Iemitsu Tokugawa in the mid-1600s, it was burnt down during the war only to be rebuilt in 1973. At 175 feet tall, it's the second tallest in Japan, the tallest being the 184 foot tall pagoda of Toji Temple in Kyoto. The Kaminari Mon itself had been burned and resurrected as well.

Japanese tourists and foreigners snapped pictures left and right. I felt comfortable strolling around gawking with my camera dangling around my neck. I loved the paper lanterns the most. They were so stereotypically Japanese, so when I saw a cheap mini version for five hundred yen, roughly six dollars, I bought it. I also bought a key chain with a makeki neko, or "waving kitty" on it. The white kitty sat upright with one paw raised and has the other resting on a cold koban, an old-fashioned coin. It's the symbol of good luck and they are in every Japan souvenir shop. But don't forget: "Neko ni koban." It's a waste to give a cat a koban!

While passing through one of the small shops, I heard a frustrated woman's voice, exclaim, "They really should learn how to speak English!"

This struck me as an incredibly stupid thing for a foreigner to say while visiting a foreign country. Curiosity got the better of me.

I ducked under a tapestry and headed in the direction of the voice to see if maybe I could help with something.

I spotted a short lady and her husband, whose nationality I couldn't quite identify. The woman was jabbing her finger at a wind charm, which hung out of reach above a glass figurine case.

"That one! That one!" the woman said to the storekeeper, raising her voice. "That one!"

"Which one? How many?" the storekeeper was saying in heavily accented English, getting upset that the customer was raising her voice.

The chimes hung above their heads. The storekeeper pointed to a blue glass crystal chime.

"No, no!" the customer said, making sweeping hand motions that might as well have indicated the entire wall. "Not THAT one, THAT one!"

The storekeeper started to pick up a bag that was hung next to the wind chime.   "No, no! That!"

Frustrated, the shopkeeper turned away from the situation completely.

"She's ignoring me now?" the distraught customer exclaimed.

I slipped through the narrow aisles to stand next to them. "Excuse me, which one would you like? I speak Japanese."

The woman had her mouth open, presumably just about to explode to her husband. She heard my offer and blinked.

"Oh! Yes, thank you! Finally. That green one hanging over there."

"Ah, okay."

When the shopkeeper turned back to us, I politely described the chime in question.

"How many?"

"One, please."

"Okay." It was brought down and quickly wrapped.

"I also want that and that..." the customer went on to me.

"Great descriptions," I thought.

"The frog and the bunny statue?" I clarified.

"Yes."

I told the shopkeeper.

"You know, they really should learn to speak English so we can communicate!" the foreign woman said earnestly to me.

"Well, we are in Japan!" I replied with a rueful smile. The man standing next to her, who I assumed to be her husband, laughed.

"I kinda assume that it's my fault if I don't understand because I don't speak Japanese," I added gently, hoping she would realize how stupid her previous statement was. The lady smiled and shook her head.

82

"Where are you from?" I asked her.

"Thailand," she responded.

"Oh," I said. I'd been sure that she had a Latin accent. True to her statement, she turned around and spoke Thai to her husband. I didn't think people spoke much English in Thailand, so wasn't she being a bit hypocritical?

The shopkeeper rang the price up. I took my leave while the couple paid for their goods. It felt good to use what little Japanese I knew to smooth out an uncomfortable situation.

I continued down Nakamise until it came to and end, spilling out into a garden of shrines and statues. Straight ahead was the largest shrine in the complex- Sensoji Shrine. As I approached the entrance, I noticed a large cauldron-like object with a roof over it set out front. Powerful, smelly gray smoke billowed out from all sides. People went up to this thing before they entered the shrine, wafting the smoke over their heads with their hands. This cleansing ritual purifies people before entering the holy shrine.

The smoke smelled pretty bad to me and I had no desire to carry the smell away on my clothes, so I skipped that step. Immediately inside there were small windows where one could buy a delicate yet expensive charm. Straight ahead was a large bin covered with metal slats. People threw five-yen coins, clapped their hands, and prayed. The coins clanked noisily against the metal, alerting the kami, or natural gods, to the presence of the worshiper so it would come to hear the prayer.

I snapped a picture and kept moving. Statues and altars sat in view directly over the moneybox area, but a netting covered the door. No one was permitted to enter there.

Once outside again, I saw some small statues of Jizo, the wandering monk, who's the protector of lost children. Someone had tied a bright red apron around the stone neck. A statue of Buddha looked like a chef with a white apron and a fluffy hat. I took some lovely nature pictures of a serene waterfall amongst grass and well-kept trees. It was almost too beautiful to stay in for too long.

Eventually I wandered out of the shrine area and went downtown for a while, past random shops, pachinko machines, and convenience stores. At two o'clock I felt worn out and headed for home.

Chapter 8 - Ueno Park and a Fight Offer
Sunday, September 28

Anytime someone mentioned sightseeing in Tokyo, Ueno Park kept coming up. It's the largest and oldest park in Tokyo, with shrines, various temples, a huge pond, the famous Ueno Zoo, and five museums.

On Sunday Cayte, Candie and I withstood the troublesome hour and a half commute to the Park. At least the trip was mostly a straight shot and we only had to change trains once. After a while of standing, a few people got up and we got to sit down. A few people glanced in our direction as we pulled out food. It's socially unacceptable to eat on the train, but we were hungry.

"Whatever," Cayte said, tearing open the plastic bag, which held her freshly baked curry bread, a curious deep-fried bread roll with curry sauce inside. "Let them think we're stupid foreigners and don't know any better."

I wasn't about to argue with her.

Ueno was indeed a happening place. The station exits right into a mini market called Ameyoko, short for Ameya Yokochi, meaning Candy Store Alley. It was lined with a myriad of shops and stores selling all kinds of foods, clothing, and nick-knacks. Hawkers screamed about how delicious their fresh fish was, and live crabs blew bubbles in their buckets.

Huge trees peered over the tops of buildings across the street. Cayte, Candie and I left the market and walked down a wide path with tall trees bowing to us on either side. The Japanese had planted them with a caring, artful appreciation, like guardians of the walkways.

We decided to walk past the Shinobazu-no-ike pond first, and then visit the shrines, which were on the way to the Tokyo National Museum, our final destination.

"So where's the pond?" I asked. My two friends shrugged.

"That looks like a map." Candie pointed to a stone tablet a few meters away. We squinted at it for a few minutes.

"It should be right over...yeah, there it is!"

The roof of a shrine called Benten Hall was visible through the thick leaves of deciduous trees nearby. Benten is the Japanese name for the Hindu Saraswati - a goddess of everything that flows: water, words, speech, music and knowledge. Over the course of history, she became one of the seven Japanese gods of Fortune and can be seen on many statues of the seven characters riding a boat, carrying a biwa musical instrument.

"But it's supposed to be in the middle of the Shinobazu pond," I said. "I don't see a pond."

Huge plants with leaves twice as big as a human head were growing in a wide circumference around the shrine

"Maybe this isn't it," I said. "Why are you smiling, Candie?"

"Look closer," the soft-spoken American urged. I walked off the gravel path and up to a plat. And almost fell into the pond! All the plants were actually floating on the surface, like a vast field of lily pads.

"So no space is wasted in Japan after all," I commented.

The shrine was the size of a two-story house, lifted off the ground by a dozen or so red poles. Such support beams lined the corners of the cylindrical building, giving it octagonal edges. The red color complimented the white walls, making it stand out amidst the greenness of the surrounding nature.

Also known as Benzaiten, it looked like a mini pagoda with roofs on two levels, separating the first level from the second. The top roof had bronze trimmings and ornaments on top and around the edges.

To approach, we walked shoulder to shoulder on a narrow slate path. Stone pillars and black marble tablets with Chinese characters stood to either side of us. Our sneakers crunched on gravel when we strayed off the path to take a closer look. On the other side, a statue of a monk calmly held a staff. Someone tied a red apron and hat into him. Old haggard trees, only slightly taller than the pillars, oversaw all the activities on the little island.

In front of the shrine was the cauldron with a roof; inside incense burned. I'd seen the same thing in Asakusa. Turns out that every shrine had one.

"You wave the smoke over your head," Cayte said.

"For good luck?" I asked.

"Maybe that or cleansing," she replied. In addition to the incense pot, we made a stop at a roofed fountain, which stood a few paces away. We followed the cleansing ritual of pouring water over our hands.

Visitors weren't allowed into the shrine itself, so we peered into the dimly lit interior. Gold and silver-painted ornaments and statues glinted and shone in what little light came in.

We passed under the large wooden tori gate, leaving Shinobazu-no-ike.

"Let's look for the Inari shrine," Candie said.

"What's that?" I asked.

"That's the shrine to Inari, the kami, or god of rice, foxes, agriculture and fertility" she replied. "Look over there! See those small, red tori gates? They always lead the way to an Inari shrine."

We followed her pointing finger. Rather than one big one, there were many little tori lined up in a row, making a very interesting photo perspective-wise. They led to the "Gojo Tenjin" Shinto Shrine, neatly tucked neatly away among the trees and nature. A long rope attached to a gong hung down in front of the entrance. We took turns tugging on the rope, which hit the gong with a resounding clang. It supposedly summoned the shrine spirits to hear our wishes and prayers. A pair of fox statues was placed at the entrance to guard against evil spirits.

"Foxes are messengers of Inari. It looks like there's a tunnel here," Candie commented, taking the lead. We passed through it into dark cave where a grimacing dog statue greeted us on a pedestal right before the entrance.

"Is that a fox or a dog?" I asked, bringing my face up really close to it. "It really looks like a dog."

Another animal statue sat on a shelf, alongside a box containing some kind of symbolic figurines and incense. It smelled musty.

"Most dogs lived in caves," Candie commented absently, as we left.

Going back outside, the gates of the zoo loomed directly ahead of us, but we got side tracked by a giant dome-shrine, a Buddhist pagoda with a cone on the top. A giant Bodhisattva face was carved into a stone tablet on my right. The face was bigger than me and kind of creepy, but it made a good picture.

After paying our six hundred yen entrance fee, I was painfully reminded that little screaming children like to go to the zoo, too! Four-year-olds were constantly jumping out in front of us the entire time, which made it especially difficult for Cayte, who couldn't see. The kids would run between her long, thin, white cane and her legs, maybe thinking it a fun game of limbo. Luckily we never actually collided with one.

"I hate people!" she fumed. "And small children most of all!" Candie and Cayte were muttering under their breaths in a type of murderous serenade. Later on, Cayte amended that she only hated kids when they tried to make her fall on her face. She went on to become a happy kindergarten teacher.

I didn't mind the mass of families, though. Just another part of living alongside humanity. It was a very nice Saturday afternoon. We glanced at birds and took pictures of the monkeys. When we went to see the giant panda, though, we were in for a disappointment.

To begin with, the cages were in terrible condition. The floors were tiled like someone's shower. As if to make up for it, there was a small potted bush next to a small bathroom tub-like recession built into the ground for holding water. The giant panda was lying on a hard shelf looking very depressed. The "lesser panda" was pacing around like an irritated wolverine. I felt sorry for all the big animals that had to live in such small cages. Only the penguins looked happy with their nice pool and waterfall. They swam merrily around, splashing and playing.

Near a rest area we got to sit down for the first time. I set my bag down on the dirt next to the benches.

88

"Do we have time to go to the National Museum, at least?" I asked, munching on a doughnut. Candie was peeling open the rapper to a Popsicle she had bought.

"Well, it's 2:30 now. They close at 4:00..."she replied.

"Wanna still go?"

The girls agreed, and we pushed ourselves up off the benches. My feet felt like lead. We followed a short path through some trees. There, across the street, was the large modern five-story building. We crossed the street and headed over to the ticket machine. A security guard stopped us. He started talking to me, possibly because I had been in the lead.

"Something something something do you understand Japanese?" he asked seriously, but politely.

I should have said "no" and let Cayte and Candie struggle with him because they had better Japanese. Unfortunately I said yes, and he rattled on for a few minutes. He apparently didn't notice my frustrated twitching smile, but Cayte finally got it.

"What'd he say?" I said in a stage whisper.

"Well," Cayte replied, "I think he's saying that since I'm blind, I don't have to pay. Roxy, I think you have to pay. I think he thinks Candie is my guide, so she doesn't have to pay either."

She spoke to the guard a bit, and after a few more minutes, he waved a hand and started ushering us towards the entrance gate.

"Uh, I think he changed his mind and we all get in for free!" she laughed. "At least I'm useful for something!"

The museum was interesting, but I've seen so many in the past that I wasn't terribly impressed. Despite being pretty tired from our trek around the park, we still enjoyed ancient painted screens, kimonos, samurai armor, statues of Buddha, ancient ceramics, and Ainu clothes and tools. The Ainu are the native people of Japan. Just as America has its Native Americans, Japan has its Ainu.

At four o'clock and ready to collapse, we headed back to the Ameyoko mini market and found a small ramen shop. I'd heard about the legendary Japanese ramen, much different from the instant *Cup Noodle* or *Top Ramen* sold in the States. In the actual shop, we get served a deep bowl of Chinese noodles with vegetables and sometimes meat on top. How the popular anime character Naruto could devour multiple bowls, I had no idea. Probably because he wasn't actually a real person.

We wolfed down ours in no time. It was a suitable end to my first out of many trips to Ueno Park.

September 29

Everyone who trains at Cross Point has to sign an attendance book when they first come in. Today just for laughs, I wrote the kanji "sixty three." It's a play-on-words with my name. "Roxanne" is pronounced "roku san" by the Japanese. "Roku" is six, and "san" is three. "San" is also is the polite ending you add to someone's name, so I could also be called "Miss Six."

Uematsu was sitting behind the desk, checking something on the computer.

"I wrote my name!" I announced.

"Yes," he said, not looking up.

"I wrote it!" I repeated.

He finally tore his eyes away from the screen and glanced at the notebook.

"Hmm?"

"It's six three! Roxanne!" I said with a grin.

"Ah!" he exclaimed. "Ah! Nice! Funny!"

I must have tickled his funny bone. For the rest of the class he walked muttering "sixty three" to himself.

He taught us some great technique, and then had us spar. I was tired, but made it through class. We did a bit of kickboxing, too. When someone's throwing their fists in your face, you surprisingly find the energy to block and defend yourself. I sparred with some guys who wouldn't hit me, but also a guy who nearly kicked my legs out from under me.

"Hey Roxanne!" Uematsu said after we finished class. "He's a Super Saiyan!" he exclaimed, jabbing a finger at Tiger-san. The short Shooto-kickboxer had died his hair yellow and it was all sticking up. We all laughed.

90

"So, do you like Dragon Ball Z?" asked a lanky shorthaired fellow, as we were taking our gloves off. He and a few friends squatted near me, shuffling through bags to find water bottles. He gestured to the Gohan, Piccolo, and Vegeta pins I had stuck on my backpack.

I had been waiting my entire Japanese-speaking career for the next fifteen minutes- fifteen wonderful minutes. My grammar sucked and my vocabulary was horrendous, yet somehow I managed to carry on a conversation. Dragon Ball Z aired in Japan in the early 90's, but was brought over to the USA in the late 90's. I watched it on TV from middle school, bought the VHS, and finished it off by DVD in college. This fighting anime about training to get stronger, acquire more strength, and defend the earth truly inspired me.

"I have eight Dragon Ball Z T-shirts, you know," I boasted.

"Really? Eight?" They were impressed. I just so happened to be wearing one that night, too. The hero "Trunks" from the future came and effortlessly sliced the bad guy "Freeza" in half with his badass sword. The best scene ever.

"Your Japanese is really good!" the skinny guy complimented me.

"No, no, I'm still learning," I protested modestly. Inside, I glowed.

We were just putting our gloves back on when the phone rang. Kotani answered it, and then motioned me over.

"It's the promoter of Smackgirl on the phone," he said.

I blinked. "REALLY?" I practically shouted.

He smiled at my delayed reaction. "Yes. How much do you weigh now?"

"Uh...about 139 pounds," I answered.

"Pounds? What's that in kilo's?" he asked. When I hesitated, he continued, "Well, never mind. How much can you weigh for the fight? Can you make 61.5 kilos?"

We did some quick calculations and I discovered that was 135 pounds.

"Sure!" I almost danced.

Kotani chattered away for a few more minutes, and then hung up the phone. I hadn't been able to catch any of the conversation.

"He wants you to fight," he told me, "but they're still looking for an opponent."

"Sweet!" I exclaimed.

The rules were slightly different from the UFC or Pride style of mixed martial arts. In both styles, the fighters wear mouth guards and start standing. They can kick, punch, and take each other down. "Smackgirl" fighters wear 8 oz open-fingered gloves, compared to the 4 oz UFC style. Once on the ground, Smackgirl fighters can strike to the body, but not the face like in the UFC or PRIDE. The all-female promotion also has a time limit for groundwork. After thirty seconds, the referee stands the fighters back up.

It didn't matter to me if the rules were different. It was my first fight, and I saw some pretty brutal ones in the UFC. I didn't look forward to being pinned and smashed; nor did I have any desire to smash someone's face into a bloody pulp.

I had over six years of grappling under my belt in the forms of submission grappling, judo, and BJJ. In addition, I had been training kickboxing and Muay Thai for a few years.

"I'm ready. I'm ready for this!" I told myself.

I returned home spiritually energized, yet physically exhausted.

"I wouldn't have it any other way," I realized, struggling to get my heavy futons and blankets out from the closet. "I love the dojo."

I knew that the camaraderie with others at the dojo motivated me to do my best. There's nothing like struggling and sweating alongside others. I also got the chance to practice Japanese and improve my language skills. Everyone tried to correct my mistakes and teach me words. People seemed honored and honestly pleased that I had such an interest in their country and their language.

Chapter 9 - Climbing to New Heights: Mt. Fuji and Tokyo Tower
October 5

There's a saying in Japanese that everyone must climb Mt. Fuji before they die. Another saying goes, "He who climbs a second time is a fool." I would find out all too well why later.

If one started from the bottom and walked to the top, it would take two days. Some extremists camp out on the mountainside, which I heard gets freezing and miserable at night. Cayte, Candie and I weren't that gung-ho. We kicked back on a nice, comfortable coach bus, which cost about thirty bucks per ticket.

"You better take your gloves because it's really cold on the mountain!" my host mother had said before I left. I'm glad I followed her advice and brought a jacket and hat. The autumn day was warm and clear in Tokyo. The higher we drove the foggier and chillier it became. The leaves became redder as we went higher, leaving Tokyo's climate.

It took about two hours from the center of Shinjuku to the "fifth stop," which was about halfway up the mountain.

Other than us three, the bus was empty save for two middle-aged ladies. They must have adhered to the saying "silence was golden" because although our voices weren't particularly loud, they seemed to resent our chatting. We received constant glares from them over their shoulders the entire trip. However, the moment they saw Cayte's dog, they were all smiles, fawning all over Yogi.

Finally, the big empty bus parked itself in a small gravel parking lot. We all piled out. We'd reached the Fifth Stop.

"Do you mind if we take a picture with your dog?" one woman asked, hopefully clutching a camera to her chest.

"Sure, I guess," Cayte said politely.

Giggling and smiling, they shot their pictures. To our surprise, they asked for Cayte's address, and went on their way. The girls and I just exchanged silent looks and shook our heads.

Later, Cayte actually received copies of the pictures in the mail. "They're some of my most prized photos from that trip to Japan," she told me later.

We stood in front of a restaurant and three large gift shops. They seemed out of place, framed in spooky fog. Enticing fragrances wafted from food stands selling takoyaki - fried octopus, fried potatoes, and yakitori – fried noodles. Right behind these buildings, the ground dropped off into a misty mix of damp fog and multicolored treetops. If one fell down back there, they'd keep rolling for a while. My friends and I hit the gift shop first, and then started up a well-trodden path of crumbled up volcanic rock and dirt.

We passed many families with small children and even a person in a wheelchair. We noticed a pair of older ladies trying to mount a horse. A young skinny man was trying to hold it still. Apparently Mt. Fuji offers that service for those who don't want to walk.

Upon closer inspection, we saw they were the same ladies who glared at us for talking on the bus, and then bothered us for a picture of Yogi. We made an obvious note of taking pictures of them struggling to mount their high and mighty horses. They pretended not to notice.

The footing was tricky. Roots and rocks protruded everywhere. We went slowly so Cayte didn't trip. Yogi could only do so much.

"How do you do it?" I asked Cayte, as she deftly stepped over a jagged stone that rose up like a shark's tooth to meet her. "How did you know that was there?"

"I don't know. I'm used to it," she replied, "And Yogi helps, of course." Then she nearly stumbled.

"This is so cool! It's like being inside a cloud!" I said at one point. Too cool, for the fog obscured a clear shot of the surrounding mountain range. At one time the inclining path we were following looked like it went into nowhere. I made sure I took a picture of that. I really liked the trees. Most of them grew horizontally off the mountain, and then curled upward. I felt like I was walking up to the house of the gods. I'm not a religious person so much as

94

believing in the strength of one's own will and spirit, yet there was something mystical about the voluminous way the mist married the clouds. There floated a cool serene zone of nothingness that wasn't nothingness at all. It was a place of soul searching, of hiding, of discovery, of peace. Only the chatter of the tourists, foreign and Japanese, pierced the stillness. It was like an annoying voice of a morning bird that wakes you from a pleasant dream.

The gravel slopes became increasingly devoid of life, and the landscape became almost gray-scale.

"Here, take my picture to prove I was here!" I commanded, thrusting my camera into Candie's hands. Scrambling a few meters up a slope, I perched on the edge of a rock and gave the peace sign.

"Look, Mom, I'm on Mount Fuji!" Fuji, the legendary giant that inspired all who caught a glimpse of its might.

I was all set to power up the slopes for another few hours, but my two friends were getting tired. We browsed through the souvenir shops until the bus picked us up at 4pm. The drive home was horrendous, complicated by rush hour traffic plus an accident on the highway.

From Shinjuku, we rode as far as Musashi Sakai together, and then they got off. I waved goodbye as the train whisked me away.

"That's the way life is, isn't it?" I thought to myself. "The train keeps going, and people get on and off along the way. It's sad, but you can't be too sad. Your friend might board at the next stop, and then you'll be together again."

Friday, October 10

Techno music suddenly erupted out of the speaker, which hung on the dojo wall in Shibuya Scramble. Today was my first visit to the new club: Paraestra's newest branch dojo. Uematsu-san shook his hips and waved his hands above his head, which provoked smiles from his students who sat off to the side stretching.

"Ret's paachi!" I exclaimed, imitating Japanese's mispronunciation of English. He pointed at me and laughed.

Zuyo had convinced me to go, even though the trip was about an hour door to door from my house. She told me that someone would be taking pictures for a promotional poster, and I'm all for pictures. I've always wanted to go to Shibuya, too. Too bad it was twice the distance from Cross Point.

Class was scheduled to begin at seven thirty, so I left the house at six. I had to change trains from the Chuo line to the Inokashira Line upstairs in Kichijoji station. I'd taken the Inokashira line before when I visited Gutsman Shooto gym, so I didn't get lost as I had dreaded.

Once I got off the train at Shibuya, the expanse of the station awaited my exploration. It was immense.

"I wonder which exit I have to take," I thought, a knot forming in my stomach. "I have to choose soon, or I'll be late..."

I had to ask two people the way, but eventually found the correct one. Upon exiting the ticket gate, I immediately collided with a mass of people.

"This place is like Shinjuku," I muttered to myself, staring about me in awe. Tall office buildings and mini skyscrapers with long colorful signs loomed up on every side. It was about seven o'clock and just beginning to get dark. People of all shapes and sizes pushed their way through the crowd. And to think, people were only just starting to make their way home. The businessmen and women that cram themselves on the late trains hadn't even come out yet.

I located my landmark: The Hachiko statue. Hachiko was a dog known for its loyalty to its master. Legend has it that everyday, the master would go to work, and the dog would sit by the train station to wait for his return. One day, there was an accident, and the master never returned. The dog continued to sit there day after day, waiting and waiting, refusing to leave. Eventually, it died. The people erected a statue in its memory, and before long, it became the place everyone met at if they went to Shibuya.

I made my way through the mob into a group of loiterers who were standing around Hachiko. There, I located a city map and compared it to my messy hand drawn one.

"Okay, I'm here, and the club is here... That way," I muttered to myself, getting my bearings.

I walked past people squatting on the sidewalks, selling cheep jewelry and handmade bags. Two teenage bands were demonstrating their skills for anyone who wanted to pause and listen. Even further down I saw people carrying boom boxes and rapping to the rhythm.

The thought struck me. "This is the nosiest city I've been in so far!"

I approached a major intersection which just so happened to be the famous Shibuya Scramble, one of the busiest crossings in the world. Streets crisscross in at least five places in all different directions. The traffic lights stop the cars for one minute and waves of people simultaneously pour over the white-striped streets. Organized chaos in its finest form.

Riding the tidal wave of people, I made it to the other side. The new dojo took its name from that famous place. I hoped just as many people would join the dojo that crossed the Scramble.

I quickly strode down the street past restaurants, bars, commercial stores, and business of all kinds. I found what I thought was the major crosswalk I was supposed to turn left at, but I was wrong. I backtracked, but wasn't sure which way to go.

I called Zuyo, and could barely understand a word she said over the phone. Somehow she helped get me back on the right road. I finally found her ten minutes later standing on the street corner in her dark blue jiu jitsu gi.

"This is embarrassing," she laughed, glancing down at herself. "This way!" she said, and took off at a trot. I quickly followed her down a side street, down some stairs, and into the new gym.

My teammates had had stressed the word "wide" when describing the new place to me. I agreed. Well, big for Japan, at any rate. Joao Amaral's New England BJJ gym near Boston was bigger, but here there were actually two separate rooms.

I signed my name in the attendance book at the front desk.

"Ah, Roxanne! Welcome to the new gym!" said a guy whose name I couldn't recall.

The room closest to the door had stiff blue mats. Heavy bags lining two walls hung from metal support beams. Rambar's kickboxing class was warming up there. Further back, I could see orange mats, which looked softer. I guessed that's where the BJJ class would be held.

"Oh, Rokusan!" Uematsu-san greeted, coming over.

"Nice place!" I commented. "Very wide!" Actually, the Japanese use the word hiroi, or "wide" to mean "big," and semai, or "narrow" to mean "small."

At first glance, I had thought they painted the walls yellow. Not exactly an aesthetically pleasing compliment to bright orange mats. After running my fingers along it, I discovered that it was actually yellow foam padding. This proved incredibly pleasing to me and my body when I was eventually slammed into it during training. Built into the walls were metal hooks that could hold boxing ring ropes and pads.

The class that day was relatively small, but not everyone knew about the club yet. Kotani-sensei still taught the Kichijoji Friday jiu jitsu class so we assumed most people went there.

Later that night as the time for sparring neared, people who just got out of work began to show up. I decided to finish a little early. My body felt exhausted from the day before, and also from biking back and forth to school three times today over a banking issue. Let me just note that it's impossible to cash an American check in a normal Japanese bank, so don't even try.

During class, Uematsu-san showed some excellent technique. A judo throw "tomo-na-ge" is done from already being on one's back in front of the opponent. I would hold onto both of the opponent's sleeves, and put both my feet in their hips. If he was leaning forward, I could pull him over me, lifting him off his feet. Then, I would make a big circle with my arms from my head to my side, which flips him over me. I wanted to try it while we were free sparing, but never got the chance. While we were free sparing, though, someone was indeed taking the pictures for promotion. At the end of class, he took a group picture.

On my long train ride home, I stood in packed between some of the thousands of commuters dragging themselves home after overtime work.

"I think my Japanese language ability has gone up," I reflected. "It's only been a month and a half, though."

Something my teacher Marty Holman said replayed itself in my mind:

When you visit Japan, you'll be speaking more Japanese in a week than you'll ever practice in the classrooms.

It was totally true. For language learners, there's always been a huge gap between recognition and production. In my college classes we tended to do more listening and absorbing than actually conversing. Although I know more complicated grammar and kanji characters, on the spot I can never remember it enough to get it perfectly right.

Language can be seen not only as a set of rules, but as recognition of set phrases. When you read a novel, you don't sound out all the words. You glance at the word "responsibility" for example, and instantly know what it is. We recognize the patterns. That's why beginners of a foreign language practice reading in monotones. They have to sound out every word and don't have time to concentrate on intonation. The same thing goes for grammar.

Not only does the Japanese language fascinate me, but the mechanics of any language do. I love studying about how words are put together to make meaning and how they are naturally learned by natives. *Linguistics is definitely a field that suits me*, I thought. *I'm so glad I decided on Japanese for a major.*

October 11

A flood of humanity flowed out the doors like a tidal wave.

"That's... a lot of people," I commented to Candie and Cayte. We stood just outside the western facade of Tokyo Station. The massive brick building looked more like a mansion, reaching about three or four stories high. Completed in 1914, Tokyo Station is the busiest station in Japan in terms of number of trains per day: over 3,000. It's the fifth busiest in Eastern Japan if you count the number of people who pass through. Shinjuku Station takes first place for the most people at around 3.7 million per day.

Tokyo Station is a huge hub connecting 13 aboveground train lines. Underground, it's a crisscross network for the five different Tokyo Metro subway lines. Passageways connect everything for passengers, who can also go shopping in a massive sprawling mall.

We spotted Mana's slender form emerging from the crowd. As usual, she wore a cute fashionable outfit, outdoing us Americans who rocked simple T-shirts and jeans.

I checked my watch. Exactly eleven o'clock. How Japanese people managed to show up right on the button, I'll never know.

Our mission was visit one of the tallest structures in Japan: the Tokyo Tower. Its triangular shape built from red and white metal beams stood out distinctly among the other high-rise skyscrapers in Tokyo. It was built in 1958 and stood at 333 meters tall, making it the world's tallest self-supporting steel tower. The Eiffel Tower in Paris is 320 meters high. It was built as a broadcast tower for radio, digital and analogue TV waves. Our destination was the observatory, found 250 meters up the tower.

The fifteen-dollar fee stopped us in our tracks.

"That's expensive," I commented. We grimly stared at the board, having trouble making a decision.

"I kind of want to go," I said slowly.

"I can wait down here if you guys want to go up," Cayte offered. "I don't mind."

Candie and Mana exchanged unsure glances. Mana hesitantly offered to wait with Cayte. I decided to be a Japanese and go with the group.

"Nah, I'd rather not split up," I said. "But to appease me, we have to stop and buy some crepes. I've never had one before."

They readily agreed. Near the bottom leg of the tower, we'd passed a small stand with delicious-looking plastic models.

The ones that attracted my attention resembled banana-chocolate burritos.

I had two.

"This is the best thing ever," I ranted, licking the chocolate syrup off my fingers. "Actually, this is bad. I'm gonna get fat!"

"I know it!" my friends chorused agreement.

"It's actually pronounced 'coo-reh-p,' not 'krey-poo,'" Candie said. "It's French."

"Oh, I see. So do they taste the same as the French ones?" I asked the group.

Nobody was sure.

After the crepe fiasco, we got slightly lost in the tiny wooded "Shiba Park" overshadowed by the Tower. I couldn't believe the contrast of the quaint little stream bubbling over rocks, the cool clean air, and the aura of peace, next to which ran a major highway.

The four of us wandered out of the park and stumbled directly into a matsuri. The festival was being held in front of Zojoji Temple, a rather large shrine of the Jodo Pureland Buddhist sect. Merchants hawked food and toys under their kiosks. The cheerfully bright multi-colored banners and sunroofs added to the festive air.

We bought takoyaki, the fried octopus dumplings, and sat off to the side to eat it.

"I can never get enough takoyaki," I announced. The statement was met with silent nodding as we chewed.

Presently, our chat was interrupted by an overweight Japanese man who wanted to pet Yogi. He was dressed in regular jeans and polo shirt, but his behavior seemed a little off.

"Excuse me, could you not pet him? He's a Seeing Eye dog. He's working," Cayte said politely in Japanese. The man ignored her and continued to reach for the dog.

"As usual," she muttered, trying to pull her animal away. The man looked offended. He turned to Mana.

"Excuse me, are you Japanese?" he asked.

She blinked and swallowed her last bite of takoyaki, probably offended. She obviously looked Japanese, and he'd heard her speak the language with a native accent.

"Um, yes, that's right," she answered carefully.

"Ah, I see," the strange man said, and proceeded to make a pass at her. "You are really pretty," he went on.

She unconsciously started inching away. We took that as our queue to say "sumimasen," or excuse me, and bolt. Luckily, he didn't follow us.

"Yabai ne," Mana said with a laugh, once we were safely away.

"What's that?" I asked.

"Hmmmm," she said, and attempted to explain. "You say it in situations when you're in trouble."

We all brainstormed and came up with the equivalent in English: 'oh, crap', 'uh oh', or even 'oh no, I've screwed up'.

In return, we taught her some fun English words, like "dork." It's difficult to explain, so we attempted to use it at every opportunity, sometimes unnaturally, making for an entertaining afternoon. It was like the old quote: *In learning you will teach, and in teaching you will learn.*

A twenty-minute train ride brought us to the city of Ikebukuro to visit Animate- eight stories of wonder and goodness. A fly would have had ample opportunity to wander into my mouth for the length of time it was hanging open. I couldn't believe all the merchandise! One could almost see the drool dripping down my face as I handled "rare" finds.

"Erin would die to have this! Caitlin would jump for joy! Oh, Kendra would love this!" I thought repeatedly. Everything seemed to have my or my friends' names written all over them in pink neon marker.

Luckily, I convinced myself that I didn't need twenty extra T-shirts, pins, or key chains. I certainly didn't need any more folders with Naruto or Dragon Ball Z on them. However, the notepad with Full Metal Alchemist was absolutely essential to my daily life.

After the shopping fun, it was dinnertime. Cayte suggested a pizza place called Shakey's and I was all too happy to agree. I hadn't had pizza in months. A branch of the popular chain was located near Sunshine City, the shopping plaza across the street

102

from Ikebukuro station. My jaw dropped when I saw the menu, though. It cost about fifteen dollars for a pizza, which was only the size of a regular dinner plate.

"This large is like an American Pizza Hut's medium size," I complained. "And …what's this? They put corn on pizza? Each pizza has a name? Is that mayonnaise? How odd…"

"That's the average price in Japan," Cayte said, flipping through the menu unconcerned. "Let's just order separately rather than share. Look, you can order half a pizza for half the price."

Half cost was roughly eight dollars. Mana ordered a bowl of spaghetti in a cream sauce with salmon roe over it. I have to admit- it looked awful. I'm sure you can do all sorts of things with pasta, but in my life as an Italian, I'd never come across such things. Show me the meatballs.

Candie and Cayte ordered "California light" pizzas with various toppings. The crusts were extremely thin, and crumbled apart when they tried to cut them with a pizza cutter. My pizza consisted of four tiny oily pieces, with no cheese that I could find. There wasn't any sauce. The dried-out crust tasted like cardboard. I have to say that it was the worst pizza I've ever eaten in my entire life. I only ate it because I paid for it.

Candie and Cayte apparently loved theirs to the extent that they raved about it twenty minutes out the door. I hesitated to show my true feelings in front of my friends. Privately I wondered what planet they were from.

"I think I have to get going," Mana said, with a regretful smile.

"Yeah, you live all the way in Yokohama!" Cayte agreed. "That's a long ride. What, about two hours?"

"Yeah," Mana said.

"But we're going to do karaoke!" I said. "My first time ever!"

"Oh really?" Mana said. "I'm sorry! Well, have fun!"

We said our goodbyes and headed in opposite directions. Cayte led us to a narrow building with a bright blue sign that said karaoke in Japanese katakana. We signed up at the front desk, which looked more like a hotel lobby.

"We have to decide on the time now," Cayte said. "How about like one hour?"

"Sure," Candie and I said together.

Cayte nodded, putting her pen to the paper.

"Kochira eh dozo! Right this way, please," the bowing staff man said with a polite gesture. He led the way down the narrow hallways to an elevator. The tacky bright blue paint of the walls struck me like a punch to the temple. Everything was loud, including the music seeping out from under the doors, which lined the corridor. It reminded me of a hotel, but one that tried to squish itself into a place too small for its bulk.

On each side of the squashed corridor were doors, which led into tiny, dimly lit rooms. Our host unlocked one and gestured us inside with a forced smile. "Yeah, I'd hate to work here, too," I thought.

We cautiously entered. Well, I was cautious. Cayte bustled in and set her bags down on the black plastic sofa that hugged the wall. It was perfectly square. From the ceiling, colored lights flashed. These "karaoke boxes" were half the size of a college dorm. In the middle was a table with the songbooks on it. Taking up almost one entire wall was a flat-screen TV. We had one hour to sing our hearts out.

My friends flipped slowly through an encyclopedia of songs that looked to me like massive phone books. Candie used a remote control to enter the song's number and hit 'send.' Cayte queued her song to play next, and then hurriedly picked up one of the three mics lying on the table.

We all sang, reading the lyrics flashing across the TV but I felt embarrassed. I was certainly no Mariah Carey.

"You choose a song, Roxy." Candie handed me the book.

"Uh, er, how about this one?"

"I don't know it, but go ahead."

"Never mind." I didn't want to sing alone. It was actually hard to find songs we all knew and liked. If I wasn't familiar with the Japanese songs Candie chose, I did my best to speed-read the subtitles in hiragana. It was good practice. However, I decided it wasn't my cup of tea. Maybe one had to be drunk in order to

104

experience the full joy of karaoke. Candie and Cayte had a little alcohol, while I sipped on orange juice.

Friends are the candy of life. We could have done anything and I would have enjoyed my day. Merely being in their presence, laughing with them, sharing memories- I would remember it forever. Positive energy nurtures the human spirit.

October 19

"Roxanne, there's a matsuri in Kawagoe tomorrow. Wanna come?" Zuyo asked me one evening.

"Tell me more," I said, licking my lips in anticipation. We settled with our backs against the dojo wall after BJJ sparring.

"It's hard to describe," she began, "but you see, there are these carts called blah blah blah." She used a Japanese word I didn't know. "They yada yada yada and also there's music and bladdy bladdy blah. The final Somethingorother starts late at night, so we'll go in the afternoon and leave after dark. Everyone likes to do blah blah blah. Do you understand?"

I combed the sweaty hair out of my eyes. Tangles caught in my fingers. "Yes," I said. "I mean, no, but it sounds fun!"

My training partner laughed. "Okay, so meet me and Jet in Ikebukuro station this Sunday at 2:30pm."

"Okay," I agreed. Just flow with the go, man!

On the appointed day, I arrived 30 minutes early. Actually, I arrived one hour early and tried to find the eight-story anime store, but failed miserably. After walking around in circles for a while, I decided to return to the station before I got lost.

Presently, I spotted Zuyo, Jet - the resident Smackgirl veteran - and two others. Cross Point member Haruki, nicknamed Luke, came with his girlfriend. The former had lived in the United States for most of his childhood until adulthood, making him bilingual. He worked as a programmer in a prestigious Japanese company. The tall Japanese-American trained at Renzo Gracie's BJJ academy in NY, and kicked the butts of people at Cross Point quite frequently. I didn't know much about his girlfriend, but she seemed nice. Luke claimed she spoke some English, but she seemed shy to try. Zuyo spoke extra to make up for her. All in all, I was excited to hang out with them outside a jiu jitsu setting.

We took the Tobu Tojyo line for about half an hour north to a city named Kawagoe. As we chatted on the train, I was accosted by a feeling of pride and disbelief. "I can't believe I'm here, in a foreign country - Japan, no less! - speaking more than one language," I thought to myself. "This is like a dream. This is my dream."

I loved listening to Zuyo talk. Her enthusiasm for everything in life made me excited, too. There's a difference in the way men and women are supposed to speak in Japanese. The way Zuyo actually chose her words broke some rules. She used "zo," an emphatic suffix tacked on to the end of sentences that usually only males use. This made her ten times cooler in my book. In English, one might compare it to, "Shall we go?" versus "Let's get goin', guys!"

I noted carefully how she converted her speech into the politer form when talking to Luke's girlfriend since they didn't really know each other. The ability to switch between polite and casual language is a skill learners have to practice. It doesn't come naturally to us, as it does to native speakers.

After arriving at Kawagoe, we emerged from the station and almost got swept away by a crowd. We saw average, modern electronics stores and convenience stores lining the streets. In front of them stood temporary makeshift food stands and kiosks with colorful canvas roofs. Cooks stood behind grills serving up things like takoyaki, candied apples, skewered chicken, and bananas. There were festival games like throwing darts. Kids tried their hands at fishing an object out of a water basin with a rod or toy fishing pole.

I spotted the crepe booth first, but behind it was a stand for "choco-banana." The middle-aged stand owner skewered a long banana and slowly dipped it into a vat of chocolate. My mouth watered as he pulled it out, casually picking up a tin of multi-colored sprinkles and tossing some over top. They stick randomly to the wet chocolate, but I knew better that it was art! With that, he stuck it in a holder. They looked quite comical sticking up like

106

flowers in a garden. I knew I had no other choice but to immediately buy one.

"I have to make sure these things are suitable to be sold on the streets of Kawagoe," I said to Luke. Everyone laughed at me.

"It sure is crowded!" Zuyo commented, as our fast-paced stride was halted by a mass of humanity.

I loved seeing so many people in one place. It's annoying if you're trying to get somewhere, though. Being smushed back to back against a complete stranger isn't exactly pleasant, but at least we were all together. We tried to relax and let the crowd carry us along. It was the togetherness I appreciated the most. In my childhood, I had a few good friends, but never experienced the camaraderie of a group.

Occasionally, the slow-moving crowd stopped altogether. It boiled and churned like a pot of vegetables. Little kids darted between us. Couples said, "Sumimasen," and cut us off, trying to reach a food stand. At 5'8" I was a little taller than the average Japanese was. I could see pretty well over people's heads.

As we got further down Main Street, we came upon a giant structure on wheels in the middle of the crowd. It looked kind of like a wagon or carnival float, with a stage raised over our heads. About four people were pulling it, hauling with all their might on ropes attached to the front. Two others stood on either side with long poles, which they occasionally shoved under the wheels, either to stop the giant from rolling forward, or to adjust its course. The wheels looked like old-fashioned wagon wheels.

The stage had two levels. On the first one, several people sitting cross-legged played the drums. Other people formally dressed in colorful kimonos played the flute while standing behind them. Finally, one masked character dressed in a costume fancier and crazier than a kimono did a dance. Sometimes people in formal clothing sat on the roofs, or if not, a statue was placed there instead. Paper lanterns hung off the corners, and colorful hanging drapery-like fabrics hung as the background.

These stages had many themes. On one, a man wore a green smock tied crisscrossed on his chest. A mask, with the mouth set wide open in laughter, covered his face. He swayed to and fro, waving a fan like a jester. On another float, someone looked like a washerwoman gesticulated wildly to the crowd. They all moved with exaggerated motions, intentionally looking a touch idiotic.

Another character who stuck out in my memory was a strong man in a sleeveless shirt. He paced back and forth in his area limited to only a few square feet, making muscles and shaking his fist at the crowd. I wondered what his problem was. I wasn't versed in understanding Japanese pantomime.

My favorite stage was a stationary one, though, and sat parked off to one side. A man in a kitsune fox costume twirled about in a wild dance. A huge mane of flowing white hair billowed out from the sides of his mask, bouncing up and down off his back. His leaping and gesturing was spectacular to watch.

When a mobile stage passed a stationary stage, those riding them stopped everything they were doing and took notice of the rival stage. The two main dancers faced each other. The musicians halted their previous tune, and immediately started playing some fast-paced battle music. The intensity of their dancing and music increased. Luke told me it was a "battle of the sounds."

"That's the main theme of this festival," he said.

"Who wins?"

He only shrugged. "I dunno, I've never been here before!"

We walked around for hours, glancing at the booths and shops and sampling foods. I tried mochi balls skewered on a thin rod. Mochi is made from sweet sticky-rice mashed into a glutinous nugget.

Eventually Zuyo led us into Koedo, a section of town that is reminiscent of the old Edo period. It really had the look and feel of an ancient city. I felt like I'd just walked into the past. Wooden buildings had been converted into stores. Maybe they'd been stores in the first place. It appeared the families lived upstairs.

The energetic Zuyo led us through a low door into a traditional Japanese restaurant. In the entrance hall, we took off our shoes and put them in a wooden cubby along with the dozens of other customers' footwear. Our table was low to the ground, and we settled cross-legged on cushions around it. There was a hole in the middle of the floor, under the table, where we could put our feet into if we wanted. On cold winter days, that space is heated

We ordered things like octopus salad, sushi, yakitori - skewered grilled chicken, and daikon sarada – radish salad. I liked the latter because the thin white slices were crunchy, juicy and sweet.

The total bill was slightly more than I wanted to pay. Everyone put in about 30 dollars at the end of the night. Nobody seemed to blink an eye. I found myself worrying that I'd have enough train fare to get home. It's so easy to underestimate the cost of things in Japan since everything is so expensive. Yet like before, the camaraderie was priceless.

After dinner at 9pm, the festival was still at its height.

"When are they going to have the 'final showdown?" I asked the group. Nobody knew for sure.

"Maybe in another hour?" suggested Zuyo.

"I really want to see, but can't wait that long. It's getting late," I said sadly. Plus I was exhausted. Everybody agreed, and we took our respective train lines back home. Big sister Zuyo always did such a good job of showing me the interesting things about Japan. Little did I know that in a few years, I would be the one playing tour guide for all sorts of friends, co-workers, and family.

Chapter 10 - Teri visits Japan!

I first met Teri Kleinberg at the Sityodtong Muay Thai gym in Boston one summer before my exchange year. She walked into the grappling class one day and much to my surprise, I soon found myself beaten up by another girl. Once she sunk in the guillotine choke and cranked, I tapped quickly.

"You've done this before," I said, stretching my neck.

"I used to wrestle," she laughed in reply.

That experience was new to me. I decided we should be friends, so I did her the favor of driving her home that night. She had just graduated from Harvard and was one of the nicest people I had ever met.

"I think my father knows you," she said to me while I sped down Sturrow Drive.

"Really? Who's your father?"

"Eric Kleinberg."

"What?!" I exclaimed. I'd been training kickboxing and grappling with Eric for the past two years. Consequently, I knew him quite well. He was about my father's age, but it didn't stop us from becoming friends.

"You're his daughter?" I blinked and stared. Her Asian face looked nothing like his blond-haired, sharp-nosed white guy appearance. She laughed.

"My mother is Chinese," she told me.

My mind reeled. Eric had always talked about his daughter doing this and that, as much as parents will. We began a friendship that lasted over the years, so when Teri made plans to do a world tour, she included Tokyo as one of her destinations.

With my host mother's permission, she planned to stay with us for a few days. I had a seminar class during the time she was scheduled to arrive, and I couldn't miss it or I'd fail the class. I gave her directions on how to find her way to Koganei herself. She could do it, proving she didn't graduate Harvard for nothing. When I finally made it home myself, we had a wonderful dinner of chicken meatball soup, plus chicken potato stew. It was like a big girl's sleepover after that. Although terribly jetlagged, she wanted to show me her pictures from her visit from Norway. I showed her my collection of Japanese snapshots so far. We ended up going to bed at midnight.

Thursday, October 23

I collected my homework assignments from the teachers in some attempt to be a responsible student. Then I skipped class to go sightseeing with Teri. The previous night we got in contact with an old high school buddy of Teri's named Cliff, who also happened to be doing an exchange program in Japan. He'd been to Kamakura once already and recommended it as one of the best places to sightsee in Japan.

Kamakura is a coastal town in the Kanagawa prefecture, a little more than an hour south of the bustling Tokyo. At one point, when Minamoto Yoritomo established a military government in 1192, he made Kamakura the headquarters. The city grew accordingly in size, and there remain many temples, shrines and historical monuments that attract tourists. It was also from Kamakura that I got my first glimpse of the Pacific Ocean from mainland Japan.

We met up with him Thursday at 11am in front of the Kamakura train station. Cliff was tall and brown-haired with a friendly smile. He was the kind of person a mother would describe as, "Well, he seems like a nice young man!" if a lady brought him home to meet her folks. We all got along splendidly. Right after exiting the station, we three adventurers began exploring the main street called Komachi Avenue. Quaint little tourist stores lined either side.

A few minutes later, Teri suddenly interrupted our idle conversation. "Hey, that looks like a pickle shop." She pointed and we followed her finger.

"Pickles?" I repeated.

"Yeah! Don't you know? The Japanese have many different of kinds of pickles!" she said, making a beeline for the shop. That shop sold exclusively the tart multicolored mixtures of vegetables. Indeed there were dozens, and I couldn't always tell what vegetable they had been made from. Free samples sat beside almost every bin, with mini chopsticks resting nearby for customers to use. I saw some that were obviously cucumbers, eggplant, some kind of root, and more. We sampled every single pickle and then left without buying anything.

At the end of the street stood a large shrine called Tsurugaoka Hachiman-gu Shrine. Hachiman is the Shinto god of war - the protector of all people in Japan - but the common person used to worship him in ancient times as the god of agriculture. Since then, he became identified as the patron deity of the powerful Minamoto clan of old.

As per custom, we cleansed our hands in the purification fountain before entering the shrine. Teri and Cliff were fascinated by the rack, which held hundreds of the little rectangular wooden plaques. Visitors to the shrine bought them for about five dollars in a Shrine shop. They wrote their wishes or prayers, and hung them on top of the others' who had come before them. The plaques branched outwards like a manmade tree of dreams.

I read out loud for them.

"This person wants to go to the University of California," I translated.

"Hey, I go there!" Cliff exclaimed, and took a picture.

"And this person... I think she wants to pass some kind of test." I squinted at the messy scribble.

"This one's in English," Teri pointed out.

"And this one looks like a little kid wrote it." Cliff took a few more pictures.

After we had our fill of that shrine, we wandered around a neighborhood in the direction of another one, eventually running into the shrine of Yoritomo Minamoto, the man who became shogun in 1192 and created the Kamakura Bakufu, a feudal style of government.

We passed through a small tori gate and climbed steep, uneven stone stairs. At the top, under tall, beautiful deciduous trees were several small stone monuments. In the middle next to some

112

flowers stood a Pocari Sweat water bottle. It looked very out of place so we took a picture. I liked how the roots stuck out in a random mess from the dark brown soil. No moss or grass covered the earth in that area. Many trees grew out of the mountain horizontally, curving upwards in an act of desperation to reach the light.

We stopped for a delicious curry lunch – my first curry shop experience! One meal cost about seven US dollars. Without delay, the elderly woman server came out of the back room bearing bowls with heaping mounds of rice. I eagerly awaited what came next, as she placed them before us. Next to our bowls, she placed what looked like Aladdin's lamp, filled with brown spicy curry with chunks of carrots floating around. We poured it over our rice.

"This is fantastic," we all agreed simultaneously.

Every time the waitress came by to check up on us and I'd reply in Japanese, she'd compliment me. "Your Japanese is so good!"

"Oh, thank you..." I mumbled every time, my mouth full of curry. I was getting kind of tired of hearing the compliments, because I knew in my heart that I had a long way to go. She meant that I was better than the average gaijin foreigner who came in her shop. Cliff spoke Japanese as well, but was one year behind me.

We had ordered too much rice, so we made a contest of daring each other to finish it. Teri won. We then rolled ourselves out the door and back to the main street.

Next on the tour was the Daibutsu, the largest statue of Buddha in Japan. Technically, it was the second largest. First place went to a similar Daibutsu statue in the city of Nara.

"According to this map," said Teri as we walked, "There's a beach right up ahead. Let's go there first! It'll remind me of my old home in California."

We adjusted our course to Zaimokuza Beach. It was beautiful, topped off by the sunny warm weather. If we'd been in America, that beach would have been packed. The sand was dark brown, with little bits of seashell mixed in. I'd never seen thick sand like that. I liked it.

Schoolboys hung out smoking. Businessmen with suit jackets slung over their arms took strolls along the paved path, which ran parallel to the shore.

Cliff smiled. "I bet that's what they did all day instead of going to the office," he joked. We laughed.

"Wow, look at that!" Teri pointed to a large group of schoolgirls in identical uniforms. They must have been on some kind of field trip.

"They look kind of out of place, don't you think?" she murmured to me, digging around in her backpack for her camera. The girls' dark navy blue sailor-style uniforms and red sashes contrasted distinctly with the tan of the sand. The way the light hit the sand made it appear lighter than up close. It made for a nice photographic opportunity.

I really wanted to move on before it got too late. After a gentle prodding on my part, we left the vacation paradise spot to sniff out the giant Buddha statue. A bus apparently ran from the station but we decided to walk. Bad move. It took longer than we thought (about 35 minutes). By the time we arrived, our legs were in pain and exhausted.

The monument was worth the suffering, though. The serene-looking Buddha sat cross-legged with his fingers pressed together in his lap. The bronze statue had turned green over time, but that merely reminded me of the Statue of Liberty. I felt a stab of nostalgia.

"I read that once a temple was built around it," I told my friends, "but a giant tsunami, or tidal wave washed it away a long time ago." That must have been a big tsunami, I thought, thinking of how long we had to walk from the sea to the statue.

For a few coins, we were able to enter the statue through a door in its base.

"Wow, it's...it's...there's nothing here," I faltered.

My friends laughed and agreed. The inside looked merely like a big cave with a little ladder leading up to the head. There was a sign prohibiting us from climbing it. It was probably there for maintenance.

Teri took a picture.

114

"It's probably not going to come out well," I said, craning my neck to look overhead. "The lighting is bad. Actually, it's not that interesting in here."

"Yeah, but at least we can say we've been inside the Daibutsu!" Teri smiled.

"You're right," I agreed, and we made for the exit. Once outside, we all said "Bus?" simultaneously, and laughed. Before long, we tired Americans joined other tourists on a bus back to the station. Once on the train, it took us another two hours to get home, with Cliff getting off midway to return to his home-stay in Yokohama.

Darkness had fallen by the time Teri and I walked through the gate of my host mother's house in Musashi Koganei. My host mother had chicken and potato soup waiting for us, along with kabocha, or pumpkin, other vegetables and udon noodle soup. We made some small talk with my host mother.

"You know, it feels so natural, you being here," I commented to my friend as we ate. "This is so great."

She agreed with me. Warm waves of friendship washed over me. We relaxed for a while, before heading over to Cross Point.

"This is my friend Teri, from the United States," I introduced her to Kotani and Uematsu sensei. "Is it all right if she practices just for today?" Without the visitor's fee of twenty dollars? I silently added, hopefully.

"Oh, nice to meet you. Sure, no problem," Kotani answered, with a gracious smile.

"She doesn't have a jiu jitsu gi, though..." I said hesitantly.

"Oh." The broad-shouldered purple belt looked troubled. "Well, in that case," he said slowly, "The Shooto class starts at 9 o'clock."

I looked at the clock. It was about seven o'clock. I did have my gi. I didn't want to wait two hours just to do one hour of practice. "Is it okay if we just practice off to the side?" I asked. "Or I can work with her since she doesn't have a gi."

I knew I was pushing it. But why not?

Kotani didn't look happy, but eventually allowed us to join the class, me with gi-pants and a T-shirt, and her with shorts and my gi-top on. We did some nice holds and takedowns, which Teri actually picked up faster than I did.

"I don't get it," I laughed, and she ended up ended up teaching me. In fact, takedowns are a huge part of wrestling, so of course she'd know them quite well. She pushed me hard since I was training for my first MMA fight. We left our two and a half hour long workout happy and tired.

"I'm going to be so sore tomorrow!" Teri laughed, as we packed up our things. Together, we bowed and thanked the teachers profusely.

Friday, October 24

I didn't want to skip class two days in a row, so on Friday Teri accompanied me by following me to school using the rickety spare bike. I used Sadako-san's nice one.

"Are you sure you wouldn't rather go sightseeing to some place more interesting?" I asked her.

"No, no, I want to see your campus. It's not too boring, don't worry!" she assured me.

My two morning classes flew by, and soon enough it was time to meet her for lunch and I invited along Candie and Cayte. It's always fun to introduce old friends to new friends. Unfortunately, that morning my Japanese teacher informed me of the test results, which were less than satisfactory. That put me in a foul mood for a good chunk of the day. Teri and I headed home, where I did homework and my friend read.

That night, we met Luke, his girlfriend, and two of her lady friends in Shibuya, a city in the bustling center of Tokyo.

"This is kind of far to come for dinner," Teri commented, but Luke had promised us a special place. He led us to an oko-no-miyaki shop. That meant literally, "cooked as you like it."

The friendly staff guided us to two wooden tables, in the middle of which was a metal skillet heated from below with a gas flame.

116

Luke grabbed a menu. "Do you like shrimp?" he asked.

"Um, yes," we answered.

"Onions? Squid?"

"Sure, and sure," we nodded, exchanging glances.

He spoke to the waitress. "Want some monja-yaki, too?" he asked.

"Sure! What's that?" we asked.

Luke ordered a bunch of things and then leaned back in his seat with a smile. We talked about this and that, and presently, a young server came over with several small bowls. Inside was a type of raw batter with things like vegetables, shrimp and meat heaped on top.

"Here, stir this up," Luke said, handing one to me. I tried to mix it, but the toppings fell all over the place.

"Apparently, I'm not skilled enough." I handed the bowl to Teri. "Here, you try." She laughed and took the dripping bowl from me, which was entirely too small to stir, in my opinion. She managed somehow.

"Okay, now," Luke began, leaning over the skillet a bit. "Pour it on the grill, and we cook it like a pancake."

Cooking our own food in this manner proved extremely entertaining. I'm glad Luke was an experienced oko-no-miyaki customer, because I would have flipped it too soon. After it finished cooking, he lathered on thick brown sweet sauce, squirted on some light mayonnaise, and sprinkled on green seaweed flakes.

The monja yaki came in a similar bowl, which also required stirring. This time you stir-fry the vegetables first, which are usually a mix of cabbage and thinly sliced carrots. After five minutes or so, we pushed the veggies into a circle to form a dam and pour the liquid batter in the middle. The challenge is to keep the liquid from leaking out. We laughed as we desperately used the metal flippers to shove back the tide. After about five minutes, the liquid started to solidify into a sticky gelatinous substance, after which we mixed everything together and ate it directly from the skillet with tiny miniature metal shovels.

The birthplace of oko-no-miyaki is Osaka, the third largest city in Japan. It's located about two hours west of Tokyo, and is famous for wide streets, outgoing people, tako-yaki and oko-no-miyaki. Monja yaki, however, is a native Tokyo food. The crispy burned part tastes the best.

"That was a blast," we all agreed afterward. I could see many more skillets of monja in my future. There's actually a whole section of the city in Tokyo called "Tsukishima," where every street is lined with nothing but monja shops. I couldn't wait to check it out.

Chapter 11 - Fight Preparation: Mental, Physical, Spiritual

The date was set: November 11. Smackgirl, against Hikaru Shinohara. As fight time became imminent, I often thought about the thing which is sport fighting.

How could I do such a thing? What would happen to me? To my personality?

I always considered myself a gentle, peaceful person. I always saved insects in the house by scooping them up in a cup and carrying outside. My mom always ran for a fly swatter. When other children teased me in elementary school and middle school, I ran to the teacher and got them in trouble, because I didn't know how to say mean things back. How could I climb into a ring and hit somebody I didn't know in the face? Team sports like soccer were one thing. Judo was another- you throw people and pin them. But MMA?

My mind continually flashed images at me. Proud and triumphant men, standing over others, beaten and bloody, being carried out of the ring on a stretcher. It was the UFC and two warriors had just fought their hearts out. They needed stitches, dental surgery, plastic surgery to fix a decimated nose, or broken orbital bone. Would I end up like that? Injury was my worst nightmare, as was hurting someone else. I would feel horrible if I broke someone's nose.

It wasn't my first time in competition, of course. I'd done many judo, Brazilian jiu jitsu, and submission grappling tournaments since I was 17 in high school. However, this was my first competition that involved striking. Somehow that made it a lot more serious.

"I won't aim my punches for her nose," I decided privately. "Instead maybe the jaw or the forehead or temple. I hope I don't break her jaw," I thought. "I want to fight clean." I wasn't the type of fighter to talk big, or hype myself up.

"Why am I doing MMA?" I wondered.

Although I considered myself competitive and always played team sports in school, fighting seemed a direct contradiction of my personality. I didn't fight to release pent up aggression. It wasn't because I liked hitting things; I didn't. When trying to find a reason, I ran into self-image conflicts. This straight-arrow girl, who is shy around guys, will soon put on 8oz gloves and try and beat another woman into submission. How do you beat someone without hurting them, or trying to hurt them?

I had a lot to learn about myself and about the sport of MMA.

Will I find the answers in the ring this weekend? I wondered. *I've been training hard, pushing myself to exhaustion in preparation for my fight.*

School-wise, I planned ahead. I decided to finish my long economics term paper one week before it was due. Who knew what state I'd be in after my fight?

"What are you thinking, fighting 'no-holds-barred,'" my mind asked me again and again, as I sat at my computer, trying to concentrate. "Shut up already!" I told it back, banging away on the keyboard. "We have to write this."

"At least I don't have to worry about weight too much. Speaking of which, I could really use a bag of rice crackers right now..."

I shook my head. "Okay, concentrate! The economic status of Japanese banks! I must finish this paper," I scolded myself out loud. "In the late 1990s, several large banks failed, and mergers were seen as one effective option. I've successfully dieted down to 64 kilos. What I am thinking, even training no holds barred?" My thoughts wandered. My fingers paused, resting motionless on the keyboard of my Toshiba laptop. "I don't want to hurt anyone."

What I've realized since then is that it's not about hurting someone versus not hurting someone. It's a sport. Fighters aren't punching someone because they hate them in most cases. They are professionals being paid to compete, just like kicking a soccer ball. It's business. But it is also a matter of the heart. It's a strange mix, in reality, where the fighter puts his or her heart and soul into overcoming pain and pressure to physically overcome an opponent.

"That may very well be, but I don't want to hurt anyone!" my heart cried out.

120

"You know," my mind spoke up. "As a fighter improves and gains more and more control, they come to understand exactly what force is necessary to defeat the opponent. Right? Take an arm lock, for example. You know how far you can stretch the arm before it starts to put strain on the joint. Then from there you go slowly until the opponent decides he or she can't bear it, so he or she taps out."

Accidents do happen, however, but all in all, it's actually safer to fight someone experienced and skilled than to fight someone inexperienced who has less control. Unless the skilled person is a jerk and is out for blood.

At Cross Point, I successfully prepared my body and went injury-free into my fight. As for mental preparation, all I could think about was the fight as the big day got closer and closer. I'd been watching a lot of Naruto of late. The plot involves a ninja village, and young members of a squadron who have to complete missions and defend their village.

That anime really does something for me. More than the plot, it's the strength of the characters that I admire. They always aspire to improve themselves, and train themselves ragged to reach the next level. They also never give up. Especially the boy Naruto. Even when broken and bloody, he always stands back up. Ironically, the latest episodes were about Naruto preparing to face another powerful fighter in a one-on-one competition, not unlike the bout I was just about to have.

Farther back in my life, another anime series touched something deep inside me. Like an invisible hand of fire, it ignited the wooden framework that surrounded my heart. As a 14-year-old, I watched the heroes in Dragon Ball Z train and suffer to become stronger. They were so cool. Their hard work, sacrifice, and pain all paid off in the end. I adopted that blind determination as my own, and threw myself into everything with abandon. I tried too hard it was almost stupid. It applied to schoolwork, sports, and personal goals. If I failed, well, that was just not an option. If the heroes gave up, their humiliation and failure would be too great to live with. Plus, their home would be destroyed. Even if they lost that battle, as long as they got back up and trained to get stronger, it would be alright.

Guts. Effort. The traits built upon themselves and turned into strength of character. What's the difference if the inspiration comes from a comic book hero, or a real life person? As far as I was concerned, Piccolo was my idol, and some day, I would become as strong as him. He was just too cool.

Of course, I didn't tell anyone this. They would laugh at me. He's just some green alien dude with a name of a musical instrument in some animation show. Right?

To me, it was a way of life. Akira Toriyama, the creator of Dragon Ball Z, was teaching us how to become good martial artists.

I sighed.

"So then the banks in Japan merged," I mumbled out loud to myself, still trying to focus on my economics paper.

My host mother called to me from the kitchen. "Roxanne, are you hungry?"

"Yes!" I hollered back, getting up from my laptop.

Neither my parents nor my host family knew about my fight. I hadn't told them. Maybe I was scared they'd disapprove and tell me not to do it.

"I gotta tell my host mother sooner or later, though," I thought.

I visualized myself entering the ring. Adrenaline spiked, and I felt energy boil inside me. It rose like fire up from my stomach.

"I wonder what that is," I wondered idly, for the millionth time. "Is it ki, the energy life force, like in Dragon Ball Z? If I tried hard enough, could I summon it into my hands and shoot fire like them? Or like Lu Kang from Street Fighter? Oh my gosh, that's so ridiculous, Rox. Of course you can't shoot fire out of your hands. Someone would have done it by now if that were the case." I laughed at myself. "Is it just adrenaline? It must be..."

I pondered and pondered but couldn't figure it out. Whatever that burning sensation was, brought on by visualization, it sometimes powered me to train for hours. It engrossed me so that

I couldn't eat. It made me twitch when I was trying to sleep. Do only other fighters feel it, too?

November 3rd

Naoya Uematsu Sensei was fighting Katsuya Toida in a professional Shooto fight: "Wanna Shooto 2003" in Korakuen Hall. My first live MMA show in Japan! I had no idea at the time, but Katsuya "Toikatsu" Toida would later become my teammate. After graduating, I would return to Japan and join the team Wajyutsu Keisyukai.

The massive baseball stadium Tokyo Dome pushed up out of the landscape like a giant mushroom. An assortment of shops, restaurants, and roller coasters surrounded it, making Tokyo Dome City. It was a playground for kids and adults alike. There were so many shops; you couldn't hit them all in one day. Indeed, a luxury hotel stood in the middle of the theme park so tourists could spend the night.

Other than the dome, the second biggest eye-catcher was the roller coaster called the Thunder Dolphin. It coiled itself over buildings and restaurants, in serpentine twists and turns. It looped around and around overhead, and even shot through a hole made in the top of LaQua, a massive eight-story shopping plaza. Too bad it cost about fifteen dollars per ride, or I'd be on it every weekend. The line is also horrendous.

In LaQua, you'd find shops with clothing, jewelry, luggage, toys, and specialty shops for baseball and anime. You could be sitting at a café on the ground level and suddenly, your tea sipping is interrupted by blood-curdling screams as the Dolphin thunders by overhead.

To top it all off, a giant Ferris wheel called The Big O slowly rotated nearby like a giant cog. It's the world's first hub-less Ferris wheel, meaning no support beams join in a focal point in the center. There was also a water slide, merry-go-round for kids, an 80-meter tower drop attraction, and a few tame mini coasters for kids.

I had yet to explore all the wonders of Tokyo Dome City, but this time I got to see the famous spot in the minds of MMA fans:

Korakuen Hall. Located on the fifth floor of the "Blue Building," it was the home to Shooto, pro-wrestling, boxing, and other MMA events.

I met Zuyo at 5:30pm at Suidobashi station, which is right next to the Tokyo Dome. I followed her through the main gate, past a Denny's diner, bowling alley, crepe/hotdog stand, and arcade.

A shop with fighting goods caught my eye, and I veered sharply to the left to look. It was a specialty shop selling mostly pro wrestling goods. I recognized a few figures, like Sakuraba, who has done both pro wrestling and MMA. They sold key chains, towels, DVDs, books, T-shirts, dolls, action figures, pens, pencils – you name it, they had merchandise for it.

Zuyo hadn't stopped, so I forced myself to hurry. A colorful horse-filled carousel spun around and around off to the side, filled with laughing children and patient adults riding side by side.

The Dome City is spectacular at night. A myriad of lights strung over trees and buildings illuminated everything in a multitude of colors. Strange decorative glass triangular structures stuck out of a fountain, which ran through one section of the park. They glowed gently among the spraying water. Droplets sparkled as they sprinkled down. It was all very magical, even romantic at times.

The time of the competition struck me as a little strange. The doors opened at 5:30 and the show started at 6:00. In the United States, I was used to the doors opening at 7:00, with a 7:30 start. Most shows never started on time anyway. I appreciated this early fight time since I had to take the train home. In the heart of Tokyo, most people took public transportation, which stopped around 12:30am. Americans, on the other hand, usually drive so they can leave any time.

The professionalism and efficiency of how the crew ran the event impressed me a lot. After thanking the man who escorted me to my seat like royalty, I let my eyes roam over the audience. There seemed to be an almost equal number of men and woman. During the fights, the cheering style differed as well. Fans shouted their

124

favorite fighter's name. Rather than, "Get 'em, George! Kick 'em in the head! Beat his face in!" or "Go, Melvin, go!" we heard single shouts of last names. "Uematsu!" people yelled. Or, "Tiger-san!" if his nickname was Tiger. No other shout was necessary. Obviously. They didn't need to be told that they should kick harder, if you think about it. I caught myself yelling techniques, but tried to refrain once I realized nobody else was doing that.

The actual fights also impressed me. Although everyone emphasized "Shooto rules," it seemed just like the MMA fighting that I'm used to seeing. The main differences were that elbows and knees to the face are not allowed. Shooto also had a knockdown rule like boxing, where the ref can stop the fight for a count of ten, if the fighter is wobbly or fell down. This gives him a moment to recover. In the end, it usually doesn't make much of a difference. Most people believe it'd just be better to let the attacker finish him.

During the entire show, I felt waves of nervousness run through my body like white water rapids. I couldn't help but imagine myself inside the ring going through what those fighters were facing. I relished that burning feeling that was there whenever I visualized my fight. Again, I wondered what it was. "Adrenaline? Ki? Chi? Fighting spirit? My imagination? As the week goes on, I'm sure it will eat me alive." I'd felt nervous before, but never scared I'd get my face punched in.

As I watched the crowd between bouts of action, I spotted other members of my dojo. We all gathered in one area and cheered together. It reminded me of when I used to work at Mass Destruction and Reality Fighting with Kipp Kollar and the rest of the guys at NAGA – the North American Grappling Association – and at my gym, Amherst Athletic Club. Experiences like these caused the bonds to grow between my new training partners and myself. I relished it.

Some time during the evening, Zuyo, who was sitting on my right, turned and asked me, "Hey, do you know Caol Uno?"

"Well, yes, I know of him. He's one of my favorite fighters. I saw him fight in the UFC. Why?"

"He's standing right behind us!"

"What!?"

Zuyo laughed at me as I turned around. Indeed it was he, seated a few rows back. I nearly jumped out of my skin, grabbing for my bag. I wanted to take a picture, but it wasn't a good shot. After the show, I couldn't find him for an autograph. Uno was also with Wajyutsu Keisyukai, and had come to cheer on Toida and two more of his teammates who I'd come to know pretty well in the future: Kenji Osawa and Hiroyuki Takaya.

Uematsu received a warm welcome from the fans. He was the second fighter to enter, but the crowd was cheering for him before the first guy's entrance music had stopped.

"He's MY sensei," I thought, laughing at myself for my child-like pride. "Not yours. Mine!" Everyone seemed to love him.

An official sitting ringside at a table banged on a metal gong. The fighters came out of their corners and met in the center of the ring. Uematsu fought so calmly, and appeared without a shred of worry. His opponent tried to stand up with him at first, and then take him down. Uematsu calmly stuffed all attempts. He stood up so straight and wasn't moving around so much. It struck me as a little odd, but he skillfully kept proper distance and then went in for the kill. A few minutes later, Uematsu heel hooked his opponent with relative ease. So cool. At the time I had no knowledge of any fighter other than those in the UFC. Toida is actually a ground submission specialist. His style, stance, and techniques are extremely unconventional, but Uematsu must have known that he'd try to take him down. However, the fact that Uematsu caught Toida in a submission hold is particularly impressive.

He was the main event, and afterward he gave a speech, none of which I could understand. I wanted desperately to understand. After the area cleared out, I waited outside along with the rest of the club.

"What's taking so long?" I asked Zuyo, after we'd been standing around for close to 20 minutes.

It was a school night.

"He's probably doing blah blah blah business," Zuyo replied, using some words I didn't know.

126

"Well, I really want to stay, but I have to be getting home."

I excused myself and made it home in time to finish some homework before it got too late.

The next day, I saw Uematsu at the dojo. Actually, I was surprised he showed up.

"You looked so cool!" I raved. "Good job! You were standing so straight, so confident. You even walked around him in a circle!"

"I fractured a rib the night before," Uematsu said with a straight face. "I was fighting like that because I couldn't move around very well."

That stunned me into silence.

"You're kidding."

He only laughed.

That blew my mind.

November 7

As the week went on, I felt more and more confident. Taking long walks, obsessive thoughts circled round and round in my mind. I constantly visualized myself defeating my opponent, in one way or another. I knew confidence and mental imagery were the keys.

In Naruto, Guy Sensei said to Rock, "All your training won't matter if you don't have confidence in yourself."

"I have confidence in my ground ability, and I've been working hard on my striking technique," I told myself. "I know I can win. I will win!"

The other night at training, Uematsu taught us a good double leg takedown. We practiced shooting in without planting our left knee down on the ground between the opponent's legs. I'd always landed heavily on my knee.

"Your knee bounces off the mat," Uematsu explained to the group. "And you simultaneously drive your ear into the person's hip. At the same time, you're cutting behind his knees with your legs. By cutting, I mean grabbing behind the knees and pulling with a hard jerk. After this, you need to swing your other leg around to the side, in this case, his right side. So when he tries to back away, the back leg, which is really hard to get, can be reached."

He demonstrated on a skinny blue belt with buckteeth. The fellow showed some resistance, but still flopped helplessly to the mat under Uematsu's practiced technique.

"You can take the person down easier if you come from the side," Uematsu finished, and then did it one more time.

I liked it. It also seemed less stressful on the body, for I don't fancy smashing my face into their stomach, or straining my neck. It happened all too often, probably due to my poor technique or style, which didn't fit me. I enjoyed learning a different takedown method.

That night, I left early because I felt a little weak. Nobody stopped me or gave me a hard time, which was nice. We all wanted me to be healthy for my fight on Monday. I returned home to work frantically at finishing all my homework.

"I think I'm finally a little homesick," I thought to myself, as I approached the gate of the home, which wasn't my own. "But I can't think about that now. I have a fight to win."

Chapter 12 – Fight Night!
November 11

My eyes slowly opened, letting in the light of a new day. Fight day. I groped around and found my mini alarm clock.

I grunted to myself. "Ten hours of sleep. Nice," I thought.

I felt no nervousness whatsoever. I simply got ready for school and went to my classes. During linguistics, I managed to pay attention for the most part, although every two minutes my thoughts drifted off to the myriad possible endings to my fight. My Japanese class presented poetry, so we met in a recording studio on the end of campus. One by one, my classmates had to stand at a podium and recite. The grade was equivalent to our final exam.

My reading could have been better. I think I got a B-minus. It would have been nice not to have exam stress the day of my fight. The class ended an hour early, so I gratefully booked it back home to where I spent the extra hour reading fight technique notes.

My host mother poked her head into my room around 1:00. "You're fighting tonight, right?" she asked me for the billionth time. "Can I make you anything?"

"Yeah, could you cook me some pancakes? I want to eat them after weigh-ins," I requested. She immediately prepared me a batch. At 2:00 I walked out the door armed with my power-food, and headed to Roppongi. On the train ride, I tried to work myself up by listening to heavy metal, and imagining myself beating on people.

I'm glad I left two hours early, since I got lost in the windy back roads trying to find Velfarre, the largest nightclub in Roppongi. My doubts as to which building it was evaporated once I saw a table being up outside.

"Is this where Smackgirl is?" I asked them in Japanese.

"Yes," one of the ladies setting up said. "But we're not open yet."

"I'm Roxanne and I'm fighting," I told her.

"Oh, okay." She turned and spoke to someone else. "Right this way!" she said, and led me into a waiting room. All smiles and bows, she gave me some last minute medical forms and asked, "Can you read Japanese?"

"Oh, yes," I answered.

"Great! Then please fill this out," she said, and left.

I looked at the documents, but could only understand about fifty percent. Around 3:45, a short Japanese woman with short black hair joined me. She looked nervous.

"This is my first fight," she said.

"Me, too!" I exclaimed.

"Oh, really?" She trained boxing and jiu jitsu at the dojo called Paraestra, the Tokyo branch.

I spoke with her a bit, and she helped me with reading the kanji and explaining the meanings of the medical background questions. I liked her a lot, and regretted not paying attention to her fight.

The fighters' meeting was supposed to begin at four o'clock, but everyone else was late. At about 4:20 Jet came waltzing in followed by Uematsu, Kotani, Luke, Genki Yamaguchi, and Shu Inagaki, my reporter friend who also trained kickboxing at Cross Point. It felt so good to have them there, talking, laughing, and making noise. I felt like I wanted to explode from anticipation.

"I'm not nervous. I'm cool and confident. Confident like a Rock. Like Rock Lee, in Naruto," I repeated to myself over and over. "I'm gonna win. This is gonna be great. Super. Super great."

The Smackgirl staff called us into the back room to weigh us in. We'd strip down to undergarments, and the athletic commission - if there is one - and promoters measure our weight. Some ladies were right on weight, but some struggled. Few fighters step on the scale at their natural weight. It's actually better to dehydrate yourself. When weigh-ins are done and you drink and eat, you have a slight weight advantage over your opponent in the ring. Since everyone thinks this way, if a fighter doesn't dehydrate, they are actually at a weight disadvantage. Wrestlers are especially good at dehydration methods, and tend to step into the cage or ring heavier than their counterparts.

After making weight, fighters run to their bags and guzzle a bottle of water, and chow down energy bars. They most likely hadn't eaten or drank anything all day. If they don't make weight, they put on sweat clothes and go jog around the building to sweat it out.

I had made sure I dieted enough so I made weight easily, even wearing jeans. Back in the waiting room, I broke out my pancakes and peanut butter. Genki laughed when he saw the little jar of Skippy and the knife I brought. I passed out bite-sized pieces to everyone.

I'd just come back from brushing my teeth, when Uematsu spoke up from his place on the couch. "Your opponent just got here!"

I went outside to take a peek. She quickly weighed in and started warming up in the ring. A few other fighters joined her, and they danced around to avoid bumping into each other. I watched her practice sparring with her coach, or training partner.

"Why would she do that in public?" I asked out loud. "She's showing off all her moves!" Luke, standing next to me, shrugged. It was extremely valuable for me. She went at him flailing punches.

"Do wide body hooks!" I heard him advise.

That doesn't sound too effective, I thought. He got her in a single leg about five times during their sparing, so I made a note to try that right off the bat. I had a feeling she didn't know a lot of grappling.

"No problem," Uematsu said to me after I came back from watching. "You'll beat her no problem."

"But I can't think that way!" I said to him, throwing up my hands. "I have to pretend she's the toughest person in the world! That way, I'll try my best."

"Okay, Roxanne," he said, grinning, and settled back against the cushiony seats. Apparently, the back room in the nightclub was one of many, and it became our corner's room. We shared the space with about five or six other fighters, plus their coaches.

Finally, they called us to the rules meeting at 5:00. We sat cross-legged, or knelt in a circle inside the ring to listen, while our coaches sat around it outside. The promoter and refs went over the

131

rules, most of which I understood. When the Japanese words went over my head, I asked Jet, who was sitting next to me. She managed to reword it. No elbows, 30-second ground rule, no soccer kicks, no face kicks to a downed opponent, no small-joint manipulations like bending the fingers back, no fish hooks or hair pulling or grabbing your opponent's clothes.

They taught us how to line up on stage after our names were called, and where to walk at what time during the opening ceremony. I felt like I was in a high school graduation rehearsal.

I managed to chat with a few of the other fighters, who were pretty nice, although naturally nervous. Maybe not the best time to make friends. After the rehearsal, one of the Smackgirl organizers with a walkie-talkie wire over one ear trotted over waving a few papers. "Okay, everyone please line up here to be checked by the doctor one last time."

We shuffled to the room he pointed to, and waited outside together awkwardly. Everyone tried not to look at their opponents. Mine, Hikaru Shinohara, was standing right in front of me. Pretty, slender and with a nice smile, she was a little bit smaller than me. Our eyes met, and I smiled slightly. I really liked her shirt. She wore a tight red short-sleeved shirt that was open in the front to reveal a black sports bra, with laces tied in front. I just wore a red spandex *Vitimins and Minerals*-brand grappling shirt I borrowed from Zuyo, along with blue Adidas shorts.

She walked over.

I opened my mouth to say "konnichi wa" but her words came out faster.

"Nan sai?" she asked bluntly. How old are you?

"Ni ju isssai," I answered, swallowing my greeting. 21.

"Aaaa? Wakai neee! That's so young," she exclaimed, half talking to me, half talking to the other ladies who might have been listening. Everybody kind of looked in a different direction. She then said something quickly about "a pretty face," "you have a tall nose, but I have a flat nose", and "zannen," which means, "it's a shame." Blinking and smiling dumbly, it took me a second to put two and two together. Unless I was totally mistaken, she was saying that she'd be okay during the fight since she had a flat nose, but I had a tall nose, so it'd be a shame once it got smashed in.

This indirect threat implication that she might break my nose shocked me. My brain chose to be amused rather than frightened, and I nearly snorted with laughter.

I made some vague response like "Oh, really? I see," and had to work to keep from smiling. Actually, it freaked me out.

She laughed loudly and moved away from me to another part of the line.

The check consisted of a few useless questions about recent injuries, how much weight one had to cut, and if we were pregnant or not. My bumps and bruises weren't worth mentioning. I only cut a few pounds, and no, I wasn't pregnant. That would be hard with no boyfriend.

After the check, people continued warming up. Jet came over and asked me if I wanted to.

"No, I'm sorry. I really don't want to show my opponent my moves. See, she's sitting outside the ring right now, watching us!"

"Oh..."

It occurred to me that Jet wanted to get some practice in, so I backpedaled and offered to be her practice dummy. She gratefully accepted. I let Jet do moves on me, and then practiced ground escapes.

"Okay, everyone, please go to your waiting rooms!" the staff instructed after a little while.

The bright Velfarre overhead lights dimmed slightly, and someone activated the flashing colored spotlights. Spectators began entering, heads bent as they checked their ticket for their seat number. Metal folding seats had been arranged around the ring, each with a number taped onto the back.

Fighters waited for what seemed like forever in our own separate waiting rooms. I occasionally peaked out to watch the place fill up. It wasn't a huge place. The ring had been constructed in the center of the dance floor.

"Shu, how many people would you say are here?" I asked my kickboxing friend, as the event seemed ready to start.

"It's hard to tell exactly," he answered, taking in the room with a practiced eye. "Maybe between 300 to 400 people."

I put my gi on over my shorts and fight shirt in order to show my jiu jitsu background to the audience when we were called out. This helped me feel more confident and proud to wear old club's patch. I displayed my "Team Joao Amaral Vale Tudo" sewn on the back.

"Hurry up and start, already!" I thought impatiently.

At 7:30 the opening ceremony finally started. Flashing lights bathed us in bursts of brilliance as we walked out onto the stage. Amidst the music and the cheering, our names boomed through the loud speakers. My heart raced, but my mind was locked in a perfect calm as I looked out onto the crowd.

As soon as we filed back into the waiting room, the first matches began. Jet was fourth on the card, and I was fifth. Impatient, I constantly paced the floor, stretched, shadow boxed, and then started the whole cycle again.

"Are you nervous?" Kotani and Uematsu kept asking me.

"No, I'm not!" I denied it. "I just wanna get out there and fight! Is it almost my turn?" A soundless TV was set up in our room so we could watch the matches.

When it was Jet's turn, we poked our heads outside the curtain, which separated our room from the back stage. The stage wasn't too far, and we had a decent view. Unfortunately, she had an accident, and dislocated her arm by falling wrong. Genki went to the hospital with her.

"I'm up next! Yay, finally!" I shouted, trying not to let Jet's misfortune get me down. "Finally finally finally, I'm next! Right now! Fight fight fight! I'm gonna fight! To show what I could do, to test myself, to punch my opponent, beat down beat down...."

"There's an intermission first," Uematsu told me.

"Oh? Oh, right. How long is it?"

"Hmmm...About 15 minutes."

"What?!"

With taking care of Jet, and taking care of lose ends, it actually stretched into 30 minutes. People kept telling me to relax, but I didn't want to. I probably made them nervous, pacing the floors as I was. It was a big deal to me. I would be in the spotlight. Strikes would be thrown. Someone was going down. My life would change.

Finally after the agonizing wait, it was my turn.

"Okay, Roxanne! Stand here," one of the staff waved at me. I put my glasses in my bag, and leaped to obey. The lights outside went dark. The audience fell silent. The staff held up a hand, signaling me to wait.

My entrance music erupted into the stillness, filling the room with heavy-metal chords. It was "Need to be Strong," from the anime Naruto.

Over the loudspeaker, the announcer introduced me in Japanese.

"Now, introducing a newcomer from America! Roxanne Modafferi!" With my blurry vision, I saw my name flash across the wall-sized screen, which hung over the stage where I would be entering.

As my song got past the intro and the cool part began, the staff member put down his hand and motioned for me to walk. I walked up the steps and out on stage.

"This is so cool," I thought, hoping desperately I wouldn't trip over something and fall down. Camera-totting men following me from behind and in front, walking backwards in front of me, filming my entrance. I walked down the steps from the stage to the floor, where Uematsu, Luke, and Kotani fell into step behind me. We went to the blue corner, and from wooden steps propped up against the ring's base, I entered the ring.

Some fighters run around the ring. Some people bounce off the ropes. Some people do a little dance. Some people hold up their arms and try to get the audience excited to cheer for them. I simply bowed to everyone and started taking off my gi. In the middle of untying my belt, my music switched off and Hikaru Shinohara's began.

I wasn't really listening to her introduction as Kotani held out a funnel for me to swish and spit water. My opponent entered, but I can't remember what she did. The audience became a blur that wasn't really important. Only my opponent was illuminated under those ring-lights. My corner's voices became small. They weren't really important either.

The referee stood in the center of the ring, as the announcer's voice boomed over the loud-speakers. "In the blue corner, coming from America, fighting out of Cross Point Kichijoji, born in the USA! Roxanne Modafferi!"

"Born in the USA? And the pamphlet said, "Blue Eyes Vibration." Stereotypical foreigner image…but I don't have blue eyes…" A wave of amusement passed through me, which immediately disappeared in tense anticipation.

"In the red corner…." Hikaru Shinohara was announced, but I was no longer listening. The ref called us to the center together and said one last reminder that there were no elbows, no punching to the head on the ground, etc. I shook hands with Hikaru and went back to my corner for the last time.

The lights, which had dimmed slightly, came on full blast. I don't even remember if there was a bell, or if someone said "go!" or "hajime!" to begin.

It was on. Hikaru and I both shot out of our corners. I tried a few testing jabs to gauge distance. Without hesitating or backing away, she lunged at me and started flurrying punches. I got socked three times hard in the face. Years of kickboxing practice translated into zero ability in the fight.

Okay, screw kickboxing, I thought. I deftly ducked under the punches and did a double-leg takedown. More like a desperate tackle. The timing was perfect. She wasn't able to sprawl at all. She didn't get guard, or wrap her legs around my waist. Better for me! I quickly passed her guard, getting past her legs to pin her from the side. Three seconds had passed. I held side control - a perpendicular pin - and tried to get a key lock. She glued her arms to her chest protectively, guarding against my arm lock attack.

"Go to the north-south position!" Uematsu called to me from my corner. "North-south!"

"But I want that arm!" I thought.

"Okay, okay! Up up up!" The ref shouted at us to stand up. Huh? Oh yeah, 30-second ground limit.

136

He pushed us apart, but like a spring, we bounced back. White Smackgirl gloves flew through the air. I couldn't see them clearly. They flashed in my vision, so I ducked down in exactly the same way as before. Her hips slammed forward into my chest, the pressure neutralizing my takedown.

She's trying to sprawl...must take away her legs!

My outside right leg hooked around hers. She couldn't resist anymore, and fell heavily backwards. I was all over her in an instant. Like before, I pressured her legs to the ground. I passed her guard, and tried to get the key lock from the side control. She defended and rolled over. I clung to her back like a monkey, pulling her up into a sitting position. My arms snaked around her neck, trying to slip under her chin.

If I could cut off her breathing, or block the arteries in her neck and stop the blood flow... I could make her tap!

Our gloves were too thick. She fought my hands off with all her might. I couldn't get by her defense.

"Thirty seconds! Stand up!" the ref called.

For a third time we faced each other. I threw a low kick to her front leg, and promptly got socked in the cheek. It didn't hurt in the slightest, but it shook me.

"Oh, I'm hit!"

I panicked and did what came naturally. I dove straight into the takedown.

"I got it! She's mine!"

She gave me her back again. I took it, but instead of trying for the choke, I shifted my grip, latching onto her arm. I yanked it straight. Her bent arm became straight. I slowly hyper extended it. Time seemed to stop a beat as I stared down at her fully extended arm. Slowly, I applied pressure.

Slowly. Hold tight. Stretch. Hold tight! One... Two...Three...

"Stop! Stop stop stop!" the ref hollered, removing her arm from my grip.

I'm not sure if she tapped or if the ref chose to stop it.

The fight was over. Over? As the ref stood us up and raised my hand as the victor, I felt pleased that neither of us got hurt. Then it struck me: I won!

One of my cornermen, I'm not even sure if it was Uematsu or Luke, came out into the ring.

"Go thank Hikaru and her corner," he said. I stumbled over, my brain still foggy, saying "thank you" in English before I managed an "arigato gozaimasu" in Japanese.

I won?!

"Here, stand other there and pose for the photographers," he said. I returned to the center of the ring and saw six photographers lined up outside the ring. I raised my fists and smiled. My hair wasn't even messed up. "I won! And I'm okay!"

Walking back to the waiting room, I tripped over a doorstep and almost fell flat on my face. Everyone laughed. Zuyo and Miyata-san bustled over from their seats in the audience and hugged me. Shu broke out a cake, soda, and chocolates be bought ahead of time.

"Now you don't have to hold back!" he laughed. "It's over! Congratulations!"

My vision improved significantly with my glasses back on. I was in ecstasy.

"I wished I'd tried more standup," I babbled to Luke, giddily. "But I knew I could get the take down whenever I wanted."

"You did well," he replied diplomatically, or something to that effect.

"And everyone back home told me not to try and stand up with a striker if she's better..." I continued chatting away.

After a while it occurred to me that I didn't undergo any major changes as an after effect of fighting. I didn't metamorphosis into a gigantic butterfly, or have any mental epiphanies, or turn into Buddha. I didn't feel like a battle-scared warrior, either. Nor had I become a ninja or samurai. Still, I just defeated another human being in my first professional match. Yet I could walk away saying that I'd never successfully hit anyone full in the face. Was that a bad thing?

138

A Smackgirl staff member poked his head in and said something I didn't understand.

"He wants to interview you," Luke translated.

We followed him farther into the depths of Velfarre. Somewhere in a back hallway, a camera stood on a pedestal under some spotlights. A few reporters clutching little notebooks stood around. I tried to answer in Japanese, and Luke stood behind us to translate the questions I couldn't understand. I felt awkward trying to use both languages, but he said that they loved it that I was speaking a little Japanese.

It was okay that I couldn't say exactly what I thought. My standup was almost non-existent, but she sucked more, so I managed to get her with my favorite move. The fight lasted almost exactly two minutes.

"I thought Miss Shinohara was very skilled and it was an honor for me to fight her," I managed in Japanese. They asked about my background and I told them I did judo for three years and BJJ for another three. "I'm looking for strong opponents to fight in the future," I added at the very end.

We hung around Velfarre until everything had finished, thanked the staff members, and then went to the hospital to visit Jet. Her arm was in a sling.

"It was dislocated, but should get better soon," they told us. Genki and Kotani assured us they'd make sure she got home all right.

I took the train back together with Luke, who lived in Mitaka, and Uematsu, who actually lived a few stops after mine on the Chuo line. For the 45-minute trip, we stood in a little circle, trying to think of a nickname for me.

"I can't believe they announced me as, 'Roxanne Modafferi, Born in the USA!'" I complained. "That's super corny!"

The train jolted to a stop, and we all reached for the hanging rings for balance.

"Probably because you didn't submit one when they asked," Luke said.

"How about 'Roxanne Armbar Queen Modafferi,'" Uematsu suggested. "Or 'Roxanne Super Saiyan Modafferi.'"

"How about simply 'Super Roxanne?'" I suggested. We all laughed. "Nah."

"How about, 'Roxanne Geisha Modafferi'? Uematsu said, obviously joking. The other train passengers must have thought we were nuts.

Finally Luke got off at Mitaka. Uematsu and I sat silently for a minute before I spoke up.

"My friends back home call me Roxy, pronounced "roku shee."

"Oh that's cool," he said. "You can always use that."

I nodded, thinking he was just saying that to humor me.

Maybe not for a ring name. That's what my friends call me.

I walked back home 200 dollars richer and with a professional fight record of 1-0. Faces and voices of all the people who helped and supported me swam around my mind in an endless circle. I wanted to tell them all that very minute. I wanted them to be proud of me.

I knew that I had a long way to go. This was only the beginning.

Chapter 13 – The Aftermath: Alone in Tokyo Tower
November 19th

Time, which had slowed to a crawl as my fight approached, burst into flight like a frightened flock of birds, flapping and fluttering furiously. I became able to think about other things, such as visiting home for Christmas vacation. It seemed like I had just left, but I'd never been away from home for more than a month until then. My parents' respective homes were within a two-hour drive from my college, the University of Massachusetts. My mother called me at my host mother's roughly twice a week, but I still couldn't wait to hold her in my arms again. My father almost never called. We'd have to work on that.

On one day during final exam week, I found myself with no tests scheduled. Rather than doing nothing, I decided to go on a random sightseeing tour around Tokyo. Some places on my list to see were Daimon, Ginza, and some other random stops on the chikatetsu – subway – and the Yamanote line, which ran in a circle through the heart of Tokyo.

I started at 10am, heading first to Akihabara, then Tokyo Tower. I decided to dish out the cash and go up to the observatory. First things first; I hit the wonderful Marion Crepe stand under the tower. After a delectable banana chocolate custard crepe, I paid the 1000 yen (about 12 US dollars) for an observatory ticket.

Soon, I found myself packed into an elevator with Japanese tourists. The courteous women operating the elevator smiled and bowed politely, saying many nice things in Japanese that I didn't catch. I did understand, however, that the Tokyo Tower was very tall. Very, very tall. She said something about France.

"Oh yeah, that's right," I thought. I'd done my homework. It was modeled after the Eiffel Tower in Paris, but stands 30 meters taller, at 333 meters (1092 ft.). I learned that the tower serves as an antenna tower for 14 local Japanese television and radio stations. It also boasts the title of "world's tallest self-supporting steel structure."

The doors slid open with a hiss. Finally!

I walked around the observatory, which was a room with windows on all sides. Here and there were mammoth-sized binoculars you had to put money into to look through. There was a small souvenir stand.

It wasn't as breathtaking as I had imagined, but still extremely cool. I bought a funny looking key chain of Tokyo tower. It was a strange little man with a huge long pink head that actually looked like a banana. He was Little Tokyo Tower Boy!

Japanese can make a cute character out of anything, I thought. I had my fill after about ten minutes.

After descending from the observatory by elevator, there were four floors above the ground floor that had some interesting attractions. The fourth floor itself had a trick art gallery, filled with optical illusion paintings and sculptures. I didn't actually enter because I didn't want to pay the ten-dollar fee.

I noted the Government Information Display Center and Exhibition Room for Statistical Information; both of which seemed so fascinating that I couldn't contain myself, and had to hurry as fast as I could to the stairs. The Wax Museum on the third floor cost six dollars, which I also didn't feel like paying, so I set that aside for later as well. A few random stores with hanging bead curtains and old rock posters sold '60s hippie music and neon lights. I glanced into them, but it was just too weird to see that sort of thing in Japan, so I continued along without entering.

Then I came to the ninja store. Yes, ninja. Little trays of knickknacks attracted my eye like colorful baubles draw in a raccoon. Metallic key chains dangled, and as I went over to look, I saw little ninja stars, or shuriken, on sale. I knew what Shinobi were from the anime Naruto. Cheap rubber nunchucks for children sat in what looked like an umbrella holder nearby, which I seriously considered getting for my cousins, but I eventually decided against it. What were twelve-year olds-going to do with those anyway, hit each other? Oh, my aunt would love that.

I wandered further into the store where a surprise was waiting for me. Along a wall was set up what looked like a carnival dart throwing game, where you win a prize by hitting a red and white bull's eye hanging on the wall. Instead of darts, you threw shuriken, ninja stars!

"Three hundred yen to throw five," a sign read. A middle-aged woman with short gray hair in the store called out "Irrashaimase!" Welcome!

I immediately pointed to the wall and said, "Yate mite mo ii desu ka?" Is it okay if I try it?

Smiling broadly, the nice lady nodded and even told me I could "renshu," or practice. I asked her to take my picture as I chucked the star. She did, then added that the shuriken were the real thing.

This is so freaking cool, I said to myself. As I held the metal weapons in my hand, I tried to imagine myself in ancient times.

I'm glad I never have to use one of these to hurt someone, I thought, smiling. For all I know, the horrible weapon may have been stained with the blood of hundreds of people. They weren't particularly heavy or light. I examined two types; one with three sides, and one with six.

The woman told me to throw overhand by flicking my wrist, whereas I would have tried sideways like a Frisbee. I figured that she knew best, so I aimed and threw. My first shuriken hit the third stripe out from the center. We exchanged shocked expressions that it actually hit. I was about ready to run to Naruto's Ninja Academy and become a Gennin - a freshman Ninja student. I threw the remaining four with varying success, but couldn't hit the center. It wasn't like throwing darts into a corkboard. These metal blades flew fast and accurately.

The woman explained that if all five shuriken hit the bull's eye, I would receive a sword as a prize. If four hit, I would get a T-shirt. Three would win me a cheap-looking plastic sword/shuriken set, two the rubber nunchucks, and one would win me a cheap-looking pin with the kanji symbol for Ninja on it.

Only one of my throws hit the bull's eye, and the others stuck in the surrounding area or bounced off the wall.

"Here's the pin!" she said with a smile. "Sorry!" I coughed up the money for four more throws and played again, not doing much better but having a ton of fun.

That game itself made my day, maybe my week. I eventually forced myself to leave. A display rack caught my eye and I paused to examine it. It had necklaces with little metal shuriken charms hung in bunches. I desperately wanted one, but knew that I'd never wear it. It screamed, "Look, everyone, I'm a stupid tourist who thinks Japanese things are cool!" The equivalent to me wearing a shuriken around my neck is probably like a Japanese person wearing a charm of an old-fashioned American rifle.

After I finished browsing through the kiosks and stores, I left the Tower. Outside, I ran into what I can only describe as a Christmas Godzilla. Little white lights were strung all over the statue - I'm not sure if it was made of sturdy plastic or metal - which loomed over a miniature statue of the Tower. On its leg hung a sign: *Gojira wo sawaranaide kudasai* (Please don't touch Godzilla). I saw some kids poking it anyway.

My next stop was Daimon via subway.

Hey, I've already been here! I realized. *Cayte, Candie, Mana and I passed by it the first time. We bought takoyaki at that big shrine.*

Ginza was next. I huffed and puffed up the multiple flights of stairs. "Ginza Times Square," built in imitation of Times Square in NY, had gigantic TV screens overlooking the wide streets. Expensive rows of shops lined each side. Ginza is known as the most expensive shopping city, so I stayed away from the goods.

Hmmm, that fish market called Tsukiji is supposed to be in walking distance, I thought.

Try as I might, I couldn't find my way. My new friend Katie from my International Persuasion class told me that night that if I wanted to go at 6am, the fish markets would be bustling.

"The sushi is the best in the country because it'd be freshly caught!" she had said. Going at 6am would mean getting up before 5:00, which wasn't in the agenda for the day.

After walking around lost for a while, I decided to go to Shinjuku and try and find a CD player. I failed to find one, almost got lost in the garden of glowing neon signs, and run over by the usual mob of people.

144

After Sadako-san's scrumptious dinner, I headed over to Cayte's dorm on the ICU campus. The next day, I would complete my last two final exams, and after that I wasn't sure what I was going to do with myself.

"Try watching *As You Like It*," Cayte suggested, sitting herself down on hardwood floor. Yogi lay like a lump, half under the narrow study desk.

"I'd rather watch anime than read Shakespeare," I laughed. Soon, Candie came over and we sat eating Japanese junk food, reminiscing about all the American cartoons we used to love.

"I'm sad that you're leaving us!" I said. Cayte's time in Japan would end with the closure of the semester. She had her junior and senior year in Cornell University to complete.

"I'll miss you!" Candie said.

We would both miss her. She'd go on to get a double degree in Linguistics and Asian studies, and start work at a kindergarten.

November 21

I made the hike to Shibuya so I could take Uematsu's class. He taught a cool defense to the double-leg takedown, and I managed to apply it in sparring twice. It's one thing to do drills and another thing to actually pull it off live. The other day I practiced some beautiful sweeps and position reversals he taught with Yukie, his girlfriend. She's truly the nicest woman I've ever met. Her facial expression is the very picture of innocence. Her eyes shine with kindness. It didn't surprise me in the slightest to learn that she was an elementary school teacher. If I were a man, I'd probably fall in love. One could say I had a girl crush on her.

She could also throw me effortlessly when we sparred judo.

I trained very hard that class. After one sparring match ended, Uematsu matched me up with a new person immediately, leaving little room for me to pick my own partner. At one point, he told me to fight this one white belt, the white being the rank of a beginner. My prideful disgruntlement to being paired with someone "lower" than I quickly changed to surprise as the man totally dominated the fight. He pinned me, making attack after successful attack that I was barely able to stave off. I believe I tapped out, or succumbed to a submission technique. Not only did this damage my pride, but also it showed that there was obviously something wrong with my gameplan. I must have had some flaw in my defense I wasn't aware of if he could clock-choke me twice.

A voice from my past flashed through my head. I was back in the Amherst Athletic club, in Massachusetts:

"If I catch you in the same thing a bunch of times, obviously you're doing something wrong," said Andrew Yao. *My cynical friend was always such a great training partner for me.*

At the Boston Top Team, too, they had a magic way of explaining things that I always seemed to understand. If I didn't get it, one of the guys would keep catching me with it. This continued until they beat the correct defense into me, and the bad habit out of me. In Japan, it just wasn't the same. Often I just didn't understand the Japanese language, or because the teacher was busy with the rest of the class.

My ire rose at my failure to crack the mystery of why I was being clock-choked. I sulked for a few minutes after our match, excusing myself to 'go to the restroom.' A thought came to me soon after, however, and with it came almost relief.

I haven't been feeling challenged enough lately, I realized. *I'm not getting beat up as much, like I did back in the US.*

True, the average Japanese person was about my size, making it physically easier for me to hold my own. I wasn't used to that. Therefore, it was rather refreshing to get my butt decimated for a change. If only it weren't by a white belt.

I missed my Brazilian friends a whole lot right then. I wandered into a corner and tried to stop the wetness from leaking out of my eyes. If anyone saw me, maybe they would think it was sweat. Clenching my mouth guard tightly between my teeth, I told myself, *You will deal with this, and get better from it! If you're not struggling, you're not growing.*

The rest of the gym probably thought I was upset because I got beat up, but I tried to make myself not care. I hobbled across the mat, feeling the fatigue of burning muscles in my legs, and started chatting with the white belt who'd just beaten me. It turns out he was extremely nice and even knew a little bit of English.

"I used to study in Milwaukee a long time ago," he said in English, but claimed to have forgotten everything.

"But your English is so good!" I exclaimed, echoing everyone's compliments about my Japanese. He waved away my compliment. I hoped he would train more often. I hadn't seen him around the gym so much. Despite the color of his belt, he said he'd been training for two years. His technique was pretty good.

November 22

Our large, gray-haired linguistics teacher lumbered to and fro in the front of the classroom, passing back our tests. All morning I didn't feel a shred of nervousness about what the score would be. After all, if you know you're going to get a poor mark, there's no use worrying about it, is there? I felt only dread. Dread and disappointment reached into the deepest part of my heart. I had tried my absolute best. I studied so hard. No matter what I did, I could not seem to score well on any of the tests he put in front of us. That's not supposed to happen.

"When you try your best, you're supposed to be able to do anything!" my heart pouted, remembering Naruto, who always stood back up even after being beaten down time and time again. I recalled many frustrating nights and afternoons spent in the comprehension of the mathematics-like linguistic formulas. What was worse, some of the Japanese students who were struggling to take the class in a second language did better than me. How could that be? English isn't even their native language! I had previously gotten poor marks on my tests – shattering for the self esteem of an honors student- and I knew this one wouldn't be so different.

The red number at the top drew my eyes immediately: 90. In parenthesis in the corner was the final grade for my semester: 120, a C.

"I was very impressed," the teacher was saying to me as he turned away. "You worked hard."

"Thank...you," I said slowly, not believing my eyes. "I got a C! I passed?" I thought.

"If you have any questions see me sometime," he said, handing the next student his test.

Wait, a 90 means an "A." I got an "A" on the test? I thought incredulously, my mouth hanging open. A fly could have done a little jig on my tongue. *I got a C for the course! I didn't fail! I got an A on the test? A genuine A?*

My brain started repeating itself.

"I defeated you, linguistics!" my heart screamed triumphantly. "You may have won the battles- all of them- but I won the war!"

I bumped into the door jam on the way out the door and promptly burst into tears walking out the building. My chest heaved with giggles. Anyone who saw me would have thought me mad.

"Hard work prevails! I'm a genius! A genius of hard work!"

Chapter 14 - Campeonato
November 23

Early morning sunlight streamed through the windows. The windows of the nearly-deserted train car were open, letting the cool Sunday morning air stream through.

Everything was quiet save for the rhythmic clicking of the wheels on the train rail. My mind was anything but quiet as I listened to heavy metal on my CD player. I had to change train lines three times, but I made it on time to meet Zuyo and a few others in Chiba, a prefecture to the east of Tokyo. There, we'd all take part in the Campeonato, the largest Brazilian jiu jitsu tournament in Japan. I wasn't sure whether to be nervous or not. Coming off my win in Smackgirl, I had every reason to be confident. After all, I wasn't going to get punched in the face.

The staff let us check in early. We claimed a spot on the ground in a corner of the gymnasium, dropping our bags in a big heap. As the gymnasium filled up, it started to look like either a big camping trip, or refugee area.

I'd been to countless judo and submission grappling tournaments in the States, namely the NAGA (North American Grappling Association) tournaments, plus the Pan-American and the Judo American-Canadians. Zuyo had been raving about how many people would show up, so I expected Pan-Am style, where bleachers were jam-packed full of fans and competitors. It wasn't as big as that. There were maybe 800 people, including spectators and fighters. My estimation could have been off, though. I only spotted two other foreigners the entire time. Being surrounded by a sea of Asian faces reinforced for me exactly where I was living and how unusual my situation was.

My blue belt division was open weight, so I didn't have to worry about cutting or dieting. It turns out I was the heaviest girl at 64 kilos, with the next heaviest girl looking about 60 kilos.

Impatience seized a hold of me, driving me to pace around. This, in turn, drove Zuyo and the others a little nuts.

"Sit down, Roxy," they kept telling me.

We passed the time chatting about nothing and checking out our potential opponents. The organizers had made a deadline to sign up so they could make the brackets ahead of time, so there wouldn't be any surprises. I would have had at least two fights if I kept winning. According to some of the stacked guys' division brackets, my teammates would have to battle through maybe five or six people to reach the top.

Finally, the event started. The ladies had to wait a while, however, and my pacing continued. We watched Yukie fight first in the ladies' purple belt division. Unfortunately she lost. I couldn't believe it! My heroine lost? It's always a shock to see one of the most skilled people in your gym face someone stronger from another dojo. Zuyo lost, as well.

At one point during the long wait, I unfortunately acquired a stalker. I'd left my group's area and was returning from a walk around the perimeter when a stocky man, possibly in his late 30's, said hello and asked where I was from. There wasn't anything outwardly unusual or creepy about him. He was wearing a casual shirt and pants. His round face with calm eyes was framed by short black hair, cut in a popular conservative style.

Maybe I was just overly cautious around men.

"I'm from Boston," I said in Japanese, picking a well-known city. It was much easier than explaining how I went to college in a small town named Amherst.

"Oh really? You're fighting, right?" he said with a smile, nodding at my jiu jitsu gi that I wore.

"Yes," I answered politely. "Are you?"

"Yes, but ah, I lost already!" He shook his head ruefully, rubbing his left arm. "I fought in the white-belt division and lost by armbar."

"How long have you been training?" I asked.

"About five months," he said. "You?"

"Oh, I'm not sure...I've done judo for three years," I explained slowly, trying to produce my best Japanese sentences. "But I suppose I've been doing pure Brazilian jiu jitsu for about two and a half years."

"Oh, wow!" he exclaimed, and ooh-ed and aw-ed over that for a few minutes.

"Are you going back to America after this?" he asked, the smile never leaving his face. It was a little strange how his expression never changed. At all.

"No, I live here."

"Where do you live?"

"Well... around here."

"Where do you train?"

"Um, I train in Kichijoji."

"Oh really! Wow. I train in Chiba Prefecture. We should train together sometime! Come to Chiba!"

"Oh, Chiba," I repeated, blinking. *Did he just tell me to go train with him?* My brain recycled the Japanese sentence and confirmed that he did indeed say that. It then played with the thought of "Chiba" for roughly two seconds before discarding it hurriedly. Even if I had the desire to, which I didn't, Chiba was too far away for me to visit. Ever. And this guy was creepy.

"What do you do?" he asked.

"I'm an exchange student," I said slowly.

"Oh really? How old are you?" he asked.

I blinked again. "Excuse me?" I said, thinking maybe I misunderstood the Japanese.

"Ikutsu desu ka?" he asked again, unmistakably the question for "How old are you?"

I decided it was time for me to pretend I didn't understand Japanese.

"Sorry, I don't understand," I said. "I'm not very good at Japanese." It was believable. Our entire conversation wasn't very fluent, and I was obviously struggling.

"Um," he cocked his head. "Age, age?" He managed in English.

I should have continued to pretend.

"I'm not telling," I said finally.

"Why not?"

"Just because," I managed some vague Japanese response.

151

He asked something else, and I fibbed that I didn't understand him. Another pause ensued. Finally I smiled and said, "Well, I have to go get ready to fight."

"Oh, okay!" His smile returned. "Good luck! I'll be rooting for you!"

"Great, thanks!" I hurried back to my group.

Tatsu was the only one there, sitting cross-legged, fixing himself some kind of protein drink.

"Tatsu, is it common for Japanese men to ask women how old they are?" I asked, switching back to English.

He looked up at me sharply. "No," he said, his eyebrows raised. "Why?"

"I just met some guy over there who was asking me a bunch of questions."

I glanced surreptitiously back where I'd come, and saw the man casually wandering around. Maybe it was my imagination, but he seemed to be meandering in our general direction.

"He seemed nice, but..."

"You should stay away from him," Tatsu said, shaking his bottle and then taking a swig. "He's a weirdo, maybe hentai." The latter meant 'pervert.' "Stay with us," Tatsu advised.

"Okay," I readily agreed, but privately thought Tatsu was being a little overprotective.

My anxiety poked and prodded at me, but I forced myself to sit next to Tatsu. About five minutes later, the man came over to us.

"Oh, hi!" I exclaimed, pretending to be surprised, but had indeed been watching him out of the corner of my eye.

"Hello! Is this your team?" the man asked, nodding a greeting at Tatsu and waiting expectantly. My Japanese friend nodded back without introducing himself.

"Yes," I said.

"Is this your boyfriend?"

"No," I said. Tatsu kept his face blank and continued taping his wrist with athletic tape.

"Ah." The man fingered the camera he held in his hands, along with the Campeonato's pamphlet. "Actually, I was

152

wondering which mat you were going to fight on. Your name is written here..." He indicated the booklet.

"Er, that one I guess." I pointed to the nearest mat.

"Well," the man smiled, "good luck with your match! I'll be cheering for you!"

"Thanks!" I said with a forced friendly smile. The man turned and walked away with a somewhat faster step than he had come with.

He'd just passed out of earshot, when Tatsu looked at me with a slightly alarmed expression. "Definitely a weirdo," he said, tearing off the end of the tape and smoothing it down on his hand. "Be careful, Roxanne!"

I nodded, watching the stocky man disappear into the crowd of gi-clad fighters.

My first match finally began at roughly one o'clock.

In the States, one could assume that majority of grapplers didn't know judo, so I never worried about being thrown head over heels. I could go out and grip and shoot for a takedown. However, Japan is the birthplace of judo. I didn't want to take a chance and get in too close too fast.

My first opponent was slender, with eyes that warned me not to underestimate her. We approached each other, cautiously reaching.

With a jolt, we connected. Our hands frantically fought for the best dominant grip on the gi lapel and opposite sleeve. I sensed her tense to jump, probably to the guard position. She'd want to wrap her legs around my waist. That would pull me down to my knees from her weight.

I backed my hips away so she couldn't close her legs around me. In that split second, she jumped! But I wasn't there! She landed on her back, me standing over her. I tore her grip from my lapel. Her legs pushed at me. I struggled to pass her open guard by holding down her legs. I faked one way, and tried to move around to her other side. She pushed me away with her feet.

Then, her hands suddenly seized a hold of my ankles. She planted both feet firmly on my hips, and pushed. I flailed, almost going over backwards. Somehow I regained my balance, and actually passed her defense. She rolled over. Clinging to her back like a monkey, I attempted to choke her from behind by using her own gi.

I was riding too high on her back. She pulled me off, escaping. This time, she managed to pass my guard and pin my back flat to the mat, chest to chest, using all her body weight. Grabbing my arm, she tried to hyper-extend it into an arm-bar. I did an escape as she tried to apply the technique. I kicked her away. Stalemated, we both stood up.

The round went back and forth between us. I thought that by being bigger, I'd overpower her. Contrary to that, she was winning with points until the end. It was a pleasant surprise to have a good, challenging fight. I tried to choke her a few more times, and almost straight arm locked her from my guard. The fight went the complete five minutes allotted. I won by decision based on position points, submission attempts, and aggressiveness.

"And the winner!" the ref called, raising my hand as we faced the score table. Elation swept over me. I could move on to the first place match.

"I wish I had more people to fight through," I told Tatsu, as we headed back to our corner to wait. The finals would be held in another hour or so.

"You still have to win first place," he reminded me.

"Good job, Sixty-three!" Zuyo said, patting me on the shoulder.

"Thanks! Be right back, I have to use the restroom," I said to my teammates, and went to use the facilities.

On the way there, my stalker met me in the hall.

"Great job!" he said.

"Oh, thanks!" I grinned, trying not to stop walking. The crowded hallways forced me to stop.

He said something that I honestly couldn't catch. I started inching away, but he struggled to rephrase.

I gleaned the words 'otoko no tomodachi' from his question. That meant "male friend."

"Uh, uh, there is! There is!" I stammered, guessing he was asking if I had a boyfriend.

154

"That guy?" he asked.

"Er, yes, I mean no, yes," I answered.

"Will you do jiu jitsu with me?" I gleaned, out of another rapid-fire sentence.

"Um, I'm going home after this," I said.

"Can you give me your phone number?"

"What? I'm sorry, I don't understand," I fibbed, shaking my head. "Well, I have to go..."

"Um, phone..." he said in English, looking at me quizzically. I thought that maybe if I stared at him awkwardly with a blank expression on my face he would stop asking. He didn't, and some kind of answer was required unless I wanted to shove past him.

"Ah. Well, I live with a host family and I can't give out their phone number," I explained, not wanting to be rude.

He asked if I had a cell phone, and I pretended not to understand.

"Cell...cell phone?" he tried, in English.

"What? What?" I said.

"Well, here's mine!" he changed back to Japanese, whipping out a piece of paper and jotting it down.

"Oh, thanks," I said, tucking it absently into my gi lapel. Maybe if I was lucky it would fall out.

"I saw you trying to choke that girl," he went on enthusiastically. "Here, let me show you something I learned the other day." He grabbed my gi lapel.

I wasn't having any of that. "Please don't touch me," I said, removing his hand, hoping he wouldn't fight me. Unfortunately, our skin touched. His hand was kind of clammy. "Excuse me, I have to go talk to my friends now."

"Oh, okay. Well, good luck with your final match! I'll be cheering you! Please call the number I gave you!"

"Great, thanks!" Smiling, more out of relief to escape, I whirled around. It took me less than a minute to weave through the crowd to my teammates. Then I realized that I'd forgotten to pee.

At last the time came for my final match. Other spectators and competitors actually gathered around the mats to watch, making me feel somewhat important. My opponent was a short, compact lady with close-cropped black hair. The information pamphlet said she practiced sambo as well as BJJ. "Sambo" is an acronym for the Russian phrase "Self-Defense Without Weapon." Practitioners train striking, throws, takedowns and submission holds in a BJJ gi top and shorts. In other words, they are badass.

The action went back and forth in an exciting matchup of strategy as much as skill and strength. As I had suspected, she was strong. I couldn't pull off any submissions from the guard. She staved off my attacks easily, and tried passes and submissions of her own. Unlike the other girl, this one seemed to have a better feel for the standup game. I therefore tried to take the fight to the ground before she could get a good grip on my gi and throw me. Even with my impeccable gameplan, I faltered once in its execution, ultimately leading to my downfall. Literally.

In the final 30 seconds, we were tied on points. The ref stood us up from a stalemate position on the ground. I should have jumped guard to take the fight back to the ground. If she threw me, she would win via points. My friends were yelling something at me, but I didn't understand the Japanese.

We lunged at each other, closing the distance. I grabbed. She grabbed. She grabbed my wrist and tore off my grip. I tore off hers. We grabbed again. I caught the edge of her sleeve and reached for behind her neck with my other hand. We bent over, trying to keep our bases and not be thrown off balance. Abruptly she released her original grip and grabbed my two lapels, falling straight to her knees directly in front of me: a drop-ippon seonage.

The second I first felt her change her grips, I tried to sprawl my hips backwards to squash down her attack. It didn't work. From my perspective, my opponent suddenly vanished. The yellow-colored mats filled my eyes. I flew over her back; the momentum and angle aiming me headfirst into the mat. It rushed up at me. Time seemed to freeze. There was no space to tuck my chin and protect my neck. I thought I was going to die.

My arms flailed outward from the sudden jerk. I tried to twist, to change the angle of my fall to anything other than the direction it was going. Anything.

156

I don't remember which part of my body hit the mat first. My left elbow exploded into fiery pain as it hyper-extended. Ligaments tore, and the elbow became burning ice. The sambo girl landed on top in a pin, but I was already giving up, tapping her back with my right hand. I tapped repeatedly, then on the mat so the ref could see.

Fear flooded my heart like lava, and then relief stilled its flow. I was alive. My neck was not broken. I felt like I could have died just then if my arm hadn't taken the impact. Then the pain wormed into the forefront of my awareness. It burned. I gulped down air and tried not to cry.

She got off of me. I tried to get up, too, but felt light-headed and fell back down. I think she said something. Probably an apology.

My judo sensei Harry Chandler's soft-spoken voice filled my mind in a flashback. I was an enthusiastic, 16-year-old white belt. "Be careful with drop seonage. It's dangerous. It can be difficult to control where your opponent lands if not done perfectly."

"Okay, then I won't do drop-seonage. Just normal seonage," I had said.

Now I was laying on the tournament mats.

"What a rotten seonage," I thought ruefully.

I rested for a moment there on my back. My teammates' faces hovered above me.

"Daijoubu ka?" they all asked at once, meaning, "Are you all right?"

"No," I said. "My...my..." My mind searched my foggy memory banks for the Japanese word. Somehow I always confused ude "arm" with ashi "leg."

"My leg...my leg...I mean my arm...my arm..." I started to feel a little bit sick. My nervous system was reacting.

Before I knew it, I was being helped up. Once upright, my head spun and the world began going white. My stomach flip-flopped in my gut. I'd felt that feeling before when I had gotten stung by a jellyfish in the waters of the Bahamas. My nervous system was going into shock.

Tatsu put my good arm around his shoulder. Zuyo held my left arm straight so it wouldn't flop or bump into anything.

Along with the ref and someone else, they guided me off the main mat to a portion not being utilized, and lay me back down. Someone ran for the medic.

"What hurts? Are you okay?" people were asking me.

"No, it hurts," I mumbled groggily. The Japanese was just not flowing. Tatsu was saying something to me. My speech was coming out a messy mix of Japanese and English.

"Ice. Ice. Can someone please get me ice?" I asked.

"What?" Zuyo said, and I realized I'd spoken English.

"I don't know what 'ice" is in Japanese," I muttered to her. "Tatsu? Tatsu what's ice? Tatsu? Tatsu?" I was blabbering.

"Kouri. You want ice?"

"Yes, kouri, get me kouri please...kudasai."

Tatsu turned to someone. "She wants ice," he said in Japanese, and the person turn and ran to get it.

Of course she wants ice! I thought. Were they not going to give it to me unless I asked?

"Can I have my medicine? Pills?" I spoke in English.

"What are pills? What pills?" Tatsu asked.

"In my bag...anti-inflammatory pills...uh, pain pills," I said through the confusion. Someone was trying to talk to Tatsu. He looked away, and then looked back as I called his name again.

"Where are they?" he asked.

"In my blue bag, in the front pocket."

"I'll go get them," he said, running off.

The world flashed on and off. The doctor arrived and saw that my elbow had immediately started to swell. A freezing flame danced from the sharp point of my elbow along the inside of my forearm all the way to my wrist. He pressed on something. I yelled. The doctor got some gauze and cloth and started wrapping my arm.

"Is it broken?" I asked, messing up the Japanese. Zuyo corrected me. The doctor said he wasn't sure. I wanted to know if he was going to set the bone.

"Why are you wrapping it?" I asked in Japanese. He just seemed to be putting cloth around it any which way. "What are you doing?" It didn't seem like he examined it very closely. I started to wonder through my slightly confused and panicked state if he was an actual licensed medic or just a volunteer.

Tatsu returned with the ice, but the doctor had wrapped the bandage very thickly and very tightly.

"I can't feel the ice," I complained.

"Well, you don't need it," the doctor said.

"Of course I need it!" I said. "It stops the swelling. Right?" I never had a broken arm before, so maybe wrapping it was more important? This guy didn't exactly inspire confidence.

I didn't know how to say what I wanted in Japanese, but the fact that I was making a big stink had my Japanese friends exchanging glances. The doctor dutifully unwrapped half of the bandage. I don't claim to be a doctor, but he used the entire thick roll of gauze, where really only half of that was necessary to immobilize my arm. I was able to feel the ice only a little bit, which disturbed me. He didn't appear too sure of himself. Or maybe he was just irritated and barely able to contain himself because I was telling him what to do.

The general excitement over my injury began to die down and matches resumed. I was able to sit up. The referee later came over to see how I was. My opponent paid me a visit to apologize and wish me a speedy recovery. I smiled at her and told her that I was fine, but secretly berated her for doing such a dangerous throw. All's fair in the fight game, though.

The move wasn't illegal. One is supposed to turn and angle their opponent in a way that they land on their back and shoulders, not head. I felt that if my arm hadn't been in the way, it might have broken my neck. That thought made my throbbing arm not seem so bad.

Ironically, my opponent, who's name was Sayaka Shioda, trained at the AACC (Abe Ani's Combat Club), where I would train six years in the future. Since then, Sayaka went on to place a few times in the Abu Dhabi Combat Championships, a professional world-class grappling tournament. She was good. Really good. And later she became my idol, once I got over my first impression.

A few minutes later, they assisted me back to our area with our bags. I reclined against the wall, using my book bag as a back support. People bustled about their own business. I tried to relax.

"Are you comfortable? Can I get you anything else?" Tatsu asked solicitously.

"No, I don't need anything," I said. My senses had returned to me.

Suddenly, my stalker appeared out of the crowd on the perimeter of our circle of bags. He didn't stop. Just giving me a tight-lipped nod and a small wave, he hurried away.

I'm not so cool now that I broke my arm, I thought to myself, a small smile playing on my lips. *He didn't even say 'get better,' or anything.*

The tournament continued. We all had to wait until all the contestants fought before the awards would be given out at a ceremony at the end. It was evening by the time everyone finished. A few people took a place, but none of my close friends.

I was just wondering when someone would take me to the hospital, when Tatsu came to stand over me.

"Hey, you got second place, remember?" he said. "They're calling your name!"

"Oh! Right!" I said, climbing to my feet.

By that time, the numbers in the gym had dwindled down to the winners and some of their teammates. Those remaining stood around the perimeter of the mat. They parted to let me step onto the mat. The announcer smiled at me as I stood before him and the heads of Paraestra, the BJJ school that helped sponsor and host the event. They handed me a box with the medal. I bowed.

After that, everyone packed up and hoisted their bags onto their backs.

"Do you know 'so and so'?" Zuyo asked, naming somebody whose name I never heard before.

"No," I answered.

160

"They trained at Shibuya once, but usually train at another branch of Paraestra."

I gave her a blank look.

"Well anyway," she continued, "They have a car so they can drive you home."

"Oh great! But can we go to the hospital?"

"Well...it's a national holiday, so the hospitals will be closed. Right?" Zuyo turned to Tatsu for confirmation.

"Hmmm, yeah," he nodded. The others standing around discussed briefly and all decided that the hospitals would be closed.

"What? A hospital closed?" I exclaimed. "No way!"

Tatsu rubbed his chin thoughtfully. "Yeah, plus it's night time. The hospitals are closed except for the biggest ones."

"How can a hospital be closed? What if there's an emergency?" I yelled.

"Okay, calm down," I ordered myself.

"There's no hospital you can take me to? What about the major ones?"

"I'm not sure. They're kind of far away." Tatsu discussed with Zuyo. "Do you know the nearest one?" I heard him ask.

"What?" I couldn't believe people weren't rushing me to the emergency room.

"You can have your host mother take you tomorrow, right?" Zuyo said.

"I want to go now!" I exclaimed.

My teammates exchanged looks.

Zuyo tried to put on a reassuring smile. "I think it'll be much better if your host mother takes you tomorrow..."

There was an uncomfortable pause.

"I guess," I answered, incredulously. *They're not going to take me!*

"Okay, then so-and-so will drive you home."

Try as I might, naturally I couldn't find a comfortable position as I bounced around in the back seat of the car. A nice man and his wife chatted with me in Japanese as we drove home. The trip took a little over two hours. The most agonizing two hours ever. It was as if someone was forcing my elbow to roast over an open fire.

They called my host mother via cell phone when we reached Musashi Koganei city, since I was unfamiliar with the roads and couldn't direct them to the house. Mitsunori, my host brother, came out to meet me on the side street where the couple stopped their car.

"Daijoubu ka?" Mitsunori-san asked. "Are you okay?" He was wearing his pajamas and robe tied over top.

"Iie, daijjoubu ja nai desu," I said, meaning, "No, I'm not."

This response seemed to alarm him very much, as it had everyone else I said it to. In Japanese, if someone asks you "daijoubu ka," you answer "yes," whether you are okay or not. But I was definitely not alright, and didn't feel like humoring anyone.

The bigger man hoisted my bag, and led the way back to his house. I profusely thanked the couple from Paraestra and followed.

My host mother stood over the stove frying korokke, or fried balls of mashed potato with meat inside.

"I'm so sorry, I can't put this down, so I sent Mitsunori...." she was saying, and then her eyes fell on my arm. She hurriedly finished her current batch and then began fussing over me.

"Daijoubi ka?" she asked.

"No, it really hurts."

"Is it broken?" she continued.

"I don't know! I think so. The medic didn't know, and nobody would take me to the hospital! They said it's a national holiday. Can you take me to the hospital?" I asked, although at that point I was pretty tired.

Mitsunori and Sadako-san exchanged looks.

"It's late," Sadako-san said, looking at the clock. The hands read eleven. "Is there a hospital open now?" Without waiting for her son to respond, she continued, "Can you wait until tomorrow? I know a clinic we can go to."

"No! I want to go now!" I said.

The mother and son exchanged glances again.

"You can't wait until tomorrow?" Sadako said again.

The silence stretched.

162

"I guess so," I said, still unable to fathom this situation. *What was wrong with these people?* I thought. "Do they have an X-ray machine at a clinic?" I asked, thinking of a small, ill-equipped office.

"Yes, yes. Are you hungry," the gray-haired lady asked.

Hungry? "A little." My arm hurt. I wanted my arm fixed, but instead, I had a korokke fried pork midnight snack.

"You know," my host mother said as I was eating. "You're probably okay."

"Oh yeah?" I mumbled irritably, with my mouth full. "What makes you say that?"

She smoothed her fluffy graying hair. "Well, I hurt my hand, you see," she said, "And the ligaments were totally cut! Look at this!" She started bending and twisting her finger in weird angles. "I can't do this!" she exclaimed. "It was terrible, that biking accident I had..."

I immediately looked away, feeling suddenly sick to my stomach.

Sadako-san laughed. "What's wrong? Does this bother you? Look!" I looked. She started bending her finger again. I looked away.

"I don't really want to look," I said, focusing on my korokke.

She laughed again and continued on about how when she had gone to the doctor, it was all floppy and dislocated. I tried to push the images out of my head.

Finally, with the help of Sadako-san, we set about laying out the futons, and I went to bed without showering. It was impossible to find a comfortable position. My elbow burned ice. My hand felt like it was going to explode. The two ice packs I kept in the freezer helped. I might have slept a few hours total, if at all. The pulsing pain kept me awake.

November 24

The next morning I waited until 7am - which was 6pm East Coast time - to call my parents and tell them what happened. My mother gushed her worry and advice, with well wishes tacked at the end. Of course, she wished me congratulations for winning second place.

After informing my father of my injury, however, the line went dead silent for a moment. I could feel the tension through the phone. His breathing rate doubled, though, as he finally expressed his concern and worry. Finally, he hurried me off the phone, ending with a phrase that now holds an element of irony.

"You aren't supposed to get hurt while you're having fun," he said firmly. "I don't expect you to get hurt over there! You're not a professional athlete who gets paid thousands of dollars to put your body at risk."

I didn't respond to that. Well, I wasn't making thousands yet. "At least I had the opportunity to challenge myself against some skilled women in one of the biggest tournaments in Japan," I told myself, when I started to get depressed. "Plus, I did take second place, even if I only won once. Actually, I did only win once, and there weren't that many people..."

I tried to be positive, but it wasn't quite working out as usual.

My first day with an incapacitated arm taught me a lot about life. *It's a miracle I haven't had a major injury before now,* I thought to myself. *Actually, no, my back injury counts.* The old muscle tear in my lower back prevents me even now from doing a lot of things. Simply running for over a minute makes me sore for an entire week. I have to be careful when practicing judo with falls and twisting motions. I've just learned to live with it. An incapacitated limb is another story.

My heart went out to anyone born without working limbs, handicapped people, people in wheel chairs, people too old to take care of themselves, and others with special needs. I couldn't even put up my hair. My host mother almost knotted it trying to make a simple ponytail for me.

Come on, you have a daughter, right? I thought, a little bit annoyed when I finally tugged the lopsided ponytail straight.

We left the house at 9am, bright and early. Luckily for me, university classes had been canceled that Monday due to the holiday, leaving me free to see the doctor at my leisure. However,

164

leisure was the last thing I wanted. I should have been in and out of the emergency room yesterday. My swollen arm was pounding and burning.

I scarfed down breakfast and I hurried Sadako-san out of the house before she finished her tea.

My host mother led me on foot towards town. About 15 minutes later, we stopped in front of a nondescript office building that sprouted up next to the rows of houses.

I hadn't been impressed when my host mother had mentioned "clinic" to me the previous night, but I trusted she knew the best place to take me. It was, in fact, the office I'd expect of a general practitioner. The waiting room was small; the size of a big living room with rows of chairs with cushioned backs. People gave their insurance card and paperwork to the female nurses sitting behind a front counter. Kids' books and magazines sat stacked up on low tables here and there. Information posters covered the walls.

Kind of strange location for it, though, in the middle of a residential area, I thought. *Well come to think of it, it's the perfect place. Families would have easy access to their doctor.*

We arrived just as it opened, and there were already a few people lined up at the door. People don't make appointments in Japan. The co-pay for public health care is dirty cheap - maybe 15 bucks for an examination - but you have to wait first come-first serve. This time, I didn't have to wait too long, however. After my host mother helped me fill out the questionnaire and first-time registration form, they sent me right in to be X-rayed.

Finally, I'm being taken care of, I thought.

A few minutes later, they sent me back to the waiting room. I sat next to my host mother for a good 20 minutes before the doctor could see me.

In his late 30's, the doctor had a comforting, patient smile. His professional and confident manner helped ease some of the confusion and anxiety I felt about the way the Japanese handled medical treatment. I doubted that my team back home would have demanded I sleep at night on a broken arm. My mom shared my disbelief and outrage. I had downplayed it for my dad's sake.

The doctor spoke slowly and I understood a good portion of what he told me.

"Please lay down on this examining table," he instructed. I complied and I explained what had happened as he slowly unwrapped the bandage. The elbow was swollen and dark purple.

He pressed gently on various parts, rotating it occasionally. He said something about X-rays that I didn't understand. I looked to Sadako-san for an explanation. She faltered, not sure of how to rephrase it. A nurse came over and put her hands on my shoulders. Before I could mentally brace myself, he gripped my wrist and elbow and started pulling and shoving. The exclamation I made was neither English nor Japanese.

"Just lay back and relax," he murmured, continuing to shove. "Blah blah blah bone."

"He's setting the bone!" I realized. "So it was broken!?"

I thought he was still in the examining mode. Apparently not. I clenched my teeth and tried to control the tears that seeped out of my eyes from the pain. It would have been nice if he had said something like, "I'm going to set your arm now. Are you ready?" But no. Thanks, Doc.

Above my head, my host mother smiled and chuckled. After it was finished, my host mother laughed at me and gently poked fun at me. I breathed heavily, tears flowing unbidden from my eyes.

How could she laugh at my pain? I thought, crossly. I later overheard her telling her old-lady friend on the phone how worried she was about me. I guess what I heard was most likely nervous laughter which covered up her own anxiety.

"So I guess it was broken?" I said, once he was finished and I could talk again.

"Only a little bit," he said, rolling his chair across the floor to his desk. X-rays were pinned up to a light. "See here, some bone was fractured and broken here in the elbow. Some of these jintai running through your wrist and down your arm are partially torn. You can still move your fingers, right?"

I wiggled them in response. "What's jintai?"

"Uh…"

166

I got out my dictionary and looked it up. It meant, "ligaments."

He and the nurse re-wrapped my arm.

"Is it supposed to be so tight?" I asked once they were finished.

"Yes," he said. I could feel the blood pulsing.

"Is it good to put ice on it?" I asked.

"Hmm." He considered. "It wouldn't hurt."

"Ah, I see," I said. Only "Wouldn't hurt?" I started to lose confidence in him.

"Blah blah damage blah blah jintai blah bone longer blah," the doctor explained.

"Um, sorry," I said, "Could you repeat that and speak more slowly?"

"Okay. I said that ligament damage is worse than a broken bone because it takes longer to heal and rehabilitate," the doctor said seriously. "But yours isn't too bad."

He proceeded to give me all sorts of doctoral advice and prescribed me some heavy-duty painkillers, which actually didn't work so effectively on my American chemistry. I should have just kept taking my Aleve. After that, my host mother returned home ahead of me, while I went to the drug store to look for hair clips I could use with one hand. None were suitable. While walking down the street, some loser bumped into my arm, rocking my world with lightning bolts.

"Shou ga nai. Ganbatte," as the saying goes in Japanese. "That's the way it goes. Just do your best."

November 28 - Thanksgiving

The ringing phone jolted me out of unconsciousness earlier than I would have liked. ICU's semesters were divided into trimesters, and the first one had just ended. I had two weeks of fall vacation before resuming school.

"Neh-san!" my host mother called from the other room. "Big sister! It's your father!"

I roused myself, pushing back the blankets with my one arm. Instead of doing an army crawl into the next room, I had to stand up and walk.

"Okay!" I called to Sadako, as I picked up the receiver.

"Happy Thanksgiving!" boomed his voice. "I'm here at your aunt's, and someone wants to say hello!"

A smile split my face as one after another, I spoke with my aunt, uncle, and cousins. It seemed like they were living in a different universe. They might as well have been. It hurt not to be able to spend important American holidays with family, but to be forgotten would have been worse.

That was nice, I thought after I hung up. Feeling loved, yet lonely, I lay back down for another few minutes. Light streamed in through the sliding glass doors on the other side of the room. Presently, the phone rang again.

"Neh-san!" my host mother's voice called, raising another octave. "It's your mother!"

I hoisted myself up and picked up the phone again, still warm from my hand.

We exchanged holiday greetings. "By the way, Roxanne," she continued in her best 'mother-knows' voice. "I read on your online journal that your upper-arm turned purple. You should go back to the doctor and see what he says!"

"Mmm, yes, I know, I'm going today," I readily answered.

A few days after my initial visit, my bicep right above where the bandage ended swelled to an alarming size. On top of that, it turned a deep eggplant-purple. I assumed it was due to poor circulation and the fact that most of my arm was tightly wrapped.

"You don't want to assume anything," said my mother. "You know that 'assuming makes an a-'"

"Yeah, yeah, I know. Hey, 'great minds think alike,'" I quoted back to her. "Anyway, it's so nice of you to call to wish me a Happy Thanksgiving! I just talked to Dad and everyone. I can tell you right now what I'm thankful for. I'm thankful for my broken arm. Better than a broken neck. But I'm sure you don't want to hear that."

168

"No mother wants to hear about her kid's injuries," my mother said sadly. "Just be careful."

"My poor parents," I thought. "It must be tough on them to have a daughter who competes in this kind of sport. And I haven't even told them that punching was allowed in that MMA fight. How AM I going to do that? 'Hi Dad, guess what…I've been meaning to tell you, but in my fights we're supposed to smash each other's faces in….'"

After hanging up, I went into the bathroom and examined my arm. The skin under my bicep bulged and sagged like a water balloon. I poked it. It didn't hurt. My stomach flip-flopped and I tried not to be nauseous. I sighed, hoping it was natural.

"How can that be natural," asked my body, or the part of my mind that represented my body.

"It's just creepy, calm down," another part of my mind tried to sooth my logical mind.

"What if this swelling does some damage?" my body continued to rant. "I'm sure it's not good to have a bubble of fluid floating around our arm for weeks at a time. Make it go away! Make the doctor re-wrap the bandage!"

"Just chill, alright? With you badgering me for a week, I've finally decided to go," my mind replied. "Maybe he can drain it or something!"

Fifteen minutes after breakfast, I found myself back at the doctor's clinic. A little old nurse shuffled through a door in the back and called me into the examining room. I had just presented my hand for merely a second, when she grabbed the pinkie of my bad hand, and started to try and get the wrapping off. The pinkie was directly connected to my damaged ligament. It hurt. A lot.

"AAH! Wait, excuse me!" I cried out, immediately withdrawing my arm. She looked shocked. "This foreigner is resisting medical attention?" She must have thought.

Does she even know what she's doing? Does she even know what my injury is? How dare she just seize a hold of my hand like that! I wondered. I breathed deeply, trying to calm myself. A culture that doesn't ice an injury immediately, and refuses to take a woman with a broken arm to the emergency room had a long way to go to earn my trust. If something went against my common sense, I would question it until I understood. Did the doctor tell her to unwrap my arm? They'd just secured it the other day. I just wanted to ask a question.

"Don't let her touch me! Don't let her touch me!" my body screamed at me.

"Shut up and calm down," my mind told my body. The lady went away. I waited. Then the doctor came over and together they unwrapped my arm slowly and carefully. Underneath the bandage, my skin was a freaky yellow with random purple and blue blotches all over. The biggest one was three inches down from my wrist. Then there was one on top of the elbow, and one just under the elbow. Well, where the elbow should be. It was so swollen you couldn't see the tip of the elbow.

So gross!

The doctor began squeezing it all over. Most of the parts didn't hurt until he pushed on the area where the ligament supposedly ripped. I yelped.

"So the swelling is okay," the doctor said in Japanese. "It's your body's healing powers. It'll be fine!"

This satisfied me, so they wrapped me back up. I paid my 2-dollar co-pay for the visit and went on my way. Once back home, I wrote the following list in honor of Thanksgiving:

I'm thankful for my misfortunes which teach me life's lessons so I can be a better person
I'm thankful for the fact that my parents have jobs and their health is good.
I'm thankful for my own health.
I'm thankful for my friends, in Japan and in the U.S. I'd be lost without you.
I'm thankful for such caring parents.
I'm thankful that my wonderful Mother calls me twice a week from overseas.
I'm thankful I'm in Japan, which is many other people's dream
I'm thankful for life itself.

December 1
Yet another visit to the doctor

"Is it time to get another X-ray?" my host mother harassed me at breakfast.

I sighed and tried to eat my oatmeal. How many times were they going to X-ray my elbow?

"It's not good to irradiate parts of your body!" I heard my mother's voice say inside my head. She always refused routine or unnecessary X-rays, while here I was going once a week. "Maybe I would grow another arm. That might be handy for jiu jitsu practice. Handy! Hahaha."

Unfortunately, it turns out that I left the doctor's that morning wanting to strangulate the radiologist. I shall hereon refer to that sourpuss as "the rento-gento-man," because the Japanese word for X-ray is "rento gen." He was of average height and weight, with nothing special about him, other than a bored expression.

After grudgingly entering the x-ray room, I plopped down on the stool next to the X-ray table machine. He grabbed my bandaged wrist extremely hard. Maybe all that fermented soy bean nato mush he ate for breakfast disagreed with him and he wanted to take it out on some stupid foreigner.

"Ow!" I protested as he twisted my arm around.

"Oh, does this hurt?" he asked with a blank expression, squeezing harder.

"HAI HAI HAI!" Yes it hurts, you spiteful bastard! I actually used my other hand to remove his fingers and glare at him. There was absolutely no reason for that. The elbow started throbbing.

"Okay, put your hand on the table here…"

"It is," I bit out, trying to align it perfectly. Jerk.

"Don't you move!" he said, not as polite as he could have been. I sat there seething as he went away to activate the machine.

After the procedure was over and I stomped outside, another patient waiting must have seen thunderclouds in my expression. She started chatting with me and my host mother, who

171

had gone with me. The elderly white-haired lady ranted that the rento-gento man did the same with her and was disrespectful about her pain. She spoke slowly, and I could understand her well.

"It's not very nice of him at all, is it?" she said. "By the way, my dear. I broke my arm before and I also had a lot of discoloration around my cast. But it eventually went away."

I felt slightly reassured to hear this. Then again, I'd asked Jet about the discoloration and she said she didn't have it. Why not?

Twenty minutes later the doctor called Sadako-san and me into his office. He snapped the thick X-ray sheets into the backlit holder, and pointed to the picture with the tip of his pen. I didn't understand very well, but he said he couldn't see a blah blah blah in the bone.

He must mean crack, I thought, wishing real life had a 'rewind' or 'repeat' button. I'm pretty sure he said that there used to be one, but not anymore.

I saw a shadow of one before, but not now.

It healed really fast!

He then squeezed it and prodded it a little, and it didn't hurt too much. The rento-gento man must have had bad karma.

The doc used his marker to circle an area on the x-ray where it looked like something was sticking out. He turned to my host mother- not me- and said, "The bone is fixed but this is nobu blah blah blah so we'll have to put a cast on it."

Mind screamed, "Whoa, whoa, whoa! Wait a minute!"

"Excuse me, what's nobu...?" I piped up.

Nobody responded.

"Sadako-san? What's nobu...something?" I asked my host mother. She didn't answer, not taking her eyes off the doctor who had pulled down the X-ray and had begun preparing for the cast.

"Bring over the something-something!" he called to the nurse, who answered him with a ready, high-pitched "Hai!" Yes, sir!

I hate it when people ignore me.

"Never let doctors do things you don't understand!" My mother's voice chimed. "Ask a lot of questions! They should explain it to you!"

That's very well for you to say, Mom, since I can't understand their explanations. I thought.

Japanese doctors are used to the patient's unconditional trust - they shut up and do whatever the doctor says. They are trained to be like this, just as my mom trained me to always ask questions. The two cultures completely clashed.

What would she say to that if she were here? Probably something like, "It's their job to make it so you understand."

"Excuse me, what's nobu-something?" I asked again. Again I received not a blink of an eye. I seethed.

"Chotto matte...." Wait a second, Sadako said to me.

Wait for what? I held my breath. Nobody was speaking. It's not like she was busy. I'd forgotten my dictionary or I would have looked up that stupid 'nobu' word myself.

Twenty seconds later, I spoke up again.

"Hey, I don't understand, so please tell me what that means!"

"Chotto matte..."

"Why should I wait?" I said, upset. When the doctor started talking again, I was so focused on calming down that he might as well have been speaking Chinese, for all I understood.

Nobody would bother to explain it to me, so I took a wild guess. Based on the X-ray visual aid and the treatment method, the bone had healed but the injured ligament still needed to heal. It was pulling open the elbow bone. The bone edges needed to touch to heal and they weren't, so the doctor had to put the cast on to make it straight again. Maybe. Most likely.

Why was there a big gap between the bones? Isn't that why you put a cast on it to begin with? Is it normal for someone with a broken arm to walk around with only bandages and a sling for two weeks?

I had no idea. Horrified, I wondered if the doctor didn't, either. I trusted him about as far as I could throw him – one armed. I reexamined my arm after the doc wiped it with disinfectant.

173

Maybe it was my imagination but it seemed to bend at a different angle. Must have been my imagination. It better have been.

He and his nurse put the cast on and sent me on my merry way. I didn't say much to my host mother on the walk home. I was kind of mad at her and frustrated at the whole situation. When we got back, she started cooing and talking to the animals. I wished she would stop those irritating noises. I was the one who needed comfort and reassurance.

"They're stupid dumb animals. They don't understand!"

And neither did I.

December 2

School was out so I had nothing to do. Feeling lonely and starved for jiu jitsu, I made a special trip to the dojo to show my teammates my cast. I sat with my back against the refrigerator. A regular dojo-mate who was tying his blue belt suddenly gestured at me and said something. I caught the words, "your boyfriend" and "your Japanese is good."

I looked over at Tatsu sitting nearby, who was taping his foot. "What did he say?" I asked.

"He means that your Japanese has gotten better because you got a Japanese boyfriend, right?"

"No, no!" I protested politely. "Minna-san no okage de!" No, no, it's thanks to all of you. I'd just learned that phrase in class that day.

Everyone said, "Oh you know 'okage de!' What a good speaker you are!"

"If only that were true. And would be nice to have a boyfriend, though..." I tried not to think about it. I always tried not to think about boyfriends. Who has the time for such things?

After I got home, I tried and failed to type in my journal. My hand still wouldn't turn over to touch the keys comfortably. I pecked out a short entry with my icicle-like fingertips. The room was the same temperature as outside: freezing! I had activated the dusty oil heater that my host mother lent me. The big clunker needed to be plugged in to an electrical outlet, plus have its tank filled with oil. The thing beeped and came to life. I huddled in front of it, trying to unthaw my hands. The winter wind whistled through the gap in the sliding glass doors.

"Lucky for me, winters are nothing like in Massachusetts," I thought. "Well, snow-wise anyway."

Although in New England temperatures plunge to negative degrees Fahrenheit, somehow it feels so much colder when you don't have indoor heating.

Do we live in the 21st century here, or what? I thought crossly, readjusting my overcoat around my shoulders. It kept slipping off because the cast got in the way.

I sighed and hit 'post' to update my simple entry in my online diary.

I stunk. It couldn't be ignored anymore. I hadn't showered in three days.

Damn it.

Gathering my pajamas and towel, I hurried through the freezing hallway into the bathroom. I stripped as fast as I could with one arm. It wasn't fast enough. My clothes lay as they fell in crumpled piles on the raised carpeted section. Goosebumps formed immediately on my skin. As quickly as I dared, I stepped down onto the tiled shower floor.

Water sprayed from the waist-high showerhead. Shivers racked my body as I knelt down on the hard tiles. Steam started rising as the warm water became hot. I tried to get under the stream and position myself so my cast wouldn't get wet.

Cold cold cold cold…!

"Can't you be more Zen?" my mind scolded. "Monks used to meditate under waterfalls, you know."

"Zen? Zen my butt, which I am currently, literally, freezing off!" my body retorted, ducking under the stream. I fumbled the soap, fumbled the bottle of shampoo, lost what little sight I had in the steam, but managed to get clean.

After I finished, I wondered how far I could stretch not showering until the next time.

December 4

My heart fell as the needle of the scale spun around and landed at 148 lbs, making my weight gain a total of 8 lbs since my initial injury. Eight pounds in three weeks. It was extremely fun, though. I love eating. It's a problem.

My mind said, "Roxy you gotta stop or you won't be able to button your pants with one hand."

My body replied, "I know, but I can't stop. Life sucks right now without training, and eating is enjoyable. Plus I feel tired and hungry if I don't eat enough."

"No, you'd be fine."

"No, I won't!"

"Then power walk to school!"

I tried it the next day and it took me 30 minutes. Not bad...not bad at all.

I found that I'd trained myself not to think about jiu jitsu all the time. The longing still existed in the back of my mind; however it wasn't tormenting me as much as in the beginning.

I tired to do as many calisthenics as I could at home after dinner. I did squats until my legs burned. It turned out to be 100.

"By the time I can use my arm I want to be able to do 200!" my body declared.

"It's nice to have goals," my mind thought idly. "Especially when you're a cripple."

"Come on, come on! Let's exercise!"

"I can't move the arm..." my mind sighed mentally.

Next, I did lunges, working the thigh muscle. It felt good, and I followed it with all kinds of sit-ups. I even tried one-arm push-ups, at which I failed miserably- even on my knees. My father can do one-arm push-ups. Following those, I used my huge hardcover kanji dictionary, which is roughly three lbs, and did bench press exercise with one hand.

December 5

Upon yet another X-ray, we saw that the bones had moved back into a better position than before.

"Excuse me," I asked the doctor. "If my ligaments were injured, does that mean the muscle is hurt, too?"

"Hmmm yes, probably. Everything is connected," he answered as he scribbled some notes on my chart.

"Um, excuse me, doctor. I have a throbbing pain in my wrist and forearm for some reason."

"Oh really? That's too bad. Try not to move it."

I just stared at him.

December 14

One chilly morning, I rolled out of my futon and went to wash my face. I tilted my head to the side, pushed my lose hair back, turned on the water. I gathered some in my cupped good hand... and proceeded to not only smack myself in the face, but to smash the glasses up the bridge of my nose. Water went flying all over the counter, on the floor, and down my shirt. I had forgotten to take my glasses off. I laughed out loud at my own stupidity.

I walked into the kitchen, chuckling to myself. "I must be losing my mind. Finally."

"Are you gonna go get your arm X-rayed after school?" my host mother asked me.

Frigging again? "I thought the doctor told me I can skip this visit?" I replied.

"Oh, I don't think so. Didn't he say every week?"

Damn, X-rays cause cancer and I have a history in both sides of the family. And the baka rento-gento man never even puts a lead vest on the patients or anything. What is up with that? I thought we were supposed to wear lead vests.

I couldn't wait to go back to the States for Christmas vacation. I'd see my Mom, Dad, family, eat Italian food, and associate with people who have actual common sense.

I decided to go and see if they wouldn't take the cast off the next day.

December 16

They took my cast off yesterday. I wondered if it wasn't too soon, seeing as I got the fracture November 23. However, the doctor had X-rayed it (again) and said,

"The bones are all healed. So please start moving your arm as much as possible. Come back in a week. Bye."

I blinked in shock. My host mother was getting up to leave. One second the doctor was sawing off the cast, the next second my tender arm was exposed to fresh air! However, I felt it was in no shape to start using it regularly. I couldn't bend it whatsoever towards my face.

"Excuse me!" I called at the doctor's back. He had turned and was walking out.

"Yes?"

What am I, just a doll in an assembly line? Next patient! Next! Next! Keep 'em coming! I thought.

"I can't bend my arm! Is this normal?"

"Oh yes, just bend it and it's normal."

"Um...what?"

He turned to face me with forced politeness. "If you bend it, it will return to normal," he said patiently. He waited to see if I had any more questions.

"Uh...hai."

I thanked him and let him go. I had so many questions that I couldn't even give them voice. However, the second I got out of the doctor's office, I whipped out the L-shaped metal splint I saved and wrapped it to my arm. It was a little more mobile than it had been with the cast, but I felt it was in danger without anything to secure it. If it got bumped, it would be forced to bend and maybe rip again.

"Hey, what are you doing!?" my host mother exclaimed. "The doctor told you to move it around!"

178

"I am moving it around," I said, continuing to wrap it.

"Don't put that on there," my host mother said, reaching for it. I moved away.

"It's not ready!"

"You should listen to the doctor," my host mother shook her head, starting down the hill, away from the clinic. "Do you want to ask the doctor if you should do that?"

I don't trust any stupid Japanese doctors, I thought to myself. *I betcha if the doc told her to start drinking iodine, she would.*

"I know how it feels," I struggled to say in Japanese, and hoped that she understood what I meant. "I know my own body."

Once home, I further examined the elbow more closely and found the point was solidly squishy. I hoped it was normal for a fractured area to still be swollen from the ligament and muscle damage. I ended up wearing the sling for the next few days. The fact that I couldn't turn my hand over to type alarmed me. I had almost no range of motion. I couldn't understand how the doctor expected me to move it.

December 19

I wanted to train. I wanted to train so hard it hurt. I wanted to train so badly that I cried every night. I went to the dojo frequently, even though it depressed me more. My feet carried me there against my will. I thought about training every day. It obsessed my thoughts. I couldn't sleep well.

The familiar stinky smell of sweat depressed me more than comforted me, when I stopped by the dojo as usual that night. Uematsu showed me a move with one arm, and tried to cheer me up. When I was sitting on the bench trying to get my coat on, he came over and squeezed my shoulder.

"Taihen da ne!" "Rough, isn't it!" He said, with a wry smile.

It was the first human contact I'd had in a month, besides the doctor and the evil rento-gento man. I wanted to hug him. Being a fighter, he knew exactly what it was like to be hurt and have to sit out. His support touched me, crossing over any racial, gender or age boundaries. Uematsu Naoya, the comic fighter. I'll never forget this.

December 20

"AAAAAH oh my god!" I screamed out loud, holding my arms straight out in front of me. Well, I had intended for them both to be straight, but it didn't quite work out. And then my body started panicking.

Night had fallen, and delicious smells wafted in from Sadako-san's kitchen. I had taken my bandages off after throwing down my school bag. The swelling had gone down a lot, so for the first time I could see the natural shape of my arm. And something looked wrong. Very wrong. There was a bump in the side where it should have been lower on my arm. I held both arms out in front of me palm up. My left arm wouldn't turn palm up, but instead turned palm down. It could only go as far as thumbs up. It was as if someone pulled my forearm off, turned it 60 degrees, and then stuck it back on.

I rushed into the kitchen to my host mother. Apron clad, she was leaning over the stove, stirring spaghetti in a frying pan with a pair of long wooden cooking chopsticks. Which was weird in of itself.

"Sadako-san!" I exclaimed, displaying arms. Tears stared to trickle down my cheeks. I sniffed. She turned to me. Her apron had tomato sauce spots.

"What?!"

"Does this ... look normal to you?" I sniffed.

"Uh... just keep doing the rehabilitation and see the doctor."

"Wha...!"

What'd you expect her to say? I thought. "Oh yeah sure..." I answered, and went back to my room to freak out some more.

"My arm healed wrong!" I thought. "They're going to have to break my arm again! I won't be able to train for even longer! How will I survive that? I can't!"

180

I dug out my cell phone and called my best friend Jessiqa from Umass. She was doing an exchange in Nanzan University in another part of Japan.

"Dear Roxy, what's the matter?" she answered, alarmed. I blubbered to her for a while, but felt only slightly better. Then I checked my watch. If I hurried, I could still catch my jiu jitsu friends before they went home.

I booked it to the club, practically running to the station, making it there in 25 minutes and beating my previous record by ten whole minutes.

I burst through the door, and spotted Jet just finishing a round of sparring. I was hot and all worked up. "Japanese, don't fail me now." I hoped. I wonder what I must have looked like, dripping with sweat and wild-eyed.

"I'm worried!" I practically shouted the understatement, for lack of a better expression. I stripped off my coat and fleece, flinging them to the ground off to the side. Finally standing in my sweat-soaked T-shirt, I presented both of my arms. "I don't think my arm healed right. LOOK!" I said. "I can't bend my arm like THIS!"

And... I bent my arm like that.

My mouth fell open. Jet looked at me warily. A few other classmates also stared. Both of my hands went palm up. Due to my mad dash, I suppose it had warmed up and loosened the muscles, becoming more flexible. My arm didn't need to be re-broken. It was fine. I needed to cry, so I went into the bathroom and let the water-works come. A few minutes later, I came out, red-eyed.

"Don't worry, Roxanne," she said to me, patting me on the shoulder. "I couldn't move my arm much at first either. And it looks weird and stuff. But it goes back," she assured me.

That night, I enjoyed a normal shower for the first time in a month. I could just barely touch my face with my left thumb if I tried really hard.

December 21

The next morning, my host mother told me, "Ara, anta futochatta no yo! Kao ni mieru yo!" "Oh you've gotten fatter! I can see it in your face!"

WHAT? How mean! Thank you so very, very much! Keep calm, Rox, cultural difference. You know you've gained weight, so just have a conversation about it. Japanese style. You know she loves you. And you love her. There's lots of love. Love love love. Love the love.

I took a few deep breaths.

"Haha yeah I did. Since the fight, I gained about 3 kilos. But it's kind of mean to say that, right?"

"Three kilos?!" my host mother exclaimed, peering at me. "Oh yeah, you did! You really did!"

Why is she so happy about it? Why is she laughing? No, it's okay, keep calm. I thought.

"You eat so many sweets and stuff," she went on.

"Actually, I don't really wanna talk about it," I finally came out and stated firmly.

"Why not?" Sadako-san asked.

"Well...I just...what do you mean 'why not?'" I couldn't keep the annoyance out of my voice. My host mother rose from her seat chuckling, and shuffled into the kitchen.

Chapter 15 - Holiday
December 20

Merry Christmas! I returned home to my Dad's apartment to find that his girlfriend (now wife) got him to buy curtains, and they'd rearranged the place.

"That's what happens when you get a girlfriend, I guess," he joked, with a big smile. I enjoyed seeing him happy.

"This is the first time you've been away for so long," Dad said, enveloping me in his strong arms. "Three months. I'm so proud of you, honey," he said into my ear. I listened, my face pressed into his big shoulder.

"You've chosen a difficult path, so you have to work harder to achieve it." He paused, and let me go. "That's alright, though. It seems to be a Modafferi trait."
It was really good to be back.

I sometimes wondered how wise it was to pay thousands of dollars for college to learn a skill that's easily forgettable, such as a language. My major was Japanese, after all. If I didn't use it, I'd lose it. I vowed to make something of myself, something great.

I enjoyed visiting my extended family, too - my father's cousins. I gorged myself on the excellent Italian food my Aunt cooked: salmon, catfish, lasagna, baked shrimp in a sweat sauce with onions over them, pasta with clam, and garlic bread. Dessert was Italian rugula, cannolis, and more.

In addition to seeing family, I stopped by my jiu jitsu club, João Amaral's BJJ Club (now called Brazilian Top Team Boston) in Everett, and watched a class for a while. João, the resident black belt and owner, listened with interest to my experiences. All my old training partners gave me big hugs. It truly felt like home.

December 30

Melting! My laptop was melting! My mom and I brought it to Best Buy, where the man behind the repair counter started spouting corporate policy about repairs. We had sent my laptop back for repairs two times, and both times it had come back still broken. Yes, it would not turn on two separate times. Is that even possible? Isn't the staff supposed to send a fixed machine back to the customer? How can staff send it back "fixed" and not "know" that it wouldn't turn on?

The policy is that they fully replace laptops if they come back from repairs four times. So that means they expect it to be sent back four times still broken? My brain must be too tiny to comprehend such logic.

Luckily for me, or not, they couldn't fix it, so we twisted their arm and I got to chose a lovely new Toshiba satellite. I caressed the shiny navy blue cover, pleased to have a more durable brand name than the previous one. With its 60 gigs of hard drive (compared to the previous 30) I felt ready to take on the world.

After our triumph at Best Buy, my mother and I went to the theater and saw *Lord of the Rings: Return of the King*. What an intense movie- one of the best I've ever seen. Following that, we had real American pizza, and then watched old classical Christmas movies, such as *Jim Henson's The Christmas Toy* and *Rudolph the Red-Nosed Reindeer*.

"Oh, honey, they're kids' movies!" my mother had protested, but agreed to watch them with me anyway. All of a sudden, preserving my customs and traditions became radically important. Now that I was living in a foreign country, all the things I took for granted were gone. The Japanese celebrated only the commercial aspect of Christmas. December 25 was "date night," where couples ate Kentucky Fried Chicken and chocolate cake. Go figure. I learned not to take anything for granted. Even tying my hair in a ponytail.

January 1, 2004

For New Years, I spent the night at my high school friend Kate's house. Another high school friend Erin, Kate, and I played Lord of the Rings Trivial Pursuit late into the night. Kate beat me, even teamed up with Erin. Easily. And we'd all read the books and seen the movies.

"Okay, last question, and we can choose it," I said to Erin in a stage whisper. "One of these four questions on this card…which is the least likely she'll know?"

Kate sat across the table, grinning at us. "Hurry up!" she said, rocking back and forth in anticipation.

"If she gets it, she'll win. If she can't get it, we get one more chance to win."

"Hmmm," Erin pondered. "I dunno? I mean, Kate knew the name of the first movie Peter Jackson ever directed when he was like 26."

"How about this one?" I suggested.

"Okay."

"Okay, Kate?" I said. "What are the names of the two horses Eomer gave Legolas, Aragorn and Gimli?"

"Uh…" Kate paused. "Arod and Hasufel."

She freakin' got it!

"How do you remember this stuff!?" Erin screamed. We all burst out laughing.

I flew back to Japan refreshed, ready to take on anything weird, challenging, and unexplainable that Japan could possibly throw at me.

Chapter 16 – Anime Expo
January 6

Clad in an elbow brace, with a wrist tightly taped with athletic tape, I participated in the BJJ class. Lightly. Just the previous week, I couldn't grab and hold onto anything with the left hand.

"You're back!" my training partners all said, giving me smiles and pats on the back. I spent the whole hour and a half worrying that I'd re-injure it, but got lucky. I relished the sore muscle achy feeling I got after class ended.

Looking down at my hands, I was surprised to see my skin peeling off, and blood on my knuckles. My skin had become weak, unaccustomed to gripping the rough gi uniform material. In addition, my face was dry and peeling, but I didn't care. It was strangely satisfying that I'd worked hard enough to make them bleed. The elbow hurt, but not too much. I just iced it when I got home, and took an anti-inflammatory. To top it all off, that night Uematsu-san received his brown belt! I was so glad I got to be there for it. I went home with a big smile on my face.

January 7

As I lay collapsed on my futon, I realized how disorganized my thoughts were. It had nothing to do with my head spinning around in circles from jetlag, or the incredibly boring class discussion I had one hour before.

"I'll try the meditation technique that my BJJ friend Dave taught me during my visit home to Boston." I thought.

"Regulate your breathing. Focus your mind on every thought that comes into your head. Recognize it, and let it go. Thoughts are clouds, drifting across your clear mind!"

Homework, food, Dave, my Brazilian friends. The only noise around me was the whirl of the heater.

I spoke out loud. "New Year's resolution. Heater noise. Warmth. I need to do my homework. I need to finish writing a

Japanese paper. Sadako cooked but I wasn't hungry. My foot is cold."

All of a sudden, I saw them clearly: thoughts coming and going like thin clouds, flowing like a river across the blue backdrop Dave had painted for me.

I sat bolt upright. With a click clack, my fingers danced across the keys, pounding out my school essay. My mind was the open blue sky.

I learned to appreciate a lot of things not only living in Japan, but having my arm broken. I used to drive everywhere in the US. When I started biking 20 minutes to get to school, I started appreciating cars. I appreciated their roofs when it rained, and gas when I was tired.

After I hurt my arm, I couldn't ride a bike so I had to walk 45 minutes to school. That made me appreciate a bike. Back in high school, I'd hurt my back in a judo tournament and was bed-ridden for a few days. That made me appreciate walking.

I used to complain that Sadako's house showerhead was too low, so I had to shower on my knees. When my arm got put in a cast I couldn't get it wet. Now, I appreciated being able to wash myself at all, without struggling to keep the arm dry. I can now put up my hair in the morning. I can clip my nails. I can tie the belt on my pants.

As human beings, we need to remind ourselves of these things once in a while. It also enables us to be kinder to others, and understand other people's perspectives. Everybody is suffering from something. It's just not always obvious.

January 8

"Can you fight yet?" Uematsu said to me, the second I stepped into the dojo. "A promoter I know needs you..."

"REALLY? Awesome!" I exclaimed. Then my face fell. I threw a few experimental jabs with my left arm. "No, not yet. Not for another two months at least. It'll probably take me another month just to get to 100% and then I'd want some real training time." Damn it...

"We're going to refocus on our training," my body told me. "We have our range of motion back. Strength returned to our hand. We can lift things again!"

"I'm still afraid to use it in training, though," my mind said. "We, I mean, YOU keep over-doing it and tweaking it, and it gets a little worse. You have to be more careful!"

"I know, I know," my body replied. "Let's make a note about our weight so we know where we started."

As of January 12, I am 148 lbs.

January 18

I'm an 'anime otaku.' That means 'one obsessed with Japanese animation.' I've seen over 50 titles, memorized which voice actors play which roles in which animes, and have tons of merchandise. In the US, I went to an anime convention called 'Otakon' a few times with my high school friends. I always wondered what one would be like in the birthplace of anime!

I found out that an anime convention called "Anime Expo" was being held in the gigantic mall called Sunshine City. It featured the cast of the popular Japanese animation "Full Metal Alchemist," one of my favorite anime so I made plans to go. It took an hour and 15 minutes to get from my house to Ikebukuro. The normally crowded streets were pretty bare so early in the morning that I didn't get lost trying to find Sunshine City. However, once I reached the immense mall, I had no idea which way to head. A map showed that there were commercial stores, offices, restaurants, meeting halls etc. The information booth which usually had friendly but bored-looking staff wasn't open yet.

At 8:30am, I wandered through some doors and found myself faced with deserted corridors and hallways. I checked my notes scribbled on a scrap of paper. Event start time: 10am. I had plenty of time to find the right room. On the floors below me were pricy fashionable clothing stores, still shut for the night. Above me were 15 or so floors of offices, and some convention halls.

After a few minutes of wandering, I exited onto a patio. The bright sunshine blinded me. I shaded my eyes, squinting.

188

Immediately, I spotted an enormous line with at least 200 people. It wrapped around building corners, curving around potted plants set up here and there. Cosplayers - people dressed like anime or video game characters - waited patiently. They chatted with their pals, checked email on cell phones, or read information booklets. At 8:30am.

"Holy crap, already?" I thought incredulously. "That's probably the line I have to be in! But I got here an hour and a half early!"

I found the end of the line, and waited in dismay for a good ten minutes. My eyes scanned over the interesting costumes and posters hung here and there. I saw the words *DigiCarat* and *Broccoli!* - the latter I guessed was the name of the company sponsoring the show. I didn't see any Anime Expo signs, though.

The girl in front of me was dressed up like the heroine "Sailor Moon" complete with waist-length blond braided pigtails. She was spacing out, holding her ticket out in front of her. I noticed it. Then noticed something else.

"Oh, that's a guy. A male sailor scout. Hairy legs and everything," I thought. "That takes guts."

His blue mini-skirt flapped in the morning breeze.

"Excuse me," I said politely in Japanese.

He turned to me.

"Do I need a ticket?" I asked.

"Yes," he said.

"Where do I get it?"

"I'm not sure," the girly man replied, pointing. "That way?" he suggested.

I decided to get out of line and take a walk. I found the room that the Full Metal Alchemist (FMA) voice actors and directors were supposed to be in. I pushed open the heavy door, and a guy standing just behind the door called out, "We're not open yet!"

"Where can I get tickets?" I asked.

"Blah blah something something go downstairs blah blah," he replied quickly. He appeared very busy.

"Sorry, I couldn't understand you. Could you say that again?" I winced.

"Go downstairs and there'll be two lines. You can get tickets there," he repeated. This time my brain translated. With that, he continued to set up a table.

When I went downstairs, I didn't see two lines. I didn't see one line. I didn't see anything. I wandered around for a little while until I found one lady sitting at a table. There were a few pieces of paper on the table, looking kind of like lists. A cardboard box sat at her feet. She stared at me.

"Excuse me, can I buy tickets here?" I asked in my best Japanese.

"Yackity yackity blah blah at 9 o'clock," she said. "Please wait ten minutes."

"Uh, okay," I said, turning away. Wait a minute. But those other people have tickets, I thought, confused.

I turned back. "Excuse me," I said again.

"Yes?" she forced an impatient smile.

"Um, well everyone is waiting outside, and I want to wait, too....well, why do they have tickets?"

"Yackity yackity yackity blah blah blah," she said.

"What?"

She rose and called over some guy. They conferred for a minute. He turned to me.

"We start selling tickets at 9," he repeated more slowly. "Please wait ten minutes. Do you understand?"

"Oh. Okay, yes I understand," I lied, unconvinced.

Ten minutes later, I bought a ticket was strolling back outside. Then it occurred to me. Wait a second. I thought the fee was 2,500 yen (about thirty dollars). This one cost 1,000 yen (about ten dollars). What is going on here?

I went back outside and asked Sailor Moon why they were waiting. He said it was to get into the dealer's room, which sold toys, videos, and other goods. Oh, I didn't want that. I wanted to see the FMA cast.

Returning to the table, I asked the man and woman, who probably hated me by then, about FMA.

190

"Oh, that's not the right ticket. That's for the Broccoli! exhibit."

"WHAT? Broccoli?!" I nearly jumped a foot off the ground. "There are two anime conventions? Right next to each other? At the same time?"

What are the chances of that? And why does Broccoli! have an exclamation mark after it? I thought.

"Yes, please go downstairs because there are two lines," he repeated what he had said before.

"I didn't see two lines," I said.

"There are two lines," he repeated.

"Two lines," the woman said.

Those people need to go downstairs and see that there ARE NOT two lines, I thought furiously.

"Fine, I understand!" I nearly yelled, even though I didn't. "Can I have my money back?" Thank goodness they complied. It would be totally Japanese of them to say, "It's your fault for buying the wrong ticket."

On the way downstairs, I snagged a young guy with an "ANIME EXPO" on a badge pinned to his shirt. I flashed him a smile and said, "Excuse me, where can I buy ANIME EXPO TICKETS?"

"Oh!" he grinned back. "Right here! To the left!" and escorted me to an area around the corner behind this curve in the wall.

Alchemists are much nicer than Broccoli! people, I decided.

I saw people without badges sitting at a table, organizing papers, tickets, and such. I turned to find the young man gone, so I confirmed with them that it was indeed a place to buy Anime Expo tickets.

"But we start selling at 9:30. Please wait ten minutes."

Fine.

I waited and got the ticket. Now, where was the actual convention? People had yet to fill the halls, so I wandered around for a while until I saw a few people standing at a door. It opened and they went inside. I grabbed a hold of the edge just as it was closing. Sticking my head through, I peered at their shirts and saw a lack of badges.

"Excuse me," I said, merely a head sticking through the door. "Koko wa broccoli no tokoro desu ka?" Which literally means, "Excuse me, is this the broccoli place?"

One of the men raised an eyebrow in a most excellent bewildered expression, as if to say, "Who the hell are you?"

He opened his mouth. "....Buro...bro...ccoli?"

I burst out laughing right in his face. He must have not been related to the convention at all. I might as well have asked about the "banana" place.

"Sorry, never mind..." I retracted my head and scurried down the hall. Crazy foreigner, right?

Finally I spotted someone holding up a cardboard sign that said, "Hagaren no renkin jitsu shi" which means "Full Metal Alchemist." There was a short line! I went to stand in it.

"Excuse me, is this the FMA line?" I asked some random guy.

"Oh, blady blady blady!" he answered and nodded.

"Thanks!" I said with a smile, and showed him my badge.

"Oh yes yadda yadda yadda," he said, and turned away.

God, I wonder how long it'll take me to understand more than 15% of what people are saying, I thought to myself, trying to see the humor of the situation.

We waited a long time. All around me, various convention goers wore the red cape of Edward Elric, the main character of FMA. I saw another male sailor scout- Sailor Mercury! He wore a light blue schoolgirl's sailor top, and pleated mini-skirt. This time it was a gaijin, a foreigner, with skinny hairy legs. I tried not to stare too long, but if he didn't dress up to be stared at, why did he? I just hoped he didn't come over and try to talk to me. After gazing at the costumes for over 30 minutes, I got really bored, so I started eavesdropping in on other people's conversations.

Right in front of me, a group of flighty girls in their late teens or early twenties was hanging out in a semi-circle formation. They were chatting and making fun of things in cute, high-pitched voices.

192

Girl A said, "So like yeah, she came over and was like, (squeak) 'I'm so sorry to keep you waiting,' and bowed like a gazillion times. I thought, "could her voice get any higher?"

She shifted her stance, and I noticed she was wearing high heels. It seemed to me that 99% of all youthful Japanese women wear high heels out in public, even with jeans.

Girl B giggled. "Yah, what an idiot. They wear their hats like this, and like this and talk like this…" she did a few strange poses. I bit my lip to keep from smiling.

"What are you talking about," Girl A laughed, giving her friend a shove. "You wear that, too!"

Girl B raised her voice a few octaves and squeaked, "How dare you!"

I wonder why I can understand random crap that I don't even need to know, but I can't understand how to buy tickets, I though remorsefully.

"It's Romi Paku! Paku-sama~! Miss Paku!" a bunch of them suddenly squealed, frantically digging around in their bags for cameras.

I heard a bunch of 'Doko doko?'s, which means, "Where where?"

Girl B grabbed Girl A's arm and started jumping up and down. I looked across the room where a crowd was being held back by staff members. Literally, staff members were joining arms and pushing away rabid fans.

Romi Paku, the voice actress for the main FMA star Edward Elric, must have been passing by. I'd never seen anything more than one profile shot on the Internet, and I was very excited. I refrained from squealing, though. Standing on my tippy toes, I couldn't see her because she was short. Fans were obstructing my view. FMA fans should be laughing right now, because height is a sore point of hers, and of the character "Ed" she plays. Ed flies into a rage whenever someone teases him about his stature.

The staff hustled Miss Paku into the hall ahead of us, and the excitement died down again.

One of the staff members standing nearby returned to his post, after having to dash to the front to hold back the fans. "Waa, bikkuri shita!" Wow, that surprised me, he muttered to himself. The Girls A and B heard and started making fun of him quietly.

Finally, at 10:30 they led us in to the high ceilinged convention hall. Hundreds of foldable metal chairs were lashed together in rows in front of a stage. I had to sit in the back. It could have been worse; a lot of people didn't get seats and had to stand sardined together for a few hours.

The staff showed the first episode of the series, which was kind of boring for me since I had watched it more than five times already. The speakers boomed painfully loudly, and I stuck my fingers in my ears during explosions. Next, we got a surprise when the popular band Yellow Generation trouped out on stage and performed the new season's theme song.

This is really impressive, I thought. Then the girl sitting next to me bumped me with her legs. Again. She had been squirming in her seat, and opening and closing her legs ever since we sat down.

Do you have a problem? I wished I could shake her and scream. *If you have to go to the bathroom, just go! Nobody's going to take your seat if you leave something on it. What's with Japanese people,* I wondered, not for the first time. Stuff like that, and also if their nose is runny, they sniff. Or wipe it. Just blow it and be done! I don't understand it.

After the music performance finished, staff sprinted out and set up few chairs on stage.

My friends back home would kill to be here right now! I thought, anxiously waiting for what came next. Fun memories of Otakon came to mind, a huge convention in Baltimore. Huge convention halls, crazy people dressed up in gigantic costumes, booths as far as the eye could see selling all merchandise imaginable – we'd all gone together. Feelings of loneliness washed over me.

Then Seiji Mizushima, the director, Sho Aikawa, the story editor, Romi Paku, and Rie Kugimiya - voice actress for Alfonse Elric - came onstage. All the women in the hall started screaming. Finally after introductions they started talking. It was the moment we'd all been waiting for. We've only heard them acting, never using their natural voices. Romi Paku actually played a young boy's voice, so that was interesting. I think I fell in love with her voice.

If my eyes could turn into animated hearts, they would have.

I want her to sing me a song before I go to bed at night! I thought in fan girl fever.

And Rie Kugimiya's voice? She also played a young boy. It was so ridiculously high, that I thought she was kidding or voice acting. She wasn't, then. My vocal cords can't even make that sound.

After the question and answer session, the show ended and the crowd dispersed. I visited another room and played video games, such as Dragon Ball Z Budukai 2 for Playstation 2, and some other fighting game. Con-goers supped at a cafe area, served by waitresses dressed up as Evangelion's Rei and Digicarat's green cat-girl. I saw a Lupin III cosplayer lounging in a slouched position at a table. Two really good Vashes from Trigun strolled by. They were tall and thin, just like the real character! I also saw a good Kakashi, from Naruto, and the guy from Gaara's group with the face paint – also from Naruto. I didn't want to be paparazzi, so I didn't snap any shots. Not having any interest in the action figure booths or a few anime shows, I ended up going home early. It was tame.

Ironically, my Anime Expo Tokyo experience was less impressive than the annual convention, Otakon, held in Baltimore, Maryland. Getting a ticket had been the biggest adventure.

Chapter 17 – Training and Health
"Your future is the result of the choices you make."

January 20

"Five…six…seven…!" I panted and huffed as I sprinted up the last step. That made my third set of eight floors, completing my workout at the Seiyu department store. In a place like Japan where space is limited, malls and markets shot vertically upward. The grocery stores were usually found on the ground floor or basement level of such stores. Ladies' clothing was the on first and second floor, men's on the third, toys on the fourth, housewares on the fifth, and services like eye doctor's offices and restaurants were on the top floor.

Seiyu followed this pattern. I found that the wide staircases in the back of the stores are always deserted since everybody always took the escalators, so I was free to run up and down as much as I liked. Yellow-stained dreary walls surrounded me, and my feet made little noise on the hard stone floor.

Gosh, I hate running stairs, I thought, briefly stretching my legs before starting the skipping decent. My knees protested. The previous day Mind, Body, and Heart rejoiced together about the further recovery of my elbow.

"I've been sparring at about 80% for a while!" I calculated. "Carefully."

Every time, I wrapped the wrist so tightly it could barely bend. That usually kept it safe, except for the over-enthusiastic white belt who latched onto me from behind, grabbed my sleeve, and pulled my arm in a funny direction. Hearing me howl, he released me, but the elbow still hurt after that.

"You're such a moron, Rox! You keep reinjuring that arm," my mind scolded.

"Yeah, Roxy, you jerk-face," my body added in support.

"But we need to work out! Must!" my heart protested.

"The only thing you should exercise is a little self-control and take more time off," my mind chided.

196

Heart wouldn't hear it. "I can't! I just can't! Especially since even working out a little brings such great mental rewards. I can't sleep well when I don't train. I get so stressed. I just have to go to the gym!"

The embodiments of my various selves seemed to be in a constant battle.

I had a lot of time on my hands to take walks before and after doing stairs.

It's funny how things change and never stay the same, I often thought to myself. *In my beloved jiu jitsu club, people moved away, new people come, and people get hurt. Zuyo hurt her foot and hasn't made it to the dojo in a while. I miss everyone.*

January 25
The Tissue Culture

In Japan no matter where you go, employees roam around the streets in front of train stations and street corners handing out fliers.

I always thought it was such a waste of paper. Not to mention the worst job ever. Like a telemarketer, it's your job to be constantly rejected, snubbed, or ignored.

Most people glance at the ads and chuck them in the trash. More often than not, I see the tiny slips of paper littered on the ground. I always refuse them (with a smile and a nod!) unless they have tissues. Yes, tissues. Businesses print their ads on little papers and tuck them in packets of about five tissues. They're very handy come winter. I also notice an increase in tissue-passer-outers during hay fever season. Thanks to this custom, I've never ever spent money on tissues in Japan. Occasionally, though, hander-outers offer them to people walking ahead of me, and then withdraw them when I walk by. That means I wasn't a target customer for that particular product or service. If that were true, though, why did I find myself with lots of 'girly service club' tissues? Maybe the staff just gave them to anybody. If I get them, I always just automatically stuff them in my pocket and transfer them into a plastic bag when I get home.

One day, I found that I'd actually run out.

"Man, I gotta collect some more!" I thought. "I can't be going out and buying them with money, now can I?"

I happened to be in Ikebukuro. The area around the huge station bustled and thrived with commercial activity. I steered myself towards a row of about three young men. They wore casual clothes, unlike others who dressed in their company's staff uniforms. The guys had baskets under their arms, tissues in their hands, and were frantically turning this way and that in the stream of human traffic, calling out "Onegaishimasu! Onegaishimasu!" which means, "Please! Take one! Here you are! Please!"

I reached for one. It was retracted. Baffled, I got the same treatment from the next two, so I made a U-turn, pretended to look in some shop windows, and then walked by them again. Again, they pointedly refused to hand me the tissues.

Gimme a tissue pack! I gotta blow my nose, I thought, irritated. That's when I realized that certain businesses tell their staff to give to target customers. A few years later, when business was slow, I was forced to hand out fliers for my English company. The manager instructed me to target businessmen as much as possible, rather than young women or kids.

So this gaijin doesn't fall into their business target group, I thought regretfully. *Now I'll have to resort to blowing my nose on toilet paper in the station bathroom. Damn you, corporate culture!*

January 26

"What am I going to do with my life after college?"

The sudden urge to decide my future came over me one night as I strolled home from the station. I zipped up my jacket tightly against the winter wind.

"You know what you want to do," my heart answered readily.

My mind was surprised. "I do?"

198

"Yes. You want to do martial arts!"

My mind scoffed. "Yeah, but I can't."

"Who says?"

"For a career? My logic. My wallet. How would I pay the bills?"

"And what if I get hurt?" my body put in, tugging my winter cap farther down over my ears. "Then we can't earn a living."

"Well," my heart began, "If you knew what you were going to do with your life before you did it, there wouldn't be much fun in struggling to attain something, now would there? That'd be like seeing the future. Who wants to know their future?" My heart spoke passionately. "What if you don't like the future? Then it's depressing living to reach that point. Silly Mind, just keep training."

"But what am I going to do with my life?"

"I just told you. Just keep going."

"But at this rate, I'm learning Japanese but it's not going to be enough to get paid professionally to be a translator," my mind said.

If my heart had shoulders, she would have shrugged. "I told you, I don't have all the answers! I can only tell you want I want to do."

I sighed and pushed open the door to my host family's house.

"Tadaima!" I'm home! I called out.

January 27

I stood crouched over him, pressuring forward with my knee. The purple belt had a hold of my pant leg and the same-side sleeve. I tried to pass his guard, but the stronger man gave me a hard yank, pulling me in close. I got sucked into his guard, kneeling while his legs were wrapped around my waste. He trapped my arm against the outside of his leg and hyper-extended it. It all happened so fast. Unable to move to even tap out, I heard the most horrible popping noises.

I just yelled. Terrified tears involuntarily sprung to my eyes. What if, when I went to move my arm, it wouldn't respond? What if it broke again? My life would be put on hold for a long time again. What would I do with myself?

"Not again, not again, not again..." The words replayed over and over, bouncing around my skull. I could barely stand it, so I went to the bathroom and cried. Carefully wiggling my fingers and flexing my arm, I decided that the damage was not severe.

"Are you okay?" he asked after I came out.

"Yeah, I'm fine," I replied, secretly irritated that he cranked it so fast.

The next day I realized, ironically, that although the elbow ached slightly, it was more flexible than it had been before the armbar. Maybe I should thank him.

January 28

"What does your name mean?" I asked Mr. Ueda, a fellow at jiu jitsu.

"Oh it's a common name," he said. "It means 'above the rice field.' So what does your name mean?"

"Well," I said, and then stopped. I didn't know how to explain my answer in Japanese. My last name is Italian- Modafferi. But it's an unusual Italian name. Its roots are Persian. In the 5th Century BC, Persians occupied Italy. In Calabria, where my family is from, there happen to be a lot of Modafferis, many who are not necessarily related. The original name is "El Modafer," although my spelling could be off. It means, "victorious warrior." Another translation I've heard is "made victorious by God."

I took a deep breath. "It's a cool name- it comes from Persian..." I said the name in English.

"Where?"

"Persia...do you know?"

He shook his head. I must have bungled the Japanese-style pronunciation.

"Anyway, it means, "winning fighter," I said, doing the best I could with what vocabulary I had.

"Oh, cool," he said. "What about your first name?"

"Um, actually I don't know," I replied.

When I got home, I wrote to my mom. She promptly wrote back:

Dear Roxanne,

I found the "baby names" book. This is what it says about "Roxanne:" Persian. Raokhshna. Brilliant One.

Roxana is famous as the wife of Alexander the Great, ancient world conqueror; Roxanne is heroine of Rostand's French classic, "Cyrano de Bergerac."

Nicknames: Roxie, Roxy. English variations: Roxana, Roxanna, Roxine.

Mom

Awesome. My name totally rules. Nice job, Mom and Dad.

January 30

Letting my feet carry me home, I allowed my mind to wander. My eyes roved through the dark buildings and shadowy streets near the train station. My hair, damp with sweat from the night's training stuck to my head.

"If you go outside with wet hair, you can catch a cold!" Mom piped up. The embodiment of her love and advice lived somewhere deep in my subconscious. I accordingly yanked my hat down further on my head to cover my hair.

"It's cold. But at least I can shower without having to worry about keeping my cast dry!" my mind thought. "I've really come to appreciate the little things."

"I've decided!" my heart suddenly exclaimed.

"Oh yeah? Decided what?"

"What I want in life!"

"Oh really. I thought you wanted to do MMA. You've decided something else since then? Do tell."

"Well...! I want to be the best female MMA fighter in the whole world!"

"WHAT!?" my mind and body chorused together.

"It totally makes sense," my heart raved on. "Luffy wants to be the next Pirate King. Naruto wants to be the next Hokage..."

If my mind had substance, she would have grabbed my heart by the shoulders and shaken her.

"So you're an anime character now? Does that mean you want to start collecting Pokémon and carry them around in your pockets?"

"What, it makes perfect sense!" my heart protested. "Of course I'm not an anime character! But they have the right idea, right? Aim for the top. You have to set your goal to be the highest challenge possible! Because people always achieve their goals or less, so if the higher your goal, the more you have the chance to achieve! Anyway, I decided, and now I feel great."

I passed the landmark 24-hour convenience store. Its striped florescent sign illuminated the sidewalk. I turned right, down the side street that led to my host family's house.

"Doing jiu jitsu won't pay the bills! You don't live in a ninja village, nor a pirate ship, and you're not Royce Gracie!"

My body interjected. "Do you guys know how many injuries professional fighters accumulate over time?" she said mournfully. "We'll have to retire and limp around by 35!"

"I'm not stupid, you know," my heart responded indignantly. "I know we'll have to find us a good job using Japanese that will pay the bills."

"I'm telling you, you won't be bilingual at the end of four years of college!" my mind said.

"But I've already decided that the best goal for me is to be the best woman MMA fighter in the world," my heart went on. "I already have tons of contacts. I'm sure Kipp Kollar from Reality

202

Fighting will give me great opportunities to fight in his organization. I'm becoming well known in Japan, too. That's why I'm training! To improve and become a world-class fighter. Why else would I do it? For my health?"

"I can't bend my arm…" my body said flatly.

"Well, seriously, I know we are slow learners in the injury department," my heart admitted.

"You're a moron," my mind chided.

"…why wouldn't you want to be the best at what you do?" my heart continued. "That's where the drive comes from. I'll always feel fulfilled if I can work towards my final ultimate goal. It used to be 'beat men in competition,' but they don't let women fight men in tournaments anymore, so might as well be content with fighting women for the gold."

"Well you know," my mind said. "There are some women who started when they were babies, who we're never going to be better than. Like Leka Vieira, the BJJ black belt."

"Don't ever say that to me!" my heart screamed. "Don't EVER admit that you are beaten! When you do that, you just mentally beat yourself. You can always improve and beat anybody if you put your mind to it!"

"Okay, okay!"

"Plus, did I ever say you had to beat Leka at BJJ? If she wants to put on gloves, then you'll punch her lights out. Did I say you had to go compete in Muay Thai? This decision is for MMA specifically. It gives you the option to take down a striker, or stand with a grappler, and use your wits to win. That's why it's so much fun. And we're going to get really good at it. Right? No more internal conflicts?"

"Right."

"The best?"

"The best," agreed Mind, Body and Heart.

February 9

My university notified me of the lack of credits I had in certain areas of my study. I wrote my father an email about my future, asking for advice. It was about three pages of ranting about all sorts of topics. I wonder if he read it all, busy as he is at work. Unlikely. His responses are usually serious and business-like for the most part. Therefore, I was amused to read his reply:

Your future !!! will be awesome !!! dude-ical !!

RPM
L. I. Company

Just great. Way to look on the bright side, Dad! Although this confirms he probably didn't read my letter before responding. Plus he signed his name with his initials. I decided to call him on the phone at a future date, and actually have a conversation.

After BJJ that night, I found that I gained approximately four inches of mobility in my left elbow. I made sure I showed everyone at the dojo.

"Look at my arm! It bends!" I walked around, demonstrating. They all smiled, humoring me. Zuyo gave me a little plastic Dragon Ball Z "ball" that opened up like an Easter egg to reveal a figurine inside. Yay, toys!

That wasn't the end to the excitement of the evening. Uematsu-san had brought a real sword to class, for reasons unbeknownst to me. He kept pulling it out at random times, assuming a stance and threatening people. I bet he was hoping for a bigger reaction out of people, but everyone went about their business, giving him the same tight-lipped smiles that they gave me when I tried to tell jokes in Japanese.

"Roxanne!" he said suddenly, pointed it at me.

"Oh, save me, Lord Uematsu!" I cried, prostrating myself on the ground. That made everybody laugh.

"It was only 10,000 yen (a hundred dollars), and not sharp," he added with a laugh. "Hiyaaa!"

204

I practice both gi and no-gi grappling. I come from a judo background where the gi uniform is the only form of dress. However, so often Brazilian jiu jitsu sparring turns into a power struggle tug-of-war. Judo and jiu jitsu fighters do tend to gain a lot of muscles around their shoulders and back. However, I found that I enjoy coming up with random escapes during fast-paced back-and-forth fights. I can move faster and escape holds better without being hindered by a thick uniform jacket.

One of my goals is to get a black belt in Brazilian jiu jitsu. Despite this, I came to the realization that I preferred no-gi grappling.

Tonight, I had a great fight with this small scrappy guy who kept trying to ankle lock me. After just barely squirming out of it, I clamped down on his foot and almost got him with it. He kicked me off and took a top position. I reversed it. We rolled over and over. Somehow during the course of our rotation, his legs shot up and went for a triangle, but missed including my arm in the lock. It turned into head scissor, with him crossing his legs tightly with my neck trapped in between. I gasped and gargled. His knees squished my face.

"It hurts...but I'm not gonna tap to something pathetic like a head-scissor! I can still breathe!" I thought.

I struggled more. Then I felt him catch a hold of my foot! He was applying an ankle lock because I couldn't move due to the head scissor. I got out by toe holding him with my non-injured hand, so he had to let go of my head. I love moves that are unconventional but I manage to get out of a pinch with them.

February 10

I received a more inspirational response from my father the following day in my e-mail inbox:

Re: your future and jobs. When we go for Chinese food we'll check the fortune cookie?!? Only kidding. It's the right time for you to be going through a thoughtful evaluation process. Do it without anxiety, though. Think. Then, think again. Don't panic, just let your gray matter absorb and evaluate. You're doing the right things.

You are more powerful than you know. Maybe I should re-phrase that. You are more empowered than you know. Don't mentally limit yourself at this point.

When you shoot at a flock of flying birds one uses a shot gun that sprays little B-Bs in a broad space. When you find a target you use a rifle with a scope to very precisely aim at the bull's eye to make sure you hit the target. You are growing now. You are putting down the shot gun and looking for a target. That's fine. Keep looking. You'll find it.

Dad

I read through it a few times, smiling. I knew if anybody could give me advice, it was him. I sighed, and then lay back down. I shoved a thermometer in my mouth, and when it beeped, I checked the temperature. Fever. I knew it. Then I got up and wandered into the kitchen.

"Sadako-san, I'm sick," I said.

"What? Do you have a temperature?"

"Yes."

"What is it?"

"Well, it's 100.1 in Fahrenheit, but in Celsius it's...uh ..."

"WHAAAAAAT?!" she screamed. "One hundred?!"

"No, not Celsius! I mean, I don't know the Celsius," I said. My thermometer was from the US and I wasn't slick enough to do the math in my head.

"You're going to be late to school," she said.

I blinked. "What?"

"I said, you're going to be late for school if you don't get going."

That's what I thought she said, I thought.

"I'm not going to school," I said. "I have a fever. And a sore throat. And, I don't know the word in Japanese, but I feel freezing."

"You can walk around, right? You know, Japanese people go to work or school anyway if they have a fever," she stated, setting the breakfast table. "Plus, tomorrow is a holiday, so you should do your best today so you can rest tomorrow."

I shook my head in disbelief. Crazy Japanese society.

"Can I have some orange juice?" I asked.

"Sure. Oh wait, we're out," she informed me.

"It has a lot of vitamins, you know," I added. "Do you think you could buy some?" I paid her a monthly fee that was supposed to be room, board, and meals. I felt entitled to ask her.

"If you drink too many vitamins, it's bad for you," she said matter-of-factly.

"Uh?"

"Are you going to the doctor?" she asked.

A Japanese hospital? Yeah, right. "Nah, I'll just rest…"

"You should go to the hospital!" she said. "Don't Americans go to school if they have just a little fever?"

"Just a little fever? Actually, no. No, they don't." Take it easy Rox, I told myself. Don't get upset at Sadako-san….

"You know the blah blah blah in the bathroom?" she continued, unfazed.

"The…what?"

"The blah blah blah. The yellow stuff in the bathroom?"

"No…what yellow stuff?"

"Yes, I mixed it with this and this and this and it tastes terrible. You can drink it. It's medicine," she said enthusiastically, slicing up an apple. "Well, it's like medicine!"

"Um, what? Bathroom?" To my knowledge, she kept cleaning chemicals and facial soap in the bathroom. I must have misunderstood something. Definitely. I really hoped.

"Would you like some?"

"Um…. no thanks? I am going to lay down now."

"Okay."

I spent my sick day reading J.R.R. Tolkien's *Silmarillion*, which I found at the ICU school library. The resident LOTR expert

Kate recommended it, calling it the "Bible of Lord of the Rings." I would say it's harder to read than the real Bible.

For example (paraphrasing): *And the Eldar worshiped Mawei, their most beloved god, and the king of the Eldar, who are also known as *insert name* and *insert name* by other tongues, is *insert name* who had five sons named *names them* who wedded *insert names of five women.**

I betcha Kate would be able to give me the lineage of Legolas at least five generations back.

February 12

Still sick.

"Let me feel your forehead," Sadako-san said that morning.

"Huh, you don't feel so hot!" she said, frowning.

Bull. I knew that I had a fever of 102, but apparently her sense of temperature is as foreign as I was. She also felt my throat. Finally she told me to stick her thermometer under my armpit. I complied. It beeped. She looked at it. And then she screamed, "Haaaaaa!"

Her outburst startled her son Mitsunori, sitting right next to her at the dinning room table. He jolted, his leg banging into the table. Glasses and plates clinked, and he looked up from surfing the net.

"I told you!" I said.

"Look! Look!" Sadako-san was jumping out of her chair now, calling out, "Look! It's THIS much past the danger mark!" She showed Mitsunori. If Nobi-chan had been around, I bet she would have shown the cat.

No kidding! I thought to myself. Then I laughed out loud. I have to laugh! She's so funny! This situation is so ridiculous! Just laugh!

"Try and find the humor in a negative situation!" Mom said in my mind. "Your attitude and the way you think about something effects the emotions you feel about them! Control your thoughts and you can control your emotions."

208

I grinned at the flustered figure of my host mother. Then I bent my arm experimentally. It cracked every time I extended it, but my range of motion had improved greatly.

I left the kitchen to the sound of my host mother ordering me to the hospital.

"You're right, Mom. Our frame of mind and attitude shapes our perceptions of reality."

So what, I have a fever? At least I can hold my book with two hands now, and type on the computer.

Chapter 18 - The Japanese Language
February 17

Confidence in my Japanese ability plummeted to an all time low. I couldn't find a simple item in a store. I spent hours bungling around, speaking caveman Japanese. All I wanted was a big solid bar of antibacterial soap, something anti-germ to disinfect myself with after a workout. No one wants impetigo or other skin rashes common to grapplers.

My first stop was a common drug store in Kichijoji. A blue cloth awning hung over carts and stands spilling onto the path. They were piled high with the day's discounted soaps, shampoos and toilet paper. I wove my way around loiterers fishing through products.

"Excuse me," I said in Japanese to a young staff-girl. Her short bobbed hair bounced as she looked up with a pleasant expression.

"Do you have body soap?"

She smiled and guided me to a wall with all kinds of soaps. Eighty percent of them were liquid. I didn't want liquid. I didn't want "face soap" and 99.9% of them said yasashii (gentle) on it. I didn't want yasashii. I wanted tsuyoi (strong)!

So I asked in Japanese, "Do you have strong soap? For after sports?"

"So-pu? Supotsu no so-pu?"

Did I get the word right? I'm pretty sure Sadako-san said 'so-pu,' so I'm saying it right. I thought.

"Hai, so-pu," I repeated. "Bo-di so-pu."

Again the staff lady smiled and said a bunch of confusing things in keigo, polite honorifics used on customers. Then she shook her head. Basically, no. No tsuyoi so-pu. Actually, I later found out that some people say "so-pu" but there is a Japanese word: "sekken."

Fine. I left, walking up and down the Sunroad, the name of the long shopping street in Kichijoji. Before long, I spotted another drugstore. It had the typical carts and medicines packed to the ceiling near the entrance. Once inside, I couldn't find any available staff.

What looked like a soap display sat a little ways down the first aisle on the left. Frustration stiffened my jaw because the soap didn't look like soap. It also didn't say "soap" in English on it, because well, I was in Japan. I could have sworn I had seen some English or at least katakana (phonetic Japanese used for foreign words) on bottles before, though. Maybe that row was really the shampoo section. I kind of felt like an idiot.

Weaving through the aisles past unwanted vitamins and feminine products, I finally I cornered a tall skinny man with bad teeth. He looked busy. Or nervous.

"Excuse me," I said. "Tsuyoi bo-dei so-pu ga arimasu ka?" Do you have strong body soap?

"Tsuyoi?" the man repeated.

"Hai. Tsuyoi."

He looked confused.

"Yasashi ja nai." Not gentle. I went on to describe how, after exercising, I would get in the shower and naturally, I needed strong soap, right? Right. Right?

The man raised his eyebrows. My smile never faded, but inside, my fists clenched. I thought my Japanese was right on. Okay, it sounded odd, but my grammar was correct. So were the words. Probably.

"Tsuyoi...?"

"Yes! Tsuyoi. Not yasashii. Not face soap. I do jiu jitsu, so I needed to kill the bad things on my body." Ok, so that last sentence came out kind of weird and unnatural in Japanese. Damn it, they must not use the word tsuyoi to describe soap! There must be another word! Like potent. I should have looked up the word for bacteria before I left the house.

"To get rid of the bad smell?" I tried hesitantly and somewhat embarrassed. Didn't even bother to throw in the English word disinfectant. That would have given him a panic attack. I'd seen it happen.

"Oh, you want scented soap?" he asked in Japanese.

"No, no!" I shook my head vigorously.

He then said a few things I didn't understand whatsoever.

"I want strong, strong! Oh never mind. That's okay." I bowed a few times, and hurried away. He obviously didn't know, and if he continued trying to help me, which was his obligation, it would just waste my time.

"Gomen nasai! I'm really sorry!" he called after me in an apologetic voice.

What a loser I am, I thought. Parking myself on a nearby bench outside, I tried not to cry.

I wouldn't let myself give up. After all, once you give up, you admit defeat.

"We shall never be defeated!" screamed my heart.

"Yeah, yeah. Calm down and let's try one more time," my mind said.

Into the next drugstore I went.

"Excuse me," I said to the next victim salesperson, and proceeded to make one long relative-clause Japanese sentence, that translates to roughly this: "Do you have strong, manly, after-exercising odor-erasing body soap?"

The woman was startled and gaped at me for a beat, and then replied with something unintelligible. She nodded. Then she shook her head. Then she took me to the shelf and handed me a bar of soap.

"Is this it?" I asked.

"...Yes," she said, after a moment's hesitation. I nodded to myself. I had no doubt that this was not the soap I was looking for. I bought it anyway. Maybe I could Jedi mind trick myself into thinking that it was the soap I was looking for. That way by the placebo effect, I wouldn't get any skin rashes.

On the way home, I bought a comic book to cheer myself up.

February 18

My eyes popped open. Had time passed at all? Was the night over? I glanced at the clock. Nope, midnight. I closed my eyes again and tried not to get upset.

I call it jiu jitsu insomnia. Without the physical exercise that clears my mind and exhausts my body, it's difficult to fall asleep. I've always had trouble getting to sleep, even as a child. Doing team sports like soccer and basketball didn't cure me. Full-contact sports did. With jiu jitsu insomnia, I wake up the next morning in the exact same frame of mind. Not refreshed, bored and frustrated, as if I hadn't slept at all.

Each day, a useless feeling began to seep in around the edges of my awareness. Any bit of training that focuses my mind will alleviate this condition. It drove me back to the dojo again and again, even if my body wasn't ready. I knew it was bad to push myself. I did it for my mental state.

And my body suffered for it.

Tonight in class, I practiced some cool leg lock techniques. The white belt I worked with was really nice. I wished I could have trained harder. I not only felt physically ill, I slightly injured my wrist. I nearly lost myself in tears when it happened.

I'd been waiting all week for the Uematsu's "Shooto" submission grappling class. I'd made it through the gi technique class, the gi sparring, and then finally at 10:30pm, an energetic young guy stuck my hand behind his knee. He sat back for the shoulder lock, and applied it. Unfortunately, it put pressure on my wrist as well. I screamed. He was very apologetic, of course, but it didn't help my wrist recover any faster. It would pain me for two weeks. Unable to find anything positive about that situation, I went home and cried for an hour.

February 22

They say Italians love to eat. Well, almost everybody does. I am no exception. Sadako's dinner tonight was Chinese dumplings called "Gyoza," and hamburger balls. Miso soup accompanied it.

The little chunks of fatty meat floating around in it made the side dish less than appetizing to me, though. Japanese love their fat. She also grated some cool radish, fried vegetables, and served burdock root mixed with carrots. The latter is called kinpira. I love it, but it's kind of oily.

"Boy, I really eat a lot," I realized, sitting back satisfied after the feast. "I should have reduced my food intake after injuring myself."

Upon stepping on the scale, I found I weighed in at a whopping 150 lbs. That was 15 pounds above my fighting weight. I don't know why I was so surprised. Over the months, I'd outgrown most of my pants and was reduced to wearing one pair of jeans I normally found loose.

Uh, oh. Diet time.

Japan is particularly particular about formality and politeness. There is a whole culture about names and ways to address people. At jiu jitsu the other night, Uematsu had just taught a technique. I wanted to know its name. I went over to Kotani-sensei who happened to be talking to Tatsu.

After getting their attention, I started explaining, "Uematsu no ashi no..." Uematsu's leg...

Before I could continue to say "technique," both their eyes went wide.

Kotani said, "Umematsu no?"

"Uematsu no!!?" Tatsu repeated,

Um...yeah? "No" just meant apostrophe S, as in to mark someone's possession.

So I repeated it ...and they repeated it again. I knew something was very weird but I finished my sentence. They blinked, told me the name of the move, and I went away. A few minutes later, Tatsu sat down on the bench.

He began to cut the tape off his ankle. I went over and said in English, "Did I say something wrong?"

"The way you called him," Tatsu replied.

"What do you mean?"

"The 'san.' You know, that means Mr. or Mrs."

214

"Wait, did I say "Uematsu no" or "Uematsu-san no?""

Tatsu replied, "You said 'Uematsu no,' not 'Uematsu-san no.'"

"Oh, really? I thought I remembered the honorary suffix! I always remember the 'san!'"

Tatsu just smiled.

So it turns out they got all worked up because I forgot the stupid honorary suffix. In doing that, it that basically implies a close relationship, or that I'm his senior. I knew about addressing someone with 'san,' but I hadn't known that I'm supposed to use it to refer to them when they weren't around.

I glanced at Kotani, who was leaning against the wall nearby, obviously listening while observing the rounds of sparring. He shot a furtive glance at me. I bowed my head and apologized. He laughed and waved off my apology.

"Well it doesn't really matter. You can call him Kotani!" Tatsu grinned. Kotani tried to ignore us.

"Yeah, right! Quit teasing me! What're ya tryin' to do, get me in trouble?" I exclaimed.

February 29

I bought a manga called *Basilisk*, in which people use old forms of speech. Compare that to a Japanese person studying Shakespeare. I excitedly showed my host mother.

"Sadako-san, this kanji isn't in the dictionary," I said. "Can you read it for me?"

"Chotto matte," wait a second, she said, reaching for her glasses next to the phone.

"Ah, that's an old one." She answered my questions. "Ooooh, terrifying!" she exclaimed, when seeing some of the pictures. "It's so violent!" She started flipping through, and I tried to retrieve it. Didn't want to traumatize her too much. I decided to ask the fellows at the dojo to help me. Genki-san loves manga. That gives us something to chat about!

March 1

Basilisk kept me up until 3:30am. I enthusiastically poured through the book, accompanied by my trusty dictionary. The next day I woke up at 8:30 and translated manga the entire morning. I enjoyed creating the corresponding English sentences. Translating was truly an art form!

I wish I could do this as a career! I thought. I knew I had a long way to go. A bilingual could probably do in an hour what I could do in a few weeks.

In the evening, we practiced spider guard and passing open guard. Pin the opponent's feet to the ground by grabbing the pant legs in a death grip. You could then jump over the knees, passing their defense, and get them in a side-control hold-down. Or, you could straighten their legs by moving backwards and then throwing your body weight forward so you land in side control. I worked with a sweet college student with the first name of Ando. She was big for a Japanese woman, and I enjoyed practicing with a female about my size.

"I belong to my University's judo club!" she said, a little shyly. "Be nice to me!"

I participated in sparring without injuries, and even did judo ronduri sparring with Ando. Because my back injury acts up if I take hard falls, it had been years since I'd done straight judo.

In addition to that accomplishment, I felt like the time put into Japanese practice was paying off. I could feel the words rolling off my tongue easier when talking to my host mother and Ando-san. This only encouraged me to study harder.

I also talked to Miyata-san a lot. Short and skinny, he looked to be in his mid 30's. He had crooked teeth, but a good heart. I loved chatting with him and he encouraged lots of conversation, trying out various English phrases on me. We may have gotten along so well because he was an oddball. I think he worked as some kind of staff that cleans offices and bathrooms before the business opens.

"I want to be a Pachinko Parlor boss!" he told me.

216

"Then why don't you?" I had responded.

"Because you have to be under 35! There's a rule!" he said, crestfallen.

"Can you lie on the application?" I laughed.

His face lit up. "Good idea!" he exclaimed.

He joked that he was so poor he didn't have a shower in his apartment, so he took a bath in his washing machine. "I go around and around and around!" he had laughed. I laughed, too, mainly at how much he amused himself.

That night after jiu jitsu, I whipped out my notebook and started asking Miyata-san questions about Basilisk. Lots of other dojo members gathered around to see what I was showing him. Once they heard me asking questions about ancient Japanese, they each added their two cents. I asked for translations. Tatsu generalized too much, Miyata was better.

"Thank you so much," I finally said, closing my notebook. People started getting changed. Miyata remained sitting close by my side.

"Now I have a question," Miyata said suddenly to me in Japanese.

"Yes?"

The jokester looked at me and hesitated. I smiled. He smiled back, showing rows of crooked but pearly white teeth.

"It's kind of a strange question," he said, lowering his voice.

"What?"

"Well. In English, do you say…" he switched to English, "Sylvester Stallone likes show naked body?'"

A little burst of laughter escaped me. "Oh, you need to say 'He likes TO show HIS naked body."

"Okay. 'Sylvester Stallone likes TO shows ....do I need to add "s" after "show?"

"No, it's just "Sylvester Stallone likes to show his naked body."

"I see." Miyata-san nodded sagely, and then repeated it more confidently. "Sylvester Stallone likes to show his naked body!"

"Yes, very good, that's it! Wait, what the hell, what kind of sentence is that?" I asked, and we both burst into laughter. He only laughed harder. What on earth was he thinking? Maybe I don't want to know.

March 4

The Cross-Point team went to SHOOTO to watch Tiger-san compete. He fought to a draw with his opponent. I wanted to see him unleash his lightning-fast front kick, but for some reason, he hesitated. Everyone agreed. We all thought he would win, but that's how it goes in the fight game. His opponent seemed the better grappler, and Tiger seemed reluctant to engage. Sometimes while watching fights, I wish I could get in there and show them what I wanted them to do. Other times, I feel lucky not to be the one in there, getting pummeled.

Chapter 19 – Fight Offer!
March 7

"Miss!" The station attendant came running over to me.

Crap, I got caught, I thought, putting on an innocent face. "Yes?"

The tall man in his 20's, dressed in a smart uniform and cap, hurried out a little office and glared down at me.

"Please show me your ticket," he said. I handed it over, having trouble meeting his eyes. "You're not a 12-year old middle schooler, ARE YOU?" He held up the child's ticket, which is discounted 50%.

I considered pretending not to know Japanese, but then dismissed it.

"Yeah...I'm sorry," I said. He nodded, and motioned back to the ticket machines. "Please go buy another ticket." He then pocketed my ticket, and escorted me back through the gates.

As a way to cut expenses, I made a habit of buying the child's ticket ever since finding out how. I was a jobless college student after all, but technically, it was wrong of me. It reminded me of the times I got pulled over for speeding in the States. Only this time, the ticket only cost about two dollars.

Chagrined that I was doing wrong, I continued on my way to Shibuya Scramble.

Almost immediately after stepping on the mat, Uematsu and Kotani exclaimed simultaneously, "Oh, Roxanne!"

"Good evening," I said, dropping my bag.

"How much do you weigh?" Uematsu inquired without prelude.

"Well, now 67 kilos, but I just started a diet."

"Can you do 64 kilos by April? You have a fight offer."

"YES!" I screamed, jumping up and down. "Smackgirl?"

"Actually, it's a promotion called Cross Section."

My spirit floated with the clouds the entire night. I was able to spar at almost 100%. Even though someone arm-barred me by accident, I recovered almost immediately.

"How's the arm?" my mind asked my body after class.

"Hmmm, well now, it's not perfect," my body answered slowly, "But by April it should be golden."

March 8th

The beautiful weekend began with my weekly chat with my mother, followed by hustling out the door to meet Candie in Kichijoji. Together, we rode the train to Shibuya and lined up to see the anime movie called *One Piece: Curse of the Sacred Sword*.

"This sure is organized," I commented to Candie, peering down the hall.

"Yeah," Candie replied, following my gaze.

The staff shooed everyone into an orderly line along the hallway. Exactly ten minutes before the movie started, we would be ushered in to specific seat numbers. Compared to the American style of first-come first serve, I felt like royalty. Except...

"And I think we're the oldest ones here. Who aren't parents, that is."

As if on cue, some little kid standing behind me started jumping up and down impatiently.

"Is it starting yet, Mommy?" her shrill voice chirped adorably.

"If you weren't here, Roxy, I'd probably be embarrassed," she admitted.

The lack of English subtitles forced me to concentrate as hard as I could on the Japanese dialogue. By the end of the movie, my brain felt exhausted. Luckily, they weren't talking about rocket science. I could understand the fight scenes without a problem. Still, I would have liked to understand what was so important about this mysterious stone, and why everyone was fighting over it and praying to it.

220

For example, one of the characters said, "The ancient legend is blah blah blah blah red moon blah blah blah." My frustration raised a notch. Then, Luffy said, "I won't forgive you for this! I'm gonna beat you up! Take that! Hahaha! You're going down! Don't underestimate me!"

Roxy all of a sudden attained native-speaker ability.

After the movie, we anime freaks - otaku – ate ramen and went shopping for manga and posters. Good times, good times. At 5:30, Candie headed home, and I found my way to kickboxing.

It didn't bother me so much to get punched in the face by one of the guys. What bothered me was that he could do it effortlessly, and I was unable to block it four times in a row, even when I saw it coming. Some part of my training was lacking, and I wished I knew what it was. It seemed like no matter how hard I practiced, I just wasn't improving that aspect of my game.

March 9

Consecutive days of late-night translations convinced me that I'd be doing it professionally some day. I could stay up all night translating and not get tired. Transforming one language into another seemed like using some mysterious power to decipher hidden code normal people can't understand. I couldn't get enough of it.

The school-free days of my spring break flew by. The Japanese school year is set up to start and finish in the springtime, unlike in the US where fall is the season. Therefore, spring break is longer in Japan and summer break is shorter.

The outdoors beckoned to me, calling me to bicycle under the trees. I glided alongside the sliver of a river that wound through the Koganei and Musashino field. The fresh air cleansed my lungs and revitalized my spirit. If only it could do the same for my aching shoulders.

Nakama. A simple word packed with so much meaning- friend, companion, group member, adopted family. I spent my early grade school years picked-on at school for being a little odd and unwilling to follow the social norm. I got called a "goodie-

goodie" and "the teacher's pet" a lot because I loved school and studying. Luckily, I could go home to extremely loving and supportive parents who more than made up for it. I had a few good friends here and there, but sometimes I just wished to be accepted by my peers, to sit among a large group of people and not feel hostility seeping in the cracks of my shield. I suppose everyone felt that way and tried to get attention in their own individual ways. Everyone wants to be special. My way was to excel in my studies and not care what anyone thought of me. As long as you like yourself, you can have fun by yourself and keep yourself company.

After jiu jitsu class, the guys all gathered around me, peering at my scrawled translations and offering their assistance. Spring bloomed into summer a few months early in their presence.

"Thanks so much for always helping me, Luke," I said to my bilingual friend, finally packing up.

"Hey, no prob," he replied, stuffing his sweaty clothes into a plastic bag.

"Actually, this is unrelated to Basilisk, but...I saw something today on the train."

He looked up.

"Do you notice how people seem to like to pick their nose in public?" I said carefully.

His eyes went wide. "I know!" he practically shouted. I jumped a little. Apparently, I hit upon one of his pet peeves.

"I notice it, too! People have no shame at all about picking their nose!" he ranted. "You're sitting on the train and you see a 40-year-old businessman just going to town on his nose! They pull it out, and flick it, too! They rub it together, let it fall on their pants, and brush it onto the person next to them! It's become like a culture! They don't even care where it goes! Everyone, I mean nobody cares!"

I had started laughing since the onset of his tirade, and was in tears by the end. It was all true! Totally true.

March 12

Boston's tall skyscrapers glowed a gentle greeting to me. I touched down on my home-country's soil today and relaxed in the rocking motion of the taxi that sped me from Logan Airport to the North End of Boston. My week of spring vacation would begin and end in one of America's original colonial cities.

My first night back, I ate a good, hearty American pizza at Uno's Restaurant with my Dad, Marion, and her daughter, now my stepsister. No matter how much pizza I eat in Japan, I still hold to the opinion that it's better without corn, mayonnaise, and a menagerie of shellfish. Japanese people put the strangest stuff on their pizza, and the crusts aren't nearly hearty enough.

March 15

I went to a Dim Sum Chinese dumpling restaurant with my father and Marion, after which we went to the Museum of Fine arts to see a Gourgen exhibition. I didn't particularly care for Gourgen's style or personality, but it felt good to spend time with family. It did seem like a family with Marion, which was nice. Kids also want their parents to be happy, and I was off living in a foreign country.

That night, I planned to visit my old jiu jitsu club, but my father said he wanted me home. Part of me wondered if he just didn't want me fighting, but I had come back to visit him, after all. Training could wait.

March 16

In Western Massachusetts, I visited my second home, belonging to my high school friends. There, Caitlin and I beat the Playstation 2 video game *Twisted Metal Black* that we'd been struggling with for a year. This event, in itself, warrants its own journal entry. It turns out that you don't just shoot the helicopter, but you have to shoot it in a certain place when it comes down and

223

lowers its shield. We were screaming with joy after we blew the damn thing up.

If that weren't enough, in addition, I killed the invincible Jared once in *Super Smash Brothers*. Of course, he killed me about 20 times, but I did get one. Various Nintendo characters use their individual powers and weapons to battle each other and try and knock them off the platforms. I can hear the music and sound effects in my sleep because my friends played it nonstop around me. However, I never got into it enough to get any good. I was always the first one to die by getting catapulted off into the abyss when I tried to join in.

For the first part of our epic battle, I died by Jared's Link's Sword a few dozen times, but then got lucky once. Once was enough. My skill is nowhere near any of theirs. Maybe only gamers can truly feel my joy. Button-smashing for the win!

March 17th

Jetlag shook me awake early with a merciless hand. Much to my delight, my mother also gets up at the crack of dawn. After enjoying a wonderful day together, and a Chinese buffet dinner, my vacation felt complete. All except for one thing.

I had rear-ended a guy in Boston on Friday, the day after I came back. Just a bump, really, but the fault was mine. From a stopped position, the light changed colors and everyone started going forward. I stepped on it a little too hard in anticipation, but when everyone stopped suddenly, I bumped the guy in front of me. We both worried about scratches, so I rubbed the dirt away from his bumper to show him the scratch-free surface. There was no scratch. Let me repeat: NO SCRATCH. I was so worried about him and what he would do that I forgot to look at my own car. We exchanged insurance information, and I tried to forget about it. I didn't tell anybody, either.

On March 18, the insurance company called my father. I got an earful when I got back from Mom's. Not telling him about the bump had not been smart, seeing as how our insurance

224

company had to pay $500 worth of scratch-damage. I vocally protested due to the fact that I wiped away with dirt with my own hands.

"There was no freaking scratch!" I insisted. We still had to pay. For what? I wondered.

At the end of the day, I went to bed glad that I didn't have to drive in Japan.

March 24
"Home is where the heart is."

"It's good to be home," I thought to myself, as the night breeze cooled the sweat on my face. After my plane touched down, I had dinner with my host family, and then went straight to the dojo. Jetlag is for wimps.

By then, the fight offer was official: April 18, in a promotion called Cross Section. The weight class: 135lbs. My current weight: 155.1 lbs.

This won't be healthy, I grumbled to myself. Lots of hunger pangs, lots of exercise, and lots of resisting my host mother's gourmet cooking. Despite that, it felt good to be away from the accident drama in the States, and back to speaking Japanese, studying, and training. In other words, living my dream.

Before the fight, though, I was looking forward to visiting Kyoto. It would be my first overnight trip that I organized myself-looking up hotels, booking them, and planning a sightseeing schedule. Even though I've traveled around the States, I always went with other people who could look out for me, and my host family took care of me here in Tokyo.

My father generously offered to finance my trip.

I want my own job, I thought, accepting his offer gratefully. Knowing I was spending someone else's money made me even more determined to be self-sufficient as soon as possible. *I want to make my own money. I want my own place. I don't want to be dependent on my father anymore. I can't wait to get a good job and work hard.*

225

March 27

Everyone always tells me that I'd better go see the sakura - cherry blossoms. They symbolize the stunning, yet fleeting transience of life. Bursting into gorgeous pink blossom, they cling to their twigs for merely a week before fluttering to the ground in scattered showers.

"You should go to Koganei Park," my host mother suggested at breakfast one fine morning. "You're always free, right?"

Always free? Put that way, it made me feel slightly useless, but she was right. At least while school closed for spring vacation.

Might as well, I thought, gulping down the last of my frosted mini-checks, a banana, and an egg.

"Is that all you're eating? Eat more!" my host mother commanded. When I shook my head, she offered, "Want some tea?"

"No thank you, and no thank you," I said, pushing away from the table. I had a strict diet to follow and 20 pounds to lose. "See you!" I hustled out the door into the garage area to get the bike.

The family's large pesky golden retriever greeted me ecstatically, jumping all over the place.

"Get down, Fortune!" I ordered him, trying to guide his dirty paws away from my clean jeans. Keeping the dog at bay, I swung a leg over the rickety black bike and waddled out the gate.

My ride took me past countless sakura trees in full bloom. It was about 65 degrees out. Green leaves would sprout later, so the springtime branches looked like huge bouquets. Sakura came in light pink, dark pink, and white. I had almost forgotten the flowering trees of Berkshire County and Amherst, surrounding my college. Thinking of the large city of Boston brought back memories of harsh, frigid winters and cobblestone streets.

Other varieties of trees with bright red flowers dipped their branches over my path. I ducked my head under the canopy, peddling hard up a slope. Off the side of the road, many families

226

with children were outside picnicking. The children roughhoused on the grass, and the adults laughed and drank sake – Japanese rice wine.

The park stretched wider than I thought, and suddenly my path lead me to a big open area of the park where maybe 100 families were spread out on blankets. Children were playing Frisbee, little three-year-olds ran around in circles. A few surprised me by darting across the bike path, laughing, and then returning to their blankets to jump on their parents.

Right about then, I started feeling sort of lonely.

"I wish I could show my parents Japan," I thought, enviously watching the families at play.

Returning home an hour later, I surfed the Internet dejectedly.

I don't wanna go to kickboxing, I thought, checking my email for the twentieth time. Nothing new. Sighing, I dutifully stuffed my clothes and gear into my gym bag. I had a fight to train for; a goal I had to achieve.

March 27
Training

In training, we did a blocking drill where one person punches: jab, cross, uppercut, over and over. The partner just puts his gloves on his forehead and blocks. Rambar, the instructor, kept asking me if I was fine, and I always answered calmly, "yes." But inside my mind, it was not so quiet.

"YES GODDAMNIT," my mind shrieked. "I'm not a paper doll that's gonna rip if someone gets through my guard, or hits my arms too hard!"

The Thai man always made me sit out when there were an odd number of people and I had no partner. He also told me to do techniques different than the rest of the class because of my gender. I tried to forgive him, but the third time he asked me, "Daijoubu?" Are you okay? For no real reason, my answer came out a screaming, "HAI, DAIJOUBU DES!" Yes, I'm FINE!

Clenching my teeth, I made sure I looked straight at the punches coming through my gloves. Rambar seemed to like my spirit. I didn't care what he liked or didn't like, though. I just wanted equality. I knew I couldn't improve if someone is punching the air in front of me rather than at my face. I needed to practice blocking, just like everyone else.

At the end of class, I sparred another girl who said she'd only been training for a month. She then proceeded to land every kick and punch me in the face. Was I really that bad?

"Yeah right, how many years did you say you trained again?" I asked.

"Well, actually I'm a dance instructor," she admitted, as if that explained everything. I didn't buy it. I also hear men claiming "baseball" as a prerequisite for joining a jiu-jitsu club. In my mind, the two aren't related, but apparently dancing certainly made her a kicking powerhouse. Maybe she conveniently forgot about having a black belt in some form of karate. Who knew?

"I want to fight pro some day!" she told me with a big smile, "But I don't know any ground work."

"Ah, you should train grappling with me!" I said, feeling some self-confidence return. Just a little bit. I sensed the fire in her spirit, and she did me the honor of sparring hard. Finally. I hated striking back then, and I still hate it now. However, I had goals to meet and I vowed to give nothing less than 100% effort.

Chapter 20 - Kyoto
March 29

After eight and a half hours of walking around Kyoto, I couldn't imagine why my knees were killing me. I got off the Shinkansen Bullet train at 11:30am and after checking into my hotel near the station, I headed over to see the Toji Shrine complex first.

I really wish I can understand these little signs, I thought, staring in vain at the plaques stuck next to various buildings and statues. Even using my electronic dictionary, I could only figure out a few words. The time and effort spent wasn't worth the reward, so I soon pocketed the machine. One of the buildings next to the main shrine hall had been turned into a kind of museum, housing various scrolls, statues, and monuments. Some scrolls appeared to be of Indian origin, along with those written in Chinese/Japanese kanji characters. Black stone Buddha and Bodhisattva statues holding symbolic instruments stood behind metal guardrails.

The noontime sun warmed my shoulders as I emerged from the museum. I headed for the gate but stopped short to snap a picture when I spotted a stone statue of the monk Jizo, the protector of lost children and animals. He carries a staff with rings attached to the top, so they clink when he walks. The small animals can hear him coming, and avoid getting stepped on when he passes by.

The atmosphere in Kyoto is really different, I thought, as a car whizzed by the gate. It was amazing how it was so quiet and peaceful inside the Toji Temple complex, but outside was a bustling metropolis. How did they do it?

Being on my own, I felt a freedom that I'd never felt before. My stamina allowed me to proceed at a quick pace. "I almost feel like I'm in a role-playing game! Exploring new places and checking off places I've visited on a map. Like Zelda," I laughed to myself. I had a few trusty ones tucked away in my backpack.

March 30

The Imperial Palace of Kyoto exceeded all my expectations. My mouth dropped open at the sight of its blue-green tiles lining the traditional pointy rooftop. Inside, painted scenes of graceful - if slightly anatomically incorrect - tigers and cranes leapt and pranced across sliding paper doors. The wood floors were polished so they shone. Tourists took off their shoes, depositing them on a shelf before proceeding.

This is right out of every feudal anime I've ever seen, I thought to myself, placing my size 10 Nikes next to a petite woman's pair of high heels. *Like Kenshin, the anime.*

"Over here, we have..."

My ears picked up the English from across the room, fading away amidst the chatter of Japanese voices. I spotted a foreign tour guide and stealthily – dare I say ninja-like? – attached myself to the tail end of their group to listen.

"This is the main attendance room, where the shogun greeted his generals," said the tour guide. The middle-aged man spoke to his group of about ten Americans or Europeans. "That's why the paper doors are so beautifully decorated." The group paused to ogle, and then proceeded on. "Over here is the shogun's room. And let me draw your attention to the floors in this area."

We all looked down. Our stockinged feet were standing on dark hardwood.

"These are the famous 'nightingale floors' built in a special way so metal clamps, nails and pins underneath squeak under the pressure of footsteps," he explained. "This was supposed to prevent assassins from sneaking up on the emperor or high officials.

So cool, I thought.

"Please refrain from talking for a moment, and let's listen!" said the guide with a smile, motioning everyone forward. We didn't speak, but other visitors chatting loudly prevented us from hearing the nightingales very well.

Inspired, I composed a poem:

230

The Floors of Nightingales

I walked with the steps of nightingales
while the strings of the harp strummed softly
as I entered the room
I felt time stop
and slowly rewind
all things became quiet
Then the nightingales voices
burst into song at my step
A page boy came hurrying by
dressed in long robes of green patterned silk
long black hair
Flowing out behind him like his robe
tied back in a tail that swished back and forth
as he shuffled by in his indoor slippers
Through the open windows
made of paper and wood
wafted fragrance of luscious gardens
of cherry blossoms and fresh pine trees
bent crooked or straight
but proudly Japanese
growing in the castle of the shogun

     The tour guide went on longer than I cared to listen, so I went on ahead at my own pace. After exiting the palace, I went to a conveyor-belt sushi restaurant for a relatively cheap lunch, and again later in the day for dinner. What can I say? It entertained me to snatch colorful plates of sushi from a belt that carry it round and round.

     After lunch, I ended up walking around the city, coming across a few minor shrines in alleys, and browsing through dozens of souvenir shops. Things started to look the same, and I realized that the goods were probably supplied by the same souvenir company. It rained all afternoon, and I returned to the hotel with squishing steps and a burning desire to re-watch the animes

Saiyuki and *Kenshin* because of their historical setting. Flipping on the TV jammed in the corner of my tiny room, I watched an episode of Pokémon.

March 31
Kyoto Day 2

How many temples can Roxy see in one day? The answer: a lot.

Bouncing out of bed at 7am, I savored a pack of gray buckwheat soba noodles and veggie salad from the convenience store across the street. A five-minute walk found me at Kyoto Station, and soon I was zooming southwestward on the Shinkansen towards Nara, the old capital.

Kyoto is a bustling city, with shrines squeezed next to modern office buildings and highways. One can walk anywhere, or hop a bus to the other side of town. Nara is greener, more spacious, more ancient, and there are fewer tourist spots in walking distance of the Nara Station. It also has deer. Lots of deer. Just as I read online, they really do come after you for food and let you pet them.

Or so you think. Rather, they pretend to be all nice and lovey-dovey until they spot the food clutched in your hands. Then they attack. Some of them do, anyway. I kept my eyes open for them as I exited the station and followed my map to Nara Park. I soon found the open grassy field in which several important shrines stood.

The Todaiji Temple housed the famous bronze Daibutsu, or *Great Buddha Statue*, that sat serenely in his state of Nirvana. At 15 meters tall, he was supposed to be a few meters taller than the statue with the same name in Kamakura, a city south of Tokyo, but I couldn't really tell. The 13.35 meter one in Kamakura lost his home in multiple typhoons and tidal waves in the 15th Century. Now he said sat outside, making him appear larger to me. This one in Nara lived in the Todaiji Temple hall. All around, huge imposing statues of warrior gods and imperial officers stood scowling.

It was all just so cool, I could scarcely contain myself. I wanted to take everything home with me. The temple building with the Daibutsu had golden ox-like horns, sticking up out of the roof. Any building with horns needs an award, in my opinion.

Inside, while I had my eyes trained on the artifacts, I nearly ran over a little girl. About five years old, she took a hold of the digital camera dangling from my arm.

Yes, dear, that's my expensive new camera, I thought nervously, preparing to yank it away if need be. *What do you want?*

"Konnichiwa," I said instead.

She turned it over and looked at the cute hamster sticker I'd stuck on the front. Looking up at me, she laughed. Her smile bloomed more beautifully than any exquisite Asian flower I'd seen on my trip so far. I melted right there on the spot. Her mother noticed and began to lead her away.

It's an angel! I thought, returning her grin. *Give me another smile, please!*

The typical image of a tourist with a camera dangling around my neck, I exited the temple and promptly ran into a herd of deer. Nara is famous for hundreds of the wild but tame animals that wandered freely around the park. They feast upon special deer-crackers handed out by tourists, available for sale in little carts. I almost mistakenly bought them for myself, thinking they were some kind of snack. The old man laughed at me when I asked what they tasted like. The cart looked like a popcorn or hotdog stand.

I refrained from spending money on deer crackers, and instead got a fellow tourist to take a picture of me standing in relatively close proximity to them. I'd been warned not to get too close because they were a bit crotchety and ill-tempered at times. I had no desire to be bitten by a deer. What a wimpy way to get hurt!

I could see it now: *"Hey, why'd you cancel your fight? What happened to your hand?" Uematsu might ask.*

"Oh, I got chomped on by an ornery deer when I tried to pet it," I would say, and then he would laugh at me until he fell off his bench.

Close up (but not too close), I saw that they really weren't very healthy. Their fur was falling out in clumps, exposing flaky skin and cracked hooves.

After seeing my fill of deer, I made my way to the nearby Kofukuji Temple just over a small hill. It was founded in 669 by the powerful imperial family, the Fujiwaras. A famous five-story pagoda stood on site. I joined dozens of other tourists in snapping a picture.

My knees started voicing complaints, but I just couldn't put a cap on my enthusiasm and take a rest. I paid about five dollars to enter the Central Golden Hall. The sheer size of the hall stunned me. I absently accepted a pamphlet from the ticket-window lady and nearly bumped into somebody in front of me.

Glancing at the pamphlet, it read: *Kofukuji is one of the head temples of the Hosso sect of Buddhism. The Hosso sect is also known as the Yuishiki, meaning, "mind only," sect. The teaching was first brought to China from India by the T'and Dynasty monk Genjo – in Chinese, Hsuan Tsang - whose travels are well known from his journal entitled Travels to the West.*

"Oh sweet!" I exclaimed out loud. "That's the story of Saiyuki and the monkey king! Excellent!"

Genjo transmitted the Hosso teachings to his disciple Jion Daishi who is considered the founder of the Hosso School in China. Craning my neck, I strained to see the ceiling of the lofty temple, but shadows veiled the wooden beams.

Yeah, very excited about that. I had to pay another five bucks to enter the treasure chamber, and my eyes feasted on ancient statues and carvings of Amida Buddha and the Goddesses of Mercy. I've seen lots of the "thousand-handed goddess of mercy" in my travels. The statues are always gesturing, gripping some symbolic object, or clasped together in prayer. In some, the arms were the same size and proportionate like normal human arms. However, a particularly eerie one had a few big arms and many tiny ones. I asked a nearby man dressed like a caretaker the reason behind that, but I couldn't really understand his answer due to the language barrier. Maybe the artists were trying to save space, but it still made my hair stand up on end.

Inevitably, everything began blending together in my mind. If I wanted to see more, I'd have to take a bus. Opting out of that, I caught the bullet train back to Kyoto at 1 o'clock, arriving a few hours later and refreshed from a brief nap. I saw Kyomizu-dera with its famous view of the foliage, and stopped by a few other small ones before they closed at four. To my chagrin, I hadn't been able to locate a certain five-story pagoda, and kept getting lost in the attempt.

Giving up, I was just about to head back to my hotel, when I turned a corner and bam: there was the pagoda poking up from behind a few other buildings. Leading up to it was a market place, looking as if it were pulled straight out of the history books. The buildings had stone roofs, cloth doors, and men pulled ladies up the hill on rickshaws. I entered the hustle and bustle with other tourists, and immediately felt one with humanity.

There's no way someone can feel lonely here, I thought, smiling to myself. A cute little souvenir shop beckoned and I ducked under the hanging cloth door.

"Irrashai! Welcome!" a little old lady called to me in Japanese, a big grin on her face. I smiled and nodded, beginning to browse her wears. She followed me. "Where are you from?" she asked, trying to make small talk.

"The USA," I replied. "I'm doing an exchange here. Well, in Tokyo."

"Oh, really! And wow, your Japanese is so good!" she said. "Here, have one of these!" She handed me a tiny Shinsengumi toy doll about the size of my thumb. The Shinsengumi were heroes of the late Shogunate period; a special police force that kept the peace. Many Japanese people even remember the officer's individual names and history.

Her kindness touched me very much and I found something to buy for my friends. Maybe it was all a sales tactic.

I got so sidetracked by the market place, which felt like an old-fashioned feudal town, that I gave up going to the Pagoda. A Pagoda is a pagoda, after all. I learned that I could find a nice angle for a picture if I stood where other people were grouped around, aiming their cameras and posing.

"Please, take us back to the hotel," my knees begged me, but I ignored the pain.

"Buck up," I ordered them. I had spotted some little pink lights strung along a bridge. I followed them over a stream and into a park of cherry blossom trees. Dozens and dozens of families spread out on tatami mats out for picnics. I saw boyfriends and girlfriends holding hands. Children ran and laughed loudly. Dusk fell, but people didn't budge. The beauty of the night scene took my breath away. Light glowed gently from nearby store windows, in addition to the park lamp posts scattered here and there.

I realized I had a smile on my face.

I love humanity, I thought.

My mind was swimming.

The next morning, I decided to head back immediately, rather than wait until noon. I've never seen so much pink in my entire life. Almost too much sakura.

Chapter 21 - The Fight Against Tama-chan
April 6

The secret to martial arts is that you have to be willing to let go of your fears and focus on the goal. This is embodied in many Japanese anime shows, where the character powers up and focuses his or her ki energy into visible light. Consider double-leg takedowns. If I don't commit fully or if I have sloppy form, I'll miss and waste energy getting back up. Sometimes I bounce off my knees, so kneepads are a must. However, it's possible I'll fall strangely and hurt my knees. If my opponent sprawls a certain way, I might jam my neck or wrench my shoulders, injuring my spine. The point being, although there's high risk, I can't be afraid of going for it 100% or it'll have no chance of success.

I have to be willing to take the risks. I have to believe I'll succeed. If there's any doubt or hesitation in my spirit, I won't be able to overcome the obstacle.

Tonight walking home, I reflected on my performance at practice.

"I think my takedown speed has increased," I applauded myself. "And I knee-barred a guy in sparring. Lastly, I managed to trip the last guy backwards, slamming him to the mat. You're on a roll, Rox."

"Gee, you look happy!" Uematsu-san had commented, as I sat there after the slam, grinning like an idiot.

I couldn't remember the last time I'd been that focused.

April 7

Today the cherry blossoms released their grip on their parent twigs. Born up by the wind, they blanketed everything in a beautiful pink. After waking up late, I biked through the park. I passed little children who were throwing tennis balls. Large dogs loped after them, dragging their leashes through leaves, dirt, and fallen cherry blossom petals, forming wavy snake-like paths on the ground. Mothers and elderly people on bikes pulled over on the side of the road to chat and watch their kids. The sun warmed my back, and I felt as if the pleasant wind could lift my bike off the road and into the air. I longed to peddle into the clouds.

What a wonderful country, I thought repeatedly. *People live amongst such beauty and keep it clean.*

The scenery and atmosphere touched me deeply. I climbed a leafy tree in the park, and read *The Lord of the Rings,* by J.R.R. Tolkien. The leaves rustled tranquilly and the branch was sturdy and comfortable. Never before had I felt so calm, my heart so peaceful. It reminded me of childhood, where I just ran around my front yard, playing make-believe without a care in the world.

April 11

I am very pleased to make a positive announcement about my martial arts skill. I've been working very on my kickboxing, and I believe I've finally achieved the level of 'average.' Yes! I'd like to think that I am not 'bad' anymore, but rather, 'average.' Now I just have to get good. I don't really enjoy it, but it can't be helped if I want to succeed in MMA. I wished more people would spar seriously with me. I have real problems finding striking sparring partners in Japan.

April 12

Finally, the spring semester classes began. The most promising one seemed to be Japanese Archeology. My teacher, Professor Richard L. Wilson, sported a neatly-cut silver-brown beard. His eyes sparkled as he described our course; he enthusiastically talked about how we'd study theory, history and do field work behind the school, where we'd actually have the chance to dig up artifacts with our own hands! Unlike the usual hour-long classes held three days a week, this was a special once-a-week course. It lasted for four hours- from about 3pm to 7.

"There's an excavation site behind the school that holds a wealth of middle-Jomon period pottery, made over 4,000 years

238

ago!" He spoke animatedly into the microphone. The large group students in the assembly hall sat still, their eyes glued to the man on the podium. I flipped through the information packet he'd handed out.

"Bring clothes you can get dirty in," he said. "Now let me just show you the area we'll be digging. You can leave your bags in this classroom. We'll be back…"

Digging! I could barely contain my excitement as he took us for a walk through the woods. Amazing plants, trees, ferns, and bamboo fought for my attention and distracted me from our professor's shouted dialogue as he led us along. I heard some girls squeal as they stepped in a soft spot of dirt, or got leaves stuck in their hair.

You'd think some people never went out in nature before, I thought, annoyed, trying to distance myself from the squealers.

Professor Wilson finally stopped and indicated a flat area covered with bushes and weeds.

"We'll be digging here," he said. We all gave the patch dubious looks, but the shed full of tools we passed on our way here left no doubt in our minds as to what was to come.

My Japanese language class turned out to be extremely difficult. I asked to be assigned to the same discussion class as my new friend Kio, but they said it was already set. When I asked, "Why can't they just change it to let me in? What's the big deal?" I was bluntly told by the head teachers to bear with it. I couldn't understand why they'd be so inflexible, especially since there was no time conflict with anything else, and it was no skin off their noses. Inflexibility and being sticklers for the rules would turn out to be a continual source of annoyance during my life in Japan.

At one point during the lesson, the head teacher held up a packet and talked rapidly for a few minutes. Then she passed them out, saying, "Minna-san, daijoubu desu ne!" Meaning, "Everybody is okay with this, right?"

This explanation met a lot of blank stares.

Embarrassed, I turned to a boy next to me who lacked the dazed confused look some of my other classmates wore, and asked, "Sorry, but what did she say?"

He leaned over. "She said to read these pages of the packets by tomorrow, memorize the vocabulary, do the questions for tomorrow, and there'll be a quiz. Then Friday you have an essay due of the summary and your opinion."

"Oh," I said. "Thanks…" A few other classmates were whispering to each other, so I had a feeling I wasn't the only one in over my head.

April 14

Cutting weight is an athlete's hell. This term refers to the phenomenon of making your body a certain weight by a certain date and a certain time, either the day before or the day of the competition. Sports that involve one-on-one competition with opponents of a similar size, such as wrestling and MMA, require weight divisions. The word "diet" doesn't quite cut the cake, so to speak. It's too nice of a word. Weight loss is accomplished by hardcore dieting to lose fat, or losing pounds of water weight by not drinking for a day, or going to the sauna to sweat it out.

Nobody had ever educated me on the proper way to lose weight without losing muscle. I figured I could just train and then not eat afterwards, which is extremely unhealthy, but I didn't know any better. Many fighters count on sweating to lose many pounds of water weight so they could drink it back and come in heavier and stronger on the day of the fight.

I had no access to a sauna, and didn't really know much about dieting. As my fight date approached, I became more and more nervous about my weight. Dieting was not going as well as I had hoped. I'd started in May at 155lbs - the highest I've ever been, thanks to my inability to exercise due to my broken arm. I weighed in the other day at a whopping 147lbs. I talked to Kotani-sensei and he said that 63 kilos (138.6lbs) would be fine. Who knew if that old dusty scale in my host family's bathroom was accurate or not? I

240

kicked myself every day for letting myself eat my way to 155 in the first place.

"Talk about lack of self-control," I berated myself, over and over.

I'd started eliminating all fat content in my diet except for what was in the milk in my breakfast cereal. My host mother nearly had a heart attack when all I agreed to eat was a tiny bowl of rice for dinner a few days in a row. My stomach growled constantly and even hurt at times. I had never experienced anything like it before. If I had only low-calorie vegetables, they felt almost prickly inside, and some force craved for more. Just physical presence, like vegetables, made almost no difference in my appetite.

There's no way I can lose multiple pounds before Sunday! I thought, already having made allowance for water-weight.

In some cases, such as grappling tournaments, a competitor can always register for the weight class above them. For example, if a man wanted to compete in the 160-175 division, but he stepped on the scale and found himself a failure at 185 lbs. He could always say, "Screw it; I'll go up a division into the 175-190 division."

For many wrestlers or MMA fighters who are given special opponents, they don't have this choice. They are required to lose the weight or they aren't permitted to fight.

After you cut weight for the first time you want to start donating to every "feed the children" or "starving orphan" organization that you come across. It's more than just "not eating." You're training and working out, so your body is screaming for nutrients. You are tired all the time if you cut carbohydrates. Yet you have no choice. The alternative is not competing, and you've been training too hard to let this opportunity pass.

I'd been controlling my weight for grappling tournaments for a few years. The dessert went first. With three weeks left, I cut out the carbohydrates at lunch because I sat in school all day, instead, eating a lot of vegetables, cottage cheese, tuna, turkey, and eggs. Naturally I made sure to get enough carbs two hours before my workout.

Inevitably, the "two weeks" rolled around, and sometimes I was still over by five or six pounds. No more thinking, "Oh, I can have a steak because I have time to burn it off."

No. It's a style of living and tortures the mind. One trick I had for weight loss was to workout hard and not eat anything before bedtime. My metabolism was revved up and burning the fat, but I didn't hear my stomach growling because I was sleeping. This is actually an incorrect method, and ensures rapid muscle-loss in addition to fat loss. I didn't realize this and lost a lot of muscle for a few years before I started noticing a difference in the size of my muscles. I also noticed my strength diminished.

I always wake up the next morning famished and think *Oh boy, can't wait for my chocolate chip pancakes and bacon...I mean Cheerios with skim milk and a banana.* However, three hours later I was starving again. Between classes, I munched on a carrot while walking down the street, thinking *I can't wait for lunchtime with a burrito and chili...I mean my salad with broccoli, tuna fish, nuts, and low fat deli turkey breast.* If I passed by a bakery or ice cream shop, I had to avert my eyes. When other people chow down their huge submarine sandwiches in front of me, I pop a stick of gum in my mouth.

Finally Monday rolled around; six days before the fight. That night, I weighed myself dehydrated. Tears ensued, followed by denial and the desire to seek out another scale, because this one must be broken.

The next morning, my mother called me.

"I read your online journal," she said in her best motherly voice. "I see you're stressed out about your weight and the jiu jitsu competition. I know you know, but I just wanted to say... don't forget to put school before jiu jitsu. You know, if your grades start slipping..."

I felt myself getting hot with anger. She was the last person I expected to hear that garbage from. My mom, my biggest cheerleader who drove me to sports practice every day in grade school, who drove me to judo class and tournaments all over the place. My mom, who knew how much martial arts meant to me.

My mom, who knew that I always got As and Bs. Just when I needed some soothing and encouragement, too!

"Mom, give me a break!" I exploded. "In the three and a half years I've been doing school and jiu jitsu, when have I ever let my grades slip because of it?"

"I'm sorry… I didn't mean to make you mad…"

I huffed for a few minutes, but forgave her almost immediately. After all, how can you blame a parent for saying that? That's their job.

April 16

"What are you doing here?" Kotani-san exclaimed in surprise as I showed up for practice. "You know, Roxanne, you really shouldn't workout because you could get injured."

"It's okay!" I protested. "Just a light workout."

After warm-ups, I partnered with an older Japanese purple belt, trying to apply an ankle lock. I've never really been good at them, and struggled to get my positioning straight.

"It's because you're a woman, huh?" my partner said. "You don't have enough strength to do it." My mouth dropped open in complete shock. I couldn't even speak. I felt my temperature rising. He didn't seem to be kidding, and I couldn't even move for a full ten seconds. Uematsu had been passing and started laughing at me and my reaction, but I seriously wanted to punch the fellow. How could he say such a sexist thing to me?

I let go of his leg and pushed myself away, having no desire to touch him or work with him anymore. He looked confused and motioned for me to come back. I didn't care and walked away to calm down.

Later on in the night while doing takedown drills, my kneepad slipped and my unprotected knee crashed to the ground. Sharp pain stabbed me like a knife, followed by a burning stinging sensation, like a thousand bees in hell. I limped home, barely able to bend it.

I repeated a silent prayer to the Universe to make my knee stop hurting by the day of the fight. I reminded myself of how Uematsu-sensei fought with a broken rib earlier that year. This was nothing! Except that I couldn't walk.

I clenched my teeth and tried to imagine myself fighting through the pain. Doubt and panic filled me and spilled out onto the dark pavement of the street I was trudging down.

It's not good for a grappler to be unable to do takedowns against a powerful striker. Tama-chan was famous for her striking ability.

Maybe I'll have to switch my stance to do a takedown, I thought, trying to formulate a gameplan.

The next day, bending my knees to pedal the bike to school caused excruciating pain. I worried about making weight, and halved my meal portions. All day, my stomach growled angrily. That night at the dinner table, I feasted my eyes and eyes alone on my host mother's delicious-looking meal; however, it looked very oily and fried. Heartbroken, I told her that I couldn't have it because I was over weight by 4 lbs. I knew how rude I appeared as I sat there and chewed my gum as my host family ate and almost drowned in my own puddle of drool.

I wondered if she didn't understand, so explained that if I wasn't exactly 135 lbs, I couldn't fight. I don't particularly care about dieting for looks. Sometimes I felt like I was going to die if I didn't have another piece of bread. The phrase I repeat to myself is *Don't eat that or you can't fight!* It's not that I stopped eating completely, but when you resist anything with any type of fat and cut the carbohydrates to a certain point, a gnawing hunger tears into your insides like a wolverine fighting for survival.

The day finally came for Cross Section. Sometimes competitors weigh in the day before, but in Japan, weigh-in time was at noon the day of the fight. If I diet right, I can wake up in the morning and actually have breakfast. If I step on the scale and find that I'm over the weight, I still have options.

I was just on weight, so I skipped breakfast but made five pancakes, and brought a jar of peanut butter and a knife.

I had planned very well and made sure I was exactly 137 lbs, just like my instructor told me. When I went to the competition hall, I saw the poster that said "Roxanne Modafferi, fighting at 135 lbs!"

Panic! It being early, no one of authority was around for me to test my weight to see if it had changed from the time I stepped on my scale that morning.

In a frenzy, an acquaintance called my instructor, who strongly implied that it might be a good idea for me to start running. But I couldn't run because I had a back injury!

Seething, I hung up on him and broke out my chewing gum. The next half an hour was spent bent over the sink spitting, receiving strange looks from anyone who came in.

Come time for the weigh-ins, it turned out someone had tweaked the scale and it was light, so I came in a pound under.

April 18

Multicolored lights flashed as Luke helped me tug the narrow-sleeved jiu jitsu gi jacket over my MMA gloves. My music faded out and I stood tensely in my corner. Abruptly, the "Can-Can" music came blaring out of the speakers. My opponent Keiko "Tama-chan" Tamai dashed down the ramp and bounced into the ring. A crazed smile on her face, the shorthaired Japanese girl dressed in a rainbow leotard ran in a circle, shaking her hands. The audience howled back at her.

"Don't be afraid," my cornerman Luke whispered in my ear. But I was smiling. This was great. I'd already made my entrance to some hard rock music. The contrast in our demeanor was amusing. I couldn't wait to get at it. Tama-chan finished her antics and returned to her corner.

The ring announcer stepped into the middle of the ring with the ref.

"And in the blue corner..."

Things began to blend together. A haze of instinct clouded my mental processes. I heard my name being announced. All I could see was my opponent, blurred due to my bad eyesight, standing on the other side of the ring. The audience wasn't even there- just a presence, watching from the darkness. The ref motioned us to the center. We touched gloves. My heart began to pound.

The bell rang. We both jumped forward. I threw a high kick at her head. It landed against the side of her face with a slap. I did it a second time. It helped she was shorter than me.

In my first fight, I ate three punches to the face and immediately went for a takedown. This time, I really wanted to throw down more. I doggedly stood my ground and exchanged. Jab-straight, jab-straight, jab-straight. I threw combo after combo. Probably horrible form, but I didn't care. My own head snapped back from her own strikes.

Suddenly, she was in my face and we were struggling in the clinch. Her hands were grabbing for a hold of my neck. I shoved her back and grabbed behind hers. We both got haphazard grips and threw knees- lots and lots of knees. I was bigger and somehow landed more. Maybe.

Were they hitting? Unsure of their effectiveness, I switched tactics. I turned my hip in and heaved her over my back judo-style. We fell heavily to the mat with a thud. I landed on top in a hold-down. Keeping my weight heavy on her upper body, I went for a shoulder lock, but she scrambled out. I twisted and kept a dominant top position.

"Hit her body!" Luke hollered at me from across the ring.

Smackgirl rules prohibited punches to the face on the ground, so I pummeled her with body blows. She nearly writhed out of my hold. I stopped pounding for a second, re-secured my hold, and then continued.

"Hit her HARD!" he screamed.

I'm trying!

I almost hit her head by accident.

Tama-chan rolled over on her belly, trying to escape. I took her back.

"CHOKE HER!" Luke cried.

I started to go for it, but she turned over again, avoiding the choke but giving me mount position.

Time ran down, with me changing positions to go for submissions, but she deftly avoided them. Unable to escape my top control, it was obvious who would win the judges' decision at the end of the two five-minute rounds.

"Winner by unanimous decision! Roxanne Modafferi!" the ring announcer called.

I ecstatically waved my hands in the air as the audience cheered. The ring announcer thrust a microphone at me, and I repeated a phrase I'd memorized about how honored I was to be there, and I'm looking forward to fighting again.

I wandered back to my corner, where Luke turned me around and reminded me to go thank my opponent and shake her coaches' hands. I numbly obeyed.

"Okay, now this way," Luke instructed, holding the ring opened for me to duck through the ropes. I followed Luke back to the dressing room, half blind, stunned and barely coherent. I'd just won my fight! I'd just spoken Japanese in front of hundreds of people!

"Nice job, Rox!" Luke was saying, handing me my glasses.

My Japanese coaches and teammates backstage were telling me "omedetou," which was "congratulations" in Japanese. Fumbling to put my glasses back on, someone caught my elbow and started leading me away. It was Uematsu-san. "They wanna interview you," he said.

"Luke?" I called. He was on the other side of the room.

"Yeah?"

"Can you help me?"

He hurried after me. Seated in the chair in front of the cameras, I couldn't understand all of the Japanese. However, it was much better than the last time, and Luke translated what I couldn't understand. The promoter and interviewers were clearly impressed that I spoke Japanese.

Finally, they seemed to be done. I breathed a sigh of relief.

"Roxanne," Uematsu said, coming up to me. "Caol Uno is a judge. You wanted to meet him, right? I'll introduce you."

"REALLY?" My eyes lit up.

"Yeah, this way!"

I followed my teacher out into the main floor where the guests had almost finished filing out. I spotted the UFC veteran with funny-looking cauliflower ears talking with some officials. We approached them and waited at a respectful distance until they were done.

Uematsu opened his mouth, but Caol Uno came forward, said my name, and shook my hand.

"I've always wanted to meet you!" I told him in broken Japanese. "You're really cool!"

He smiled and looked down, a little embarrassed. Or shy. My head felt like it was filled with fluffy clouds.

"Can I get a picture with you?"

I proudly gave the peace sign as Uematsu used my camera to take a picture. After that, my teammates from Cross Point and I all went out to eat at a cheap dinner. To top it all off, a fanboy asked for my autograph and picture with him outside the event hall. I was officially a star.

Chapter 22 - My Fight Against Kikukawa
April 22

I happened to glance up from my cornflakes and got to see possibly the best commercial of all time. An elderly Japanese couple maybe 70 years old were walking in a beautiful park together. Neither spoke; melodious music filled the air. Birds sang. The wife was pointing to the flowers, as if to say, "Look darling, aren't they pretty?" The husband gazed back at her as if to say, "Only as beautiful as your eyes."

All lovey dovey, right? In the background, you could see some teenagers playing soccer. Then suddenly a soccer ball flew straight at the old woman. In slow motion, the old woman's face broke into an expression of horror. The camera focus flashed from the ball hurdling at her, to her face, back to the ball.

The pretty music cut out with a scratch. Just as it was about to hit her, the old man dove in front of the ball, and headed it out of the way. The head-ball was so powerful that it flew over the entire field and into the woods. The teenagers followed its course in silent awe and dismay.

The old man was like, "YEAH! TAKE THAT." Then his exuberant voice suddenly softened. He looked back at the old woman lovingly. The old woman's facial expression said, "Oooh my hero! You just saved me from an awful death! I only wish to be embraced by you!" The old man's face clearly replied, "My darling, I shall love you until the end of time and die protecting you. Always..."

They got up, not quite holding hands but walking close together, and shuffled away down the garden path.

I'm not even sure which product the commercial was advertising. I suspect either chewing gum or some power drink. The Japanese make the best commercials.

April 23

    Despite sharp knee pain, I dragged myself to jiu jitsu class. Kotani-san interrupted my mental cheerleading with the question I wanted to hear the most.

    "By the way, Roxanne, Smackgirl would like you to fight on May 16. Can you do it?"

    "YES!" I cried, jumping up and down. "Yay!"

    Kotani smiled. "They asked this girl Kikukawa, and she still has to agree."

    "Kiku-who?"

    "She's good at kickboxing, but Kikukawa. You fight at 135 lbs, right?"

    "Yes," I replied, confident that I would make the weight easier this time.

    "And by the way," the heavy-set instructor added. "Did you see your picture in the magazine?"

    "What?!"

    "Yeah, a shot of you and Tama-chan fighting."

    I'm in a magazine! I thought, thrilled. "I'll pick it up tomorrow in the bookstores! Thanks for telling me!" I grinned widely.

    I practically skipped home that night.

April 29

    Where's my home? Who's my team? Foreigners living in another country often struggle with national identity. Fighters sometimes jump from gym to gym.

    I tend to be the kind of person who's inspired by those who I train with, or those I look up to. I enjoyed Zuyo's big-sisterly concern, Uematsu's joking around, Kotani's knowledgeable character. In the Japanese anime that inspire me, the main characters have nakama – like teammates and friends, except the

250

word implies a closer bond. I longed to share that bond with others, but I seemed to be always moving around.

"I was raised in the Dalton Judo Club," I reflected, thinking about the tiny local dojo I spent three years at. "Then I trained submission grappling for three years at the Amherst Athletic club. I also went to Jeremy's School of Self Defense, the Adam's Royce Gracie Association, the Hartford Royce Gracie Association, and Joao Amaral's BJJ team."

I'm so proud of those guys, I thought, bringing to mind the large team of mostly Brazilians living near Boston. *They just became an affiliation of The Brazilian Top Team.*

They became. We became? Was I part of the team?

They all like me and respect me there. I wanna get good and be able to stand up tall and say, 'Yes! I'm part of the team!' When I win, I want to thank my nakama for always supporting me. I don't care about being famous as long as I get to fight strong people! But I'll only fight strong and especially skilled people in MMA if I become well-known.

Kotani-sensei confirmed my next fight that night at practice: Natsuko Kikukawa, at 61.5 kilos, in Smackgirl May 16.

"This time don't hurt yourself before the fight!" Kotani joked. I grinned, choosing not to mention how my knees were acting up and I was limping around everywhere. They should heal in time, I assured myself. No excuses!

After stumbling home, I decided to write a letter to the family pets.

Dear dog and cat,

I have many things to tell you. However, since you don't understand people-talk, I'm going to tell my Journal and maybe the Journal-god can communicate it to you. I'm going to be very nice.

To Fortune the dog. Firstly, when we go for a walk, peeing on a bench is not a good idea. The fact that my jacket was right there was definitely not a good thing either. There are plenty of bushes or trees around, so why the bench? Please use some more common sense.

Secondly, pulling me when we walk used to be tolerable. However, when you pulled me so hard I fell and hit my bad elbow, I was definitely not excited about that. Pulling me into the river is not acceptable either.

Thirdly, howling when you want me to walk you doesn't make me a happy person. Fourthly, jumping is most certainly not permissible. When your feet catch on my headphones wire and breaks my headphones, you are nearing the end of your doggy life. Therefore, all things considered, yesterday when you were looking behind you but walking forward and smashed your head into a pole, I was very amused. I believe I actually laughed out loud.

Nobi-chan the cat,

I really don't like you at all. In fact, I dislike you intensely. I'm one short step away from hating you, so stay the hell away from me. You're very ugly, but that in itself is tolerable. I don't discriminate. But it sucks when you dislike something AND it's ugly.

Secondly, you make weird noises. That in itself is acceptable. Again, I don't discriminate. But when the noises are a combination of farting / snorting / gagging / choking / coughing / gargling noise, I get so grossed out I lose my appetite. Neither can I concentrate on my studies. This end result is something I have a little problem with.

Thirdly, you meow SO MUCH that it wakes me up at night, distracts me from studying, and my anime. I can hear it through my headphones even when I turn up the volume. I could watch anime through my college roommates playing Nintendo's Smash Brothers, but not when you're around. Your snorting even passes through the friggin walls! So shut up!

Fourthly, trying to jump up on my chair, table or my lap while I'm trying to eat, will most certainly get you kicked. I'm not my host mother. I don't coo and cuddle you like she does. In fact, whenever you come within five meters of me, I shoo you away and shut the door, so get a clue already.

Fifthly, following me is NOT appreciated. Especially into the bathroom and washroom! I DON'T want to be in your presence when I am *doing my business. If I recall correctly, I have petted you TWICE in my entire life! All of a sudden you think I'm your best friend?*

Finally, I DID NOT like you peeing on my kneepads! You do that again and you're one dead cat.

The end.

Sincerely,
Roxanne

May 6

"Kickboxing is so boring," I thought glumly to myself.

"Come on! Ten more!" my partner was screaming at me, in an attempt to motivate me.

I hate repetitively kicking pads and bags. It's so tedious! I dug down and summoned a burst of energy to complete the set. *I should be thinking positively...* I thought.

Somehow, positive thoughts were flowing away faster than I could generate them.

"I'd rather jump on someone and choke them." No amount of trying to convince myself striking is useful was going to change my feelings. Today I chose to join the kickboxing class in our sister school Shibuya Scramble. Turns out the kickboxing coach Masuda-san was good. And pretty hot. Too bad he never got into grappling or MMA. He showed us what I considered advanced moves, and pointed out my mistakes.

"Actually, you're doing your hook wrong," he said to me helpfully.

"Oh really?"

"Yes. See, you don't angle your elbow downward, like that," he said, taking a hold of my arm and straightening it out. "Do it like this."

I felt kind of silly. "Oh...really? Thanks..." I said, testing it out on the pad my partner was holding. It felt like I had twice as much power as before.

"Wow."

"Ya see?"

Masuda-san also had cool hair. It was kind of longish, and fell down over his forehead in spikes, kind of like a hero in a Japanese animation series.

"Also, you are forgetting to turn your hip over when you do a middle-kick," he coached a few minutes later, passing by me and then hurrying over to the next pair to correct their form.

Fifteen minutes into the class, another person joined, making the numbers uneven. When we changed partners, I suspected that, as the only girl, I'd get stuck without a partner.

"Uh, okay you work with me for this round," Masuda-san said to me. My heart leapt. This guy rocked so much harder than Rambar already. To top it all off, when we practiced slipping, he actually aimed for my face, making it necessary for me to actually move to avoid the punch.

I repeated his advice over and over in my mind to try and commit them to memory. I was feeling so grumpy, though, that I suspected they wouldn't sink in.

I stepped on the scale after training. The verdict: 65 kilos (143lbs).

After showering, I emerged from the bathroom, navigating around other students milling around in the ten-minute break between classes. Masuda-san was standing by the front counter. I couldn't resist.

"You have really cool hair," I told him boldly. My Japanese ability didn't allow me to be anything but blunt anyway.

He laughed, absently running a hand through his sweat-slicked hair. Half the dirty-blond locks fell back, and half stayed sticking straight up. He had nice biceps.

"It reminds me of an anime character," I continued, grinning.

"Oh yeah? Do you like anime?" he asked.

"Yeah! I love Dragon Ball Z!" I exclaimed.

"Me, too!" he said, leaning against the front counter on his elbow.

254

"Really? Cool! Look, I have a DBZ keychain on my book bag." I showed him. "I also like Naruto. Have you seen it?" I asked him.

"No, is it good?"

"Yeah!"

Masuda-san suddenly stepped away from the counter and started making a goofy Ginyu Force pose, taken from the anime. People around us chuckled.

"Kaio ken!" he exclaimed, doing another pose, of Goku this time. He sounded 100 times cooler than the English voice actor of Goku did.

"You are so cool!" I cried, scarcely able to contain my excitement. He laughed and said something I couldn't understand, holding his hands in a triangle shape, and doing Tien's solar flare technique. To top it all off, he did the "Kamehameha" move. I wanted to propose to him right then and there.

I left just as the advanced kickboxing class was starting. Pushing open the door, I glanced back over my shoulder. Masuda-san had tied a bandana on his head to hold his hair back. So cool.

May 15

After a full day of studying, I went to Shibuya for Masuda-san's kickboxing class. Afterward, I sat with my back against the wall, chatting with Uematsu-san and this guy he called Megane-kun, meaning "Glasses-boy." Nearby, some other muscular fellow was stretching following the BJJ class that had gone on simultaneously to my kickboxing class.

He has really cool socks, I thought. I admit, I have a sock fetish and love collecting interesting ones. His looked like soccer shoes, but who would wear shoes on BJJ mats?

After a moment, he noticed me staring.

"Are you checking me out?"

I couldn't understand his Japanese so well, so he may have said something totally different.

"Your feet," I said.

"You mean 'socks?'" he corrected my Japanese.

"Ah yes, 'socks.' They're cool!" I said. "I thought they were real shoes, but..." I couldn't think how to say what I wanted to in Japanese.

"Do your feet hurt?" he asked me. I think.

"Sorry, one more time?" I requested.

"You kicked the pad really hard...." he said something about kicking, and feet.

"Uh, no I'm fine!" I replied.

We chatted for a few more minutes before I excused myself to get changed.

At about 10pm I emerged from the dojo, just about to put my headphones on. The fellow came rushing out behind me, and asked me...something.

"Sorry, could you repeat that?" I asked.

"Do you want to get something to eat?" he asked.

"Oh, sorry, I can't. I'm on a diet for my fight," I said.

He paused. "Uh. How about a beer?"

"Oh, I don't drink. Thanks!"

At 22-years old, I was too dense at the time to realize he was trying to pick me up, or at least make friends.

"How about tea?" he finally suggested.

"Oh..." I thought about not drinking caffeine too late at night. Then it hit me that I was being unsociable.

"Okay, let's find a café," I agreed a little hesitantly. He seemed older than me, and I didn't want to get involved with any Japanese men, especially since my exchange year was almost up.

He bought me orange juice in Excelsior Café in front of Shibuya Station.

"I want to be a pro MMA fighter!" he said to me, "But for now I'm just doing jiu jitsu. I'm also working for the Self Defense Force," he said. "Where are you from?"

With my limited Japanese and support of my dictionary, we had an interesting conversation about anime, fighting, and traveling. He assured me that he would go to my fight.

After talking for about an hour, during which he called me pretty, and asked if I had a boyfriend. He seemed pretty cool, but

256

I'd never gone on a date before. It was my first ever- my orange juice date. I was pleased and impressed that he didn't try to get my phone number or email address. It wouldn't work anyway – I knew my communication skills definitely couldn't support a relationship.

We went our separate ways with a handshake.

May 16

The elevator lifted me up to the sixth floor of Gold's Gym in Oomori. As soon as I stepped out, a lady wearing a Smackgirl staff T-shirt thrust my fighter's pass under my nose.

"This is so you can get in and out," she explained, immediately turning back to another task.

The promoter popped up next to her. "By the way, you'll have to make a speech during the entrance ceremony," he said.

"Oh?" I managed to exclaim before he hurried away to take care of other fighters.

I stood dumbfounded at the entrance in front of the ticket tables. As usual, things were hectic on fight day. Guests and coaches squeezed past me on either side. *Why do I have to make a speech? Maybe it's because I'm the main event,* I thought.

Located on the seventh floor of Gold's Gym, the Fighting Room usually held small-scale local events on Sunday. A ring stood in the center of a big open space, mats on either side, heavy bags hanging everywhere. The Gold's Gym boxing club, various karate schools, and the MMA gym Abe Ani's Combat Club rented the space at various times of the day.

Staff had taken down the heavy bags for the event. Metal fold-up chairs lined the hardwood floors around the ring and extended onto the mat space. In the far corners, huge curtains hung from the ceiling beams to create makeshift changing rooms; one red, and one blue.

Someone directed me to the blue side. I dumped my stuff in the corner and started to change into my fight gear.

"A little early, no?" commented another fighter with a smile, unpacking next to me.

"I want to be ready early!" I said, putting on my shorts and rash guard. Emerging, I spotted Luke and nabbed him to help me compose my 'speech.' I repeated it close to 30 times to etch it into my forgetful brain.

Guests gradually filled up the area, clutching their bags and Smackgirl information pamphlets and brochures. Tension rose in the air. I swallowed my nerves. Other female fighters changed into their fight clothes, taped hands, and bounced around to warm up.

"Want me to find someone to tape your hands?" Luke offered.

"No, thanks," I said.

"Almost time for the entrance ceremony!" someone's voice rang out.

Lights dimmed. A staff member stuck his head in our room.

"Okay, ladies!" he called out, reading off a clipboard. The lights went darker, forcing him to bring it closer to his face to see. "Please line up over here in order when I call your names! You'll march into the ring, and then when I give the signal, march out again!"

Music boomed almost painfully, reverberating in our chests, penetrating to our very hearts. Colorful moving spotlights flashed all over the ring, spilling out onto the audience as if it couldn't be contained. We heard our names shouted over the loudspeaker. One by one in single file, we walked into the ring which was about to host our battles, the ring where our futures would be decided. I wore my jiu jitsu gi, as usual. A glance over at my opponent showed a pretty, black-haired Japanese lady about my size, maybe a little shorter and slimmer. She sported Budweiser fight-shorts and a black spandex fight shirt.

Budweiser? Why? How?

The announcer, dressed in a smart black suit, said a bunch of things in Japanese I couldn't catch. The audience clapped.

"And now, Roxanne-senshu will say a few words to the crowd," he said, holding out the mic to me.

258

"That's my cue," I thought, stepping forward to take it. I looked over the crowd. Not very many people came- maybe 250 or 300 at most. What was I supposed to say again? Oh yeah.

"Honorable guests, thank you very much for coming to Smackgirl today. This is Roxanne Modafferi. It's an honor to be here. I will do my best, so please cheer for me."

The spectators applauded politely. With that, I handed mic to the announcer, and returned to my place in line. A few more words were said and we were ushered out of the ring, back to our changing corners.

A strange feeling tickled the back of my mind. After we got back, Kotani-san told me I had said, "Please production me" instead of "please cheer for me." Apparently I mixed up a kou, ou, and n somewhere.

"Don't worry, Roxy. Everyone knew what you meant," Luke encouraged me, as I was lamenting backstage.

"But it was only like four sentences!" I sighed. "Oh well. Not bad for my first Japanese speech in front of a large crowd of people."

"That's right!"

As the main event, it was my honor to fight last. And wait the longest. The night melted together into a hodgepodge of entrance music, cheering, and battle cries. I bounced around in the changing area to keep warm, occasionally emerging to watch a round or two of the matches. One by one, my fellow fighters staggered through the curtain, either elated or crushed.

Then it was my turn. My mind shifted into fight mode as I entered the ring. Luke was saying something to me, reminding me of something. But my brain could no longer absorb it. I wonder if such tense situations make the brain operate on short-term-memory mode only.

After removing my glasses, I couldn't see Akiko Kikukawa so well as she entered the ring. She seemed so far away. Not for long.

"Come here! Touch gloves!"

The ref repeated the rules. I stared hard at my opponent, clenching my teeth, biting down hard on my black mouthpiece.

Almost time. Everything around me vanished except for my opponent. Did I have a gameplan? Who cared?

"Get back to your corner," he said. "Ready? FIGHT!"

The gong sounded. Kikukawa and I burst out of our corners and met in the middle. With no feeling out period, we started exchanging immediately. Living up to her name, Kikukawa threw a lot of kicks and I hurled my own back at her.

My middle kick connected with her side, hard. I tried not to swing blindly. I landed another middle kick, but didn't retract fast enough. She caught my leg and pulled, trying to off-balance me. I managed to stay on my feet. Hopping on one foot, I pummeled her face with three hard hooks. She let my leg go. I hopped to the side, executing a nice left low kick.

The crowd cheered at the hard slap as foot connected with thigh. Kikukawa then followed me, going on the attack. My head snapped back as punches connected. Where was she? Where? On the other end of the punches.

I tried to clinch and do a judo throw, but she braced herself and wouldn't allow it. Once, twice, I failed. She slipped away. Clinching me, she actually took me down. Once the fight hit the mat, I managed to stay safe, improving my position, getting side control a few times. The ref stood us back up after 30 seconds, in accordance to the Smackgirl limited-ground rule.

Most of the actual fight blurred in my memory, although I did note that my head was cooler than my previous two fights. After three five-minute rounds, I was awarded the unanimous decision for dominance. My elation glowed stronger than the spotlights as I posed victorious in the center of the ring while photographers snapped my picture.

My raised hand had signaled the end of the night. Spectators rose from their chairs and shuffled over to the elevator. Once the photographers finished, I followed Luke back to the dressing corner.

"Roxy." Tatsu stuck his head through the curtain just as I was taking my shirt off.

"Oh, sorry." He ducked back out. "Some folks from Samurai Sports Channel want to interview you," he said through the curtain.

Grinning foolishly in ecstasy, I followed Tatsu over behind the seats, out of the way of the folks who were breaking down the ring.

One slender fellow dressed in jeans and a T-shirt stood with bulky camera equipment balanced on his shoulder. Other equipment was strapped to his back. Two other nicely-dressed people shifted from foot to foot. A short, slightly chubby man wearing a multicolored polo shirt laughed and joked loudly.

"Hi, I'm Takablahblab and this is Mr. Yadayada and Mr. Somethingsomething with Samurai TV. We blah blab blah!"

I blinked. My Japanese lexicon was clearly not up for this challenge.

"Three TV employees and one comedian," Tatsu supplied for me in English from where he was standing off-camera.

"Oh. Nice to meet you!" I shook their hands.

Instead of "Nice fight, how do you feel?" they machine-gunned strange questions at me. If I was lucky enough to understand their Japanese correctly.

"Didn't it feel great to kick her leg?" the comedian asked. "Kimochi yokatta desu ka?"

Feel great? I thought, running the phrase through my mental translator again.

I wanted to say, "I don't like inflicting pain, but I was glad I did the technique right, so....is that a yes?"

What came out was, "Uh...well, I, uh so, yes?"

"Uh, huh," the comedian said, and spoke really fast to one of the reporters. They both laughed. I laughed, too. A little. They said something else and looked at me expectantly. "Right?" he finished.

"Uh, right..." I smiled back.

"Hey, I know! Kick me!" the comedian said, turning around and showing me his rear-end.

"Huh!?"

"Yeah! Right here!" he slapped his butt. I glanced at the cameramen, who had the camera trained on both of us. I glanced at Tatsu and Uematsu, who exchanged amused looks.

"I'm not gonna kick you! That goes against my code as a martial artist," I wanted to say. What came out was, "Uh....do I have to?"

"He wants you to kick him," Tatsu offered in English.

"Yes, I can see that," I said in English, my smile fading. "But...I don't want to?" I squeaked back, starting to get annoyed.

"It's for the camera..." Uematsu said, crossing his arms. Everyone must have been aware of my discomfort. "Just do it!"

"Ugh, fine," I said, and did a light kick to the comedian's proffered derriere.

"Aaahhh!" the chubby man screamed, and sprang forward. I had barely touched him.

"Wait a second, that didn't hurt at all!"

One of the cameramen snickered.

"No, no, no, really kick me!" he said. "Come on!" he taunted.

"It's okay to do it harder," another interviewer said.

I did the light one again. The comedian smiled and laughed, but it was a fake smile. He was clearly annoyed with this stubborn foreign girl who wasn't cooperating with his comedic act.

"No, REALLY KICK HIM for real, Roxy!" Tatsu said.

Embarrassment heated my cheeks. The situation has quickly become not funny anymore. Everyone watched. Just to get them to leave me alone, I gave them what they wanted and kicked him almost full power. As I was worrying about whether my form was good or not, he staggered and collapsed, crying, "Oh, oh, American's kicks hurt so much!"

I immediately felt like a bad martial artist. I succumbed to the psychological pressure of "just following orders." So I am human after all. I felt ashamed of myself. To this day I have no idea if that part was shown on TV or not.

I soon found myself enjoying cheap pizza and pasta at a diner called Saizeria together with my coaches and friends who'd come to watch me fight. At about 11pm, I stepped off the train at my home station. It took me ten minutes to walk home.

"My third fight, my third win," I thought as I got the hidden key and unlocked my host family's front door. It opened with a squeak. I tried to not clunk around as I removed my shoes and tiptoed into the kitchen. My caution proved unnecessary, as everyone was still awake in the dining room.

"What happened?!" my host mother demanded, jumping up. Mitsunori-san looked up from his computer screen. The TV news hummed in the background.

"I won! And I'm okay!" I added, remembering that she was like my "mother" after all.

Smiles of relief spread across their faces as they congratulated me.

"Are you hungry?" Sadako-san asked. "No? Then go take a rest! Sleep well!" She turned to her son as I left the kitchen. "Her face isn't bruised up or anything. That's great, I was worried that…." I heard my host mother saying, as I moved away into my room.

My pro fighting career was well underway. As I'd decided earlier, it was time to finally tell my parents exactly what I was doing. My "competition" wasn't exactly a BJJ tournament. And I was undefeated.

I dialed them up that very night. Eleven o'clock Saturday night was 10am Saturday morning on the East Coast.

"Hello?!" boomed my father's voice.

"Dad," I said, "I'm calling to tell you I won my competition!"

"Very good, honey! Did you win by ippon?" (One point, a perfect judo throw)

"No, by decision," I said, and then paused. "But Dad, actually, I want to tell you something. In this fight, well, it wasn't a Brazilian jiu jitsu tournament."

"A what?"

"Bra…Like judo."

"Oh. So…?"

I spoke slowly. "Yeah, it's a "mixed martial arts" competition. That means you can punch and kick."

"Oh." Silence fell on his end.

"Dad, I didn't want to tell you that part until I was sure I knew what I was doing. I didn't want you to worry."

"Okay...well. Now I'll worry about you. But good work." He paused. "You're okay?"

"Yes, I'm fine! I'm great!"

"Okay..."

"I just got home, so I'm going to bed now. Goodnight!"

"Goodnight, honey."

That went great! I thought happily, hanging up. Years later, I brought up this phone conversation and he remembers it quite differently. I guess reality is truly different for everyone.

Next, up: Mom. I figured that she'd understand better, though. After all, she was the one who drove me to tae kwon do and kempo class for four years, then judo practice for another three. Then again, there was motherly worry. I wonder how many hours of my training she watched from the sidelines. My parents got divorced when I was in middle school, so my father never really saw me train or compete firsthand. He had been a soccer dad instead.

I got pretty much the same reaction from her as with my father. I don't think they quite realized what MMA was. If they had seen it rather than heard my words, I'm sure my host family in the other room would have been able to hear their reaction through the phone.

Many years later, I asked my parents what their initial thoughts were.

"I was very much dismayed, actually," my mom had said. "Dismayed and concerned for your safety. It seemed you were ratcheting up your risk a notch by kicking and punching."

My father said he really found out I did MMA after I had won a title in the US. Oops.

Chapter 23 – Days Following My Fight
"The people who appreciate you will find you." ~Rachel
May 17

My eyes popped open at 4:30am, head spinning around and around like a whirling Dervish. I'd thought I'd been knocked out, sleeping well into the next day. Instead, my mind was screaming, "GO GO GO!"

My entire body ached. My back cracked upon sitting up, and joints felt stiff. I took a moment to stretch, bending over each leg. My gaze happened to fall on the tops of my feet. Ugly blue bruises decorated the top. Both ankles swelled fat and red from kicking Kikukawa.

On Monday, I did pretty badly on the Japanese vocabulary test. The most important test, however, had been passed in flying colors. On to the next challenge!

May 18

Fighters are the most critical about their own performance. My training partner Ando developed action pictures for me she took with her camera. Upon seeing them a few days later, my emotions plummeted.

"I can't see good technique in any of these action shots!" I said to myself in dismay. Every little mistake I made seemed painfully apparent.

"No, don't worry! You were awesome!" gushed my friends, who had come to cheer me on. "You're so cool!"

I only shook my head. Back at the dojo, I sat stretching before class next to Uematsu-san. I asked for his honest opinion.

"Good job, but you have a lot to improve, of course," he said, pulling his arm in front of his chest. "But really, when she had your foot, and you punched her face in like that, it looked like a pro wrestling move!"

I halted in mid-motion of taping my foot. "Pro...wrestling?"

Blunt and brutal, as always.

"How were my punches," I asked. "Were they crisp, or like flailing?"

"Kind of like flailing around," the short Japanese man admitted. Upon seeing my depressed expression, he added, "Well, it was better than your last fight!"

The last thing I wanted what to be 'pro-wrestler-esque.'

"Did anyone take a video?" I queried.

"Not that I know of. Don't worry! You won!" he said.

I would have to wait five years to see it. By then, I would be on a different level, and the footage would only serve as a laugh at how bad I'd been.

"It's only your third fight, after all," he repeated, his eyes twinkling, his smile kinder.

"How many fights have you had?" I asked him.

"Hmm...." His eyes searched the ceiling.

"Hmmm, you say?! You don't even know?!" I exclaimed. A fight is such a major deal. How could somebody not remember each one?

"Let's see...15 amateur fights and 15 professional fights," he finally responded.

"That's a lot! That's so many!" I exclaimed, my eyes popping out of my head. I forgot to ask his win-loss record, but maybe that would have been rude.

"How old are you? Uh, I mean, do you mind if I ask you how old you are?"

He laughed. "I'm 25."

Twenty-five. My goal was to be there at 25. I had four years. It turned out that at 25, I had acquired a record of 12 wins and 4 losses, totaling 16 pro fights.

He wandered away to chat with other students. Frowning, I thought good and hard about my training. Genki-san instructed us to snap our punches out and back. I noticed that so many students just whaled away recklessly as hard as they could, but Genki-san didn't correct them. Does that mean that if I were doing it wrong he wouldn't correct me?

266

Uematsu-san and Kotani-san told me my transitioning from striking to takedowns needed work, but we didn't practice them so much in class. How was I supposed to improve if the teachers don't make us time to train them?

I wish they'd train more 'pure MMA' instead of just BJJ or kickboxing, I thought.

May 20

Fat, almost-naked men pushing each other out of a ring drawn in a sandbox – to the uneducated, this is all sumo appeared to be. But no; this ancient, classical sport dates all the way back to the 16th Century and developed into a more professional sport in the early Edo period.

After a delicious yet cheep sushi lunch with my host sister, Takae-san, we trekked to The Sumo Hall, in Ryogoku, Tokyo.

Passing through the widely yawning gates, we entered the main hall. After purchasing tickets and scrumptious yet unhealthy fried sembei (rice crackers) and nuts, we wandered around looking at photographs of famous sumo wrestlers. There are six Grand Sumo tournaments per year, three being in Tokyo.

Sumo fighters are ranked into divisions according to merit, and those in turn have their hierarchy. In the highest Makuuchi division, the highest-ranking sumo wrestler is called the Yokozuna, or Grand Champion. A tournament day is structured so the lower-ranking fighters compete first in the morning, with the top fighters and Yokozuna fighting last.

Takae-san and I entered with the main crowd who wanted to see the high-level action which took place in the late afternoon.

We took our seats on hard bleachers located on the middle level of the funnel-shaped arena. Above us were more hard benches, and below, actual seats and tiny tables were built for the wealthier folks who could pay through the nose for a closer view, a comfortable cushion, and a place to put down their cup of coffee. In the center, we could see the fighting area called the dohyo – a ring, four and a half meters in diameter. It lay on a platform of clay mixed with sand, which stood raised on bales of rice-straw.

High-pitched chattering directed my attention behind me, as dozens of identically dressed middle school students poured in to the seats like chocolate into a mold.

"Is that a class field trip or something?" I asked my host sister.

"Um hmm," my host sister replied, crunching on a sembei.

I turned my attention back to the ring. Apparently, the tournament was having an intermission. I squinted at the house-like object hanging above the ring, suspended from the ceiling.

"What's that?" I asked my host-sister.

"Oh, that's like a replica of the roof of a Shinto Shrine," she answered. "The origins of sumo are wrapped in Shinto custom and ritual. Even the Yokozuna's entrance mimics some rituals performed in a Shinto shrine."

"Oh, I see. It's pretty cool," I answered.

"Yeah. Do you know the rules?" she asked, brushing some brown hair out of her eyes.

"One guy pushes the other guy?" I offer.

"Yes. A fighter wins by pushing the other out of the ring, or forcing his opponent to touch the ground with anything other than the bottoms of his feet."

She proceeded to explain the division system, but I didn't understand and had to do research when I got home. One thing I understood and found incredible was the lack of weight divisions. Sometimes, a fighter faces someone twice his size. We actually got to see such a match that day.

Eventually, something seemed to be starting. People were stirring in their seats and became quiet.

"It's the entrance! Look, here come the top 18 fighters!"

We watched as they walked out in a single file procession- 18 very, very large men, wearing colorful silk-embroidered aprons decorated with various patterns, or designs of dragons and such.

"Do they fight in those?" I asked, incredulously.

"No, they fight in only a mawash," – loincloth – she answered.

268

I sensed a quiet pride in their obvious strength. They slowly lined up around the ring, standing tall with square shoulders, noble warriors waiting to test their strength. Although unaccustomed to staring at a man's naked butt and bulging stomach, that observation became insignificant almost as soon as it registered. The sumo fighters were beautiful.

One qualm about watching a sumo tournament was the time -- everything took so damn long. I chaffed for the bouts to start already, bouncing impatiently in my seat as the announcer said something, the group filed back out, and then the first fighters climbed up the dohyo.

The bout preparation rituals are more than just foot stomping. First, the wrestler faces the audience, claps his hands, and performs the side-to-side leg-stomping exercise to drive the evil spirits from the dohyo. After that, the wrestler steps out of the ring to his corner, takes the offered ladle full of water and rinses his mouth. He then returns to the ring, squats down and faces his opponent. They both clap their hands and spread them wide, to indicate they have no weapons.

I sat on the edge of my seat, waiting for them to spring forward in a mass of muscle and unstoppable force.

Instead, they slowly stood up and returned to their corners.

"What? What are they doing?" I said.

Takae-san smiled, pulling another sembei from the bag. "They're tossing sand into the ring to purify it." We waited as they scattered the sand, and then returned to the center of the ring once again to stare each other down.

"Now?" I asked.

"Maybe."

"What do you mean, 'maybe?'"

They stood up from their squat, and returned to their corners.

"You see? Here, want another peanut?"

"Yes, please. Mmm... yummy. But why?"

"More mental preparation."

"What? How much mental preparation do they need?"

"Sometimes they do it a few times."

"A few times?"

I glanced at my watch. We had been waiting on this pair for above four minutes.

They threw more sand, and stared each other down some more.

"Lower-ranks should start immediately, but higher-ranks can do it a few times. Okay, watch now!"

In a burst of action I almost missed because I was looking at the bag of nuts, the big men lunged at each other. The crowd went wild as hands shoved at chests. One fellow was driven backwards, slipped, caught himself, only to be pushed one more time, sliding partway down the sloped dohyo. If I were a judge sitting ringside, I would have feared for my life. The match lasted about 15 seconds.

The actual matches proved very entertaining when they actually got down to it. As the afternoon wore on, the stands filled up more and more. Finally, in the 'main event,' so to speak, the current Yokozuna lost, and everyone in the lower rows threw their cushions into the ring.

Takae laughed at my horrified expression. Cushions flew this way and that like confetti. I couldn't believe people in such a polite culture would actually throw things at these dignified athletes, especially after all the traditional rituals we were forced to witness.

"They're supposed to throw the seat cushions if the Yokozuna loses," Takae-san explained, as we gathered our things to go. "That's part of the tradition. Some people pay extra money to sit on the cushioned seats just so they could throw them."

All in all, most entertaining.

After returning home, I read on my favorite website, mixedmartialarts.com, that a man named Jeff Osborne was looking for fighters for his next show in November. He promoted an all women's MMA event in the States called HOOKnSHOOT, so I sent him my mixed martial arts resume. Excitement bubbled up as I typed out a message. It appeared other skilled fighters would be on the card, and if I could at least be a preliminary fight, I could become much better known and have more opportunities.

270

I received a response less than a day later:

Roxanne,

I'm extremely impressed. Kirik has told me about you in the past. I've kept your info and resume and will definitely keep in touch.

I believe the show is overbooked right now but you never know what can happen. What months will you be home? I know Uematsu. HOOKnSHOOT is a Shooto sanctioned event. Thanks,

Jeff

What a fast response! I babbled to all my friends, hoping someone canceled so I'd get to fight.

A Few Months Later

"We might have a cancellation," Jeff wrote to me.

"I'll fight anybody!" I wrote to Jeff. "Even Jennifer Howe!" I referred to the most respected woman fighter to date, even though I didn't really know much about her. I kept hearing her name floating around, so I figured I'd mention her

He responded, "That's great. But it's not like I'd have you fight Howe yet."

"Why not? I will!"

A Few More Months Later

"Will you really fight Howe?" Jeff wrote.

"Yes, of course, I responded. "Just let me fight."

"Then you are fighting Howe," he wrote back. "Good luck."

I could have flown home without an airplane.

May 21

Saturday morning, I showed up at jiu jitsu class.

"You're able to do handstands?" Uematsu commented, watching our warm-ups from off to the side. "That's unusual. How's your elbow?"

"Well, it's healed, but it bends differently and hurts sometimes," I complained, adding a comment about it being the doctor's fault.

"Shou ga nai," he said, crossing his arms. It can't be helped. "People get hurt doing MMA. Plus, you were training a lot after you hurt yourself. You didn't let it heal properly, so you did it to yourself!"

I swallowed hard. It was true. I had many accidents where someone touched or bumped it. Every time this happened, it set the healing process back weeks. I knew it, but I just couldn't help myself. Although I pride myself for mental toughness, I just couldn't keep myself away from the dojo.

"I'd go insane. I was starting to go nuts for a while there," I reflected. I had nights I could barely sleep.

His brutal honesty struck hard, yet refreshed me. I loved that directness about Uematsu-san.

That night I hobbled home with a sore back, bumped knee, and aching elbow. It made me want to cry.

"It's only physical pain," I told myself. "My heart is happy. I have people who love me, a promising career, good grades, and health. Well, it could be worse."

I turned down the final side street leading to the house. The dark bushes sticking out from behind people's gates stood silently in the windless night.

"Physical pain is nothing compared to emotional pain," I said to myself. "I just went to jiu jitsu, didn't I? I can walk, can't I? I learned some new cool moves, didn't I? I just had a wonderful time with friends the other night, didn't I?"

"So shut up and take care of yourself!" My inner self chided.

"Everybody goofs up sometimes," the first me said. "It's nothing to be ashamed of."

"That's right. As long as you learn from your mistakes. So we blew it, and now we'll have a funky elbow for maybe the rest of

272

our life. But we made the decision, so no use regretting it. Like Uematsu said, 'shou ga nai.' The harder life is, the stronger we'll become."

May 24

Zuyo and her boyfriend led me down narrow, nondescript side streets outside Kanda station. Tall gray buildings with the occasional colorful ramen sign loomed up all around. We'd left the neon lights a while back.

"You're sure it's this way, right?" Zuyo's boyfriend asked her.

"Yes, yes," she said a little impatiently. "Ah, here!" A toothy smile broke out on her round face. She gestured at a one-story building on the corner, standing sandwiched like a kindergartener next to two high schoolers. Cultivated plants lined the stone walkway, strange in the world of gray concrete and pavement. We walked up wooden steps and slid a wooden door open sideways.

A chorus of lady's voices cried, "Irasshaimase," welcoming us inside the oldest, most famous soba shop in Tokyo. Gray buckwheat noodles, found dirt-cheap in your local super-market, become a traditional delicacy when served with flair by kimono-wearing ladies.

A young waitress, constantly bowing her head, guided us humbly to a low table. We sat cross-legged on embroidered cushions on the floor.

"So what kind of soba do you want?" Zuyo asked us, accepting the proffered menu and flipping through it.

"Um..."

"Soba...with what else? Hmmm..." Zuyo and her boyfriend sat side-by-side across from me, scanning the menu.

"I can't really read the kanji. What else is there?" I asked.

"There's tempura! You know about fried vegetables and fish and stuff like that?" Zuyo said, pointing to a few things written in flowing kanji script. I peered over and understood nothing.

"Yes, I know tempura, but oh! Does that say 600 yen? For once piece? That's so expensive."

"Don't worry; big sister Zuyo will treat you," she said, and spoke quickly to her boyfriend.

Feeling guilty, I said, "Well, maybe I'll just get soba."

"Hmmm, okay...excuse me, waitress?" Zuyo called out to the young woman, who shuffled over, bowing as she came. The couple ordered this and that, and before long, it was brought out by smiling, accommodating servers on big wooden trays. The soba came in a neatly twirled pile of noodles on a little wooden palette. Various other tiny side dishes with vegetables sat arranged nicely on my tray.

Zuyo took the top off a tiny bowl filled with dark liquid, and lifted her chopsticks.

"See, you take the soba and dip it in this tsuyu sauce. Then eat it."

"I know," I said, slurping down my first bite.

"Oh! You can slurp!" she exclaimed. "She can slurp!" she directed at her boyfriend.

"'It's amazing!'"

I chuckled inwardly to myself. It's considered polite to slurp noodles in Japan, but most foreigners are conditioned not to, it being rude in their own cultures. This slurping rule does not apply to spaghetti, however. Think about it: sauce and cheese would go flying all over the place. I often shook my head at my host mother when she slurped spaghetti, and then spluttered and coughed when the grated cheese went down the wrong pipe.

Between bites, I glanced around the restaurant. Hanging plants complimented the wooden, old-fashioned theme. In addition to low tables, the regular-height western tables sat on the other side of the room. Elderly couples, and a few groups of old ladies enjoyed a classy night of soba. They came dressed in nice kimonos and dresses. There I was, sitting in jeans and a T-shirt. Oh well.

The crunchy tempura complimented the soft noodles nicely. However, we soon finished and realized the tiny portions of soba didn't quite satisfy our fighter stomach.

274

"Delicious, expensive, but not very filling, right?" Zuyo confirmed. "Wanna go to Yoshinoya?"

Loosely translated as "beef bowl," we ordered the mounds of white rice in a huge bowl, topped with beef and onions.

"Don't tell me it's your first time!" Zuyo said, digging in and watching with surprise as my eyes bugged out.

"That's...it doesn't look so healthy," I commented. The "beef" sloshed over my rice looked to be 80% fat.

Zuyo and her boyfriend laughed. "It's like Japanese fast food," she said, cracking an egg over top.

I didn't think my eyes could have gotten any wider.

"You...you just put a raw egg over that?" I gasped.

"Oh yeah! What, you don't want one?" she asked. "Oh yeah, Americans don't eat raw eggs, right?"

"Um, no...not really...not unless you're Rocky..."

"Pass an egg," Zuyo's boyfriend said, and she handed one over.

I picked up my wooden disposable chopsticks and poked an unappetizing string of beef.

Would it be rude to try and pick off the fat? I wondered, and tried to do it discreetly. However, it proved impossible to separate the strands. It tasted okay, though. Zuyo and her boyfriend were shoveling it down. With the raw egg on top. Japanese love their beef bowl.

"Sure you don't want a raw egg?" Zuyo asked, offering me one of hers.

"Uh, I'll pass," I answered, my mouth full of rice flavored with beef sauce. Zuyo laughed and said, "I thought so!"

I wasn't Japanese yet.

May 25

I lugged my video camera to school with the intention of filming Candie's koto performance. She'd joined the koto club, and had spent the last few months practicing playing the classical stringed Japanese instrument. Before that, however, I'd have to get through the day, including the three-hour archeology go-ro-chi class.

Something told me to bring the camera to the excavation site.

We'd been poking around in the dirt for about ten minutes when I came across a find.

I flicked on my Fuji Film Camcorder. "Hey, could you film me digging this up?" I asked a classmate digging next to me on the upper level of the site.

Video running, I switched from trowel to stiff brush, clearing away the wet dirt around the edges of a protruding shard of Jomon pottery.

"So... I'm here behind ICU on May 25th," I narrated as I worked. "I'm digging up 4,000 year old Jomon pottery made by the people who used to live here. Wow, it's a big one!"

Gripping a corner, I lifted it from the ground.

"This hasn't seen the light of day for thousands of years. You can tell the time period by examining the method of decoration. You see, the ancient people twisted a rope or twine, and pressed it into the surface of the wet clay. This forms patterns that are baked in," I said. Brushing the wet dirt away revealed a reddish color.

"See?" As I smiled up at the camera, a commotion behind the cameragirl caught my eye. Other students were starting to flock to the lower level of the dig.

"Okay, thanks," I said, getting back my camera. "What's going on?"

We saw our teacher stand up from out of the crowd, gesture animatedly, and then crouch back down. Trowels and brushes fell to the ground as everyone swarmed around to hear his explanation.

I stood on my tiptoes to peer over shoulders, not a big feat considering I was as tall as the average Japanese man. The professor had his back to me, so I struggled to hear.

"So, you can see here, that this was the center. Poles were probably inserted here," I heard him say. I moved to get a better view, also trying to position myself in front of him. All 20 of my classmates had arrived.

"Remember, class, we've seen this pattern of clusters of rocks in other sites."

Someone had found a pit dwelling! Ten times better than mere pottery, it was the site of an actual residence! What a find!

"The fact that you-" Professor Wilson nodded at a student next to him, "found large quantities of broken fragments over there, probably signifies a dumping ground, or a garbage area, basically. They are commonly located on the edge of a village." He had his shirtsleeves rolled up to his elbows. Picking up a brush, he continued from where the student had left off, briskly sweeping away the lose dirt from the center cluster of stones with a skilled hand.

I switched on my camera and filmed his entire explanation – worthy of the discovery channel. The fact that the real deal was right before my eyes made it a thousand times more fascinating. I think we were all sad when it got dark and we had to get back.

After thoroughly enjoying playing with history in the dirt, I rushed to the Culture Fair held behind the school tennis courts.

Not a single cloud marred the clear beautiful night sky. A chilly breeze danced through the crowd of onlookers. Everyone sat on various blankets and plastic sheets, spread like picnic blankets on the grassy yard. I regretted not bringing a jacket.

The show featured a professional dance troupe that executed some traditional Japanese dances, followed by amateurs, my classmates, with their fan dances and plays. Finally, my classmates – including Candie – played the traditional song "Sakura" on the long stringed instrument. Slow yet clear notes twanged across the gathering. Simple and clear – somehow that's what made it so perfect.

I'm so lucky to be in Japan, I thought, not for the first nor last time.

May 29

After my archeology go-ro-chi, I met Rachel and Skye –
who wore the most amazing hot pink leopard dress – and went to
the Second Men's Dorm for a Spring Festival.

Glowing paper lanterns hung strewn through the tree
branches surrounding the area. Table-sized food stands lined the
walkway leading up to the dorm building. A terrible rock band set
up in the hall blasted something they considered music, so we
abandoned the idea of going inside.

"Wanna get some tako yaki?" Rachel asked, referring to the
delicious fried dough balls with octopus chunks.

"Good idea!"

Skye and I got our food first, and saved some places at the
picnic table placed next to the walkway. I chatted with Skye as
Rachel stood in line.

Suddenly, one of my male classmates - "John" - plopped
himself down next to me. I could smell the alcohol on his breath.
He sat very close. For a girl who only studied and trained, it was
quite a new and rather uncomfortable experience.

"Just like anything else, I gotta train myself," I told myself
sternly, trying not to inch away from him. "This is life. I gotta
train...I gotta practice and then I'll feel comfortable talking to men-"

"Hey, are you listening?" John said, scooting a little too
close to me.

"Yes, of course," I fibbed, grinning nervously.

"So ya do anythin' intrestin' lately?" he asked, speech
slightly slurred. I told him about Izakaya, a restaurant, I went to
with my Cross Point teammates last week.

"Ah, we should go sometime!" he exclaimed.

"Sounds good," I said carefully.

"We should go!" he said again.

"Ah," I said. *Is there something else I should say? Gosh, I suck
at social situations,* I realized. *I should force myself to have more
experiences, rather than just go to the gym all the time. Or should I?*

"So what are you doing this weekend?" he prodded.

"Uh, just training." I said, thinking, *Oh, I get it. I'm supposed
to make a suggestion! But...*

"Maybe... we can all go to that place," I said haltingly.

278

He laughed, "Oh, everyone....like you and me, for example?"

"Uh...."

"Not alone!" My inner self screamed. "Men = scary!"

I thought he was kidding, since I knew he had a crush on Skye. I got really confused.

"Do you drink?" John asked, purposely sounding exasperated.

"No."

"No?!"

"Yeah, no."

"Do you dance?"

"Uh, not really."

"WHAT?! How about smoking? Bet ya don't smoke, either."

"No. I mean, yeah, I don't smoke. Maybe I'm not that fun to be around?" I offered a weak laugh, starting to hope that he'd leave me alone.

John giggled and put his hand on my shoulder.

"...Roxy when you're talking to a guy, you don't say 'Duh, I'm not fun to be around!' because then what is the guy supposed to do?" His intense gaze held mine captive.

"I guess you're right." I felt like an idiot.

He continued, "So that means A) you're basically telling me to get lost, B) you're so unsure of yourself that you don't know what to say, or C) you want it so bad. So which is it?"

Want what so bad? I wondered. "Uhh....well, I guess maybe B."

"Roxy, how many boyfriends have you had?"

"Boyfriends?"

"Yeah. Up to now."

"Um, none."

He laughed. "That's a challenge!"

"For you? I mean, for somebody?" I stuttered.

He took his hand off my shoulder and laughed loudly, mirth shaking his entire body.

"Yes, for 'somebody,' Roxy," he said, turning away to talk to Skye and her sexy pink leopard dress.

I heaved a sigh of relief as he turned his back. I felt a little sweaty despite the cool evening. This was not my usual environment.

"See you later, Roxy," the Australian beauty said to me, and left the table with the drunken John.

"Bye!" I said.

Just then, Rachel came over tako yaki in hand, and followed my gaze. "You okay?"

"You don't learn social skills doing jiu jitsu or playing Twisted Metal Black every night, do you?" I asked.

"Nope," she said, popping a ball into her mouth.

I spent more time chatting with Rachel, and then rushed to kickboxing class.

June 1

Morning found me exhausted from the previous night's training class. Staying awake for classes proved the biggest challenge of the day – I nodded off in every single one of them.

"Must…go…to…jiu jitsu," my inner voice said.

"Come on, Roxy, you are like…passing out," my other self said. "Just stay home."

"But I'd promised Zuyo that I'd come and meet a new girl!" I thought. "You know how rare it is that a new woman joins the dojo."

I ended up staying home and watching some anime. In reality, I didn't care so much about meeting a new girl. Zuyo was working hard to promote women's jiu jitsu classes and make beginners feel at home. Someday I'd like to take part in that effort, but at the moment, I felt I needed to focus on myself.

June 9

Early in the night at jiu jitsu, a white belt snapped a surprise armbar on my bad arm. I felt something rip. Immediately, tears welled in my eyes. It wasn't from the embarrassment that it was a white belt, or from the physical pain. It was from fear- the terror- of taking time off again waiting for the damn arm to heal.

I prayed to the Universe as I sat on the side of the mats, icing it. "Heal. Heal. Heal!"

It stiffened up, but the next day, I found that to my surprise I could bend it farther than I could before the white belt had popped it.

Bizarre.

The part of me that spoke for my body wagged a finger at my mind. "You better do a better job of rehabilitating me this time, so it'll be normal in the future!"

That night I couldn't get to sleep until 1:30. Jiu jitsu insomnia again. Not tired enough to sleep. So I studied, as a hard-working college student should. I began to despise my elbow, and blamed it personally, as if it had a mind of its own.

"You're acting all ornery just to spite me. You jerk. It's all your fault. Damn elbow, causing me to pack on the pounds," I'd say, downing more chocolate Pocky crackers, and melon-pan sugar-bread.

Apparently, I wasn't the only one. A week later, I found out that Zuyo had gone to the doctor for tweaking her knee, and Genki-san limped into the dojo one day on crutches.

"Of course you get hurt doing MMA," Uematsu had said. "Live with the pain. Shou ga nai."

Despite all my sho ga nai-ing, when I was injured, I was in a constant state of being ticked-off at the world. If only I could train, just one class of jiu jitsu! I could get a fix then. Like a drug. I was a jiu jitsu junkie.

I watched lots of Dragon Ball Z on my computer, enjoying watching the heroes beat the snot out of the bad guys in a flurry of punches, kicks and ki blasts.

"Don't forget, Rox, it's not how far you fall, but how many times you keep getting up. Just like your heroes. You've gotten hurt a ton. When have you not come back?" my heart coached me.

I knew I had to endure. That in itself was tough mental training necessary to forge an MMA fighter.

Chapter 24 - Saying My Goodbyes
June 10

"Big Sister!" Sadako-san called to me that morning from the kitchen. "Your mother's on the phone!"

Not having slept very well, irritation still hung over my head from the previous day. Heat had replaced cool spring air. Even early in the morning, I could feel the temperature rising. I did an army-style crawl off my stacked-up futons, my legs getting tangled in the sheets.

"Thank you!"

I picked up the receiver in the next room, and lay on my stomach on the tatami mats to take my mother's call.

"Hi Mom," I said.

We chatted for a few minutes about the weather.

"You know," my mother said suddenly, "You shouldn't be fighting men."

What? Why all of a sudden...? Bad move, Mom. Very taboo topic.

"I was talking to one of your previous martial arts instructors," she continued, "and he says that you really shouldn't be fighting men. Even in training."

My mouth literally fell open in shock.

After a brief silence, my mother continued, "They're stronger and it's more dangerous..."

"I can't BELIEVE you just said that to me," I burst out. I thought she of all people understood me and accepted what I was doing. After all, she was the one who drove me to karate and judo practice since I was 13.

Another dangerous moment of silence. I never raised my voice to my parents.

"You might think you're a professional, but he is also professional. He's been doing judo for years and years, and you've been doing it for only few years or so..."

She trailed off.

I didn't get it. I used to train with men in the judo club every day. Blinking a few times, my next sentence came out in a seething, halting monotone. "So. Who exactly. Should I train with. According to my previous instructor?"

"Um, well," she faltered, suddenly sounding less sure of herself. "You should try and find women…"

"There. Are. None."

I wanted to scream, "Don't you realize what you're saying?!"

My inner mind soothed, "No, no, no, Rox. Don't get mad at Mom, she doesn't know any better. She remembers the judo dojo with many other ladies. She doesn't know what it's like nowadays. She just loves you and is trying to help. She loves you! She's your mother! What else is she supposed to do? You're her beloved daughter.

I took a deep breath.

My heart howled, "But she just said you're weak! She said you're weak because you're a woman! She said you got hurt because you're weak, weaker then men! Weak weak weak! And you shouldn't ever train with men because you'll never be as good as a man, because you are weak-!"

"She never said that!" my mind cut in.

I exhaled and took another deep breath.

"Weak weak weak!"

"Oh my god, shut up," I ordered myself.

"Sorry, honey, I didn't mean to make you upset," came my mother's voice, but not particularly apologetic.

"Yeah. I know," I managed. *You can tell him to…!* "Don't worry, I'll be fine. But I don't want to hear that advice anymore, okay?"

"You're going to discredit all of his advice just for that?" said my mom, incredulously.

"Yes," I bit out. Suddenly, all the thoughts swirling around my head solidified like concrete.

At that moment, I suddenly decided. Mom said something but I didn't hear her.

"I will become so skilled at martial arts that I can beat any man, trained or not trained, whatever weight. I will become the best mixed martial arts female fighter in the world. No one will call me weak. They will call me strong. Actually, I don't care what 'they' call me. I will know deep inside myself that I am strong."

Whether these were actually achievable was beside the point. If you don't shoot for the moon, you'll never reach the sky.

Mom said something else about finding women, but I hung up on her and cried for five minutes straight, shaking with fury.

"I will make it happen!" I swore. "It will happen. I will be the best. I'll show everyone, and myself, that I can do anything I set my mind to. Anything."

June 11

Only final exams remained in my last term at ICU. While I enjoyed the days spent in Japan, I knew my time was up. The United States beckoned me home. Part of me cried, but another part looked forward to going home and being American again. It really sank in after I canceled my health insurance, and closed my bank account.

June 17

Countdown: eleven days left. I spent many of them studying kanji and trying not to overeat. Our Japanese teacher decided to give us a classical Japanese poem and have us memorize it as part of the final. Thanks! Just what I needed.

As I sat in my room, I noticed an insect invading my personal space. Wham! No more. After wiping its unfortunate remains off the heel of my palm, I grabbed the 'mushi bye-bye' bug repellent sitting on my table. I aimed the spray can at my arm but missed. Vapor erupted into the room with a hiss. I inhaled a big lungful, gasping and hacking. My nose stung and tingled.

"Does that count as doing drugs?" I wondered. "Am I going to get high on mushi-bye-bye?"

June 23

The Archeology final exam was really hard. Even though I'd studied a lot, details got me scratching my head. Were the pits of seashells found in middle Jomon period or early Yayoi period? In which period did we find the circular twisted twine pattern on the pottery?

Who remembers this stuff anyway? I thought in frustration, jotting down a guess. I was able to redeem myself somewhat by writing an essay talking about Jomon activity in the Eastern Kanto region, from what we learned on the site behind ICU.

I ended up getting a C.

I trained hard at jiu jitsu, thanks to my recovered elbow. My last day at Cross Point ended on a happy note. I started going around saying goodbye to people.

Luke caught me just as I was heading for the door. "Wait, can you go to a celebration party for Kotani? For getting his brown belt? We're going to the Chinese restaurant across the street," my tall Japanese-American friend said.

"Uh, okay," I agreed. I waited impatiently by the door for everyone else to pack up. Our group of roughly twelve members entered the restaurant at about 10pm. Much to my surprise, a few other teammates were waiting for us. A bunch of tables had been pushed together in the back of the room, and appetizers were on the table.

Turns out the get-together wasn't for Kotani. It was a surprise farewell party for me.

Sitting cross-legged on cushions around the low table, we toasted to a fun year of training and friendship. The staff served a variety of Chinese cuisine dishes: dumplings, salty crunchy deep-fried river shrimp, and fried chicken, among other things.

"Now it's after your fight, so you can eat all you want!" Miyata-san said. I laughed, not mentioning that I hated to eat before bedtime. This was a special occasion. I loved the little shrimp- we ate them, head, tail, shell and all!

"Guess what, Roxanne?" Uematsu-san said at one point. "You're on the Smackgirl Volume 4 DVD. I saw it in the store the other day."

"Oh cool!" I exclaimed.

"Yep. Make sure you pick it up before you head back to the US!"

Before long, a few dojo members who hadn't come to class popped in to see me.

"I can't believe you guys made a special trip here, out of your way!" I kept saying, very touched. Miyata kept trying – and failing – to speak English. Zuyo laughed and made sure I got to try all the dishes. Kotani-san and his stiff manner softened a little, as he asked me my plans for the future. Their smiles filled my heart, their words a blessing I could never have imagined.

Suddenly, just as the waiters were placing the desserts on the table, I notice my watch said 11pm.

"Oh my gosh, I have to catch the train!" I nearly jumped up.

"Ah, me too!" Luke said, "But the last one is at twelve something, right? We have a little time."

"Roxanne," Miyata said to me, leaning sideways into me a bit. I could tell that he had drunk a little too much beer. "If we get married, I can live in the States, right? I can get a green card or whatever, right?"

"Haha I suppose," I answered.

"I want to live in the States! Marry me!"

The whole table laughed.

"What's in it for me?" I wanted to quip, but couldn't find the words in Japanese.

The joy of that moment of camaraderie remains forever stamped into my heart.

Human life bursts into existence like a firecracker, yet slips away as quietly and silently as the tide. My grandmother "Nanny" passed away

287

today. She was born in America, making her an American citizen, but went back to her parent's country of Lithuania as a baby. She returned to America at 13 years old to continue her life. She worked hard all her life, doing various jobs, one being waitressing. She married my grandfather, who, in the same way, was born in America but grew up in Lithuania. They had four kids, my mother being the youngest. I didn't know Nanny very well, but she was a sweet woman who always had a cat on her lap, always smiling quietly. May she finally rest in peace after 93 long years. I'm honored to have her name as my middle name, Vincenta. It's too bad I couldn't make her funeral.

June 24

Reflection filled the days before my departure from Japan. As much as I wanted to go home, as much as I missed my old way of life, I found that I didn't yearn for it at all. What awaited me back in the suburbs of Massachusetts? What could be more exciting, more stimulating, than living in Tokyo?

The familiar UMass campus, studying, familiar restaurants, familiar roads, familiar towns. At the same time, everything familiar called to me, welcoming me back, like the loving parents that were indeed waiting for me with open arms. However, there'd be no adventure as great as Japan. No hopping off the train line at a random stop. No more exploring nooks and crannies of some alleyway. No popping into tiny shops, where trinkets and do-dads dangled all around. What I yearned for was to continue my cultural adventure.

I'm living in a dream, I realized. *Living in the college playground provided by my parents, through wise investments and saving since I was born. I didn't pay my own bills, like some. When I get back, will I settle down, or will my spirit cry out for Japan?* I wondered.

Japan, with its tera temples and tori gates in the middle of the metropolis. Busy Shinjuku, with its little traditional ramen, sushi, yaki niku, shops, Izakaya and all. Cell phone shops with booths that spilled out onto the street; store clerk ladies dressed in gaudy plastic dresses screaming about bargains. College kids with

288

part-time jobs, or company employees handing out tissues with fliers.

Cross Point Kichijoji with big sister Zuyo teaching me everything and looking out for me. The comedic fighter Uematsu, his eyes twinkling as he demonstrated a leg lock, yelling at people in the dojo with his tough-guy male slang. Kotani-sensei, the stocky jiu jitsu sensei who although always seemed a little tense, got me all of my fights and supported me. My nakama – my companions – going out together and supporting each other. Genki-san and Tiger-san, the kickboxing teachers. I could never understand a word they said. Ever. From Day One to the day I left. But the togetherness! Taking care of each other. Accepting me, a foreigner, into their group.

"Someday! I'll return someday, and I'll understand everything," I vowed.

A red moon was out tonight. It shone through the clouds, lighting up nothing, but illuminating my mind as I peddled down the quiet street. I pushed my bike up the hill, only to turn around and walk it back down the hill for exercise. An old man did a double take at me as I passed him for a second time.

I thought about all the people I've met. How many thousands of people lived in Tokyo?

"Wait, is that...?" Suddenly, I recognized a dojo-member Yoshi by his bald head. I peddled up next to him. Garbed in a sharp business suit, he had a cell phone to his ear. Upon seeing me, he told the person he'd call him back, and clicked his phone shut.

"Yoshi!" I exclaimed.

"Roxanne!" He gave me a little bow.

"That's right, you live in Koganei," I said, hopping off my bike to walk next to him.

"Yes. I'm on my way home from work," he answered with a smile.

Continuing to chat in Japanese, I mentally patted myself on the back. It took a lot of hard work to get to the point of being able to communicate in a foreign language.

"You know, you've come a long way since you got here. Kotani-san was also saying that your Japanese improved a lot. He said you always try so hard."

"If I improved, it's all thanks to you," I answered humbly. "But I make so many stupid mistakes."

We turned off the main street, and headed towards the residential district.

"Shou ga nai," Yoshi said, "When you first came here, you couldn't really understand anything I said, could you?"

"Hmm. Yeah, I guess not," I answered.

Yoshi nodded, and smiled again. "So really, it's quite amazing. I can't speak English at all. And you've gotten this far."

"Now I'm embarrassed!" But it was true. His compliment made me feel a little better about the "C" I'd just received in my Japanese class.

"I'm far from perfect. But someday I will be perfect!" I exclaimed.

"That's the spirit!" Yoshi answered.

The more I learned, the more I realized that language is just a tool used for communication. As long as your listener can understand what you want them to, you've succeeded.

Mosquitoes hummed around our heads as we continued to chat in the cool summer night. We eventually went our separate ways at an intersection, and I hopped back on my bike to ride for a little while longer.

I thought: *I have to stop struggling to hold onto everything. I always do that. I run into people who I think I'll never meet again. Someone I plan to meet goes away suddenly. Should I cry? But maybe I'll run into him again by accident. Then, would I cry all over again at the next parting? Life was too unpredictable to get worked up over everything. Emotions are the frosting on the cake of life- sweat, enjoyable, but sometimes bad for the health. This is true of many things in life. Don't look back- enjoy the present and plan for future possibilities.*

The shining moon winked at me. I smiled back. I'd always see one everlasting friend again.

I think I've grown.

June 27

My last full day I went souvenir shopping and spent time with my host mother.

"Do your best back in the US!" Sadako-san said. It almost felt like any other day.

I wondered if she would miss me. She hosted an exchange student every year. I wondered how I compared with her other ones. Two years later, after I moved to Japan permanently, we'd have lunch together occasionally. Much to my amusement, she'd tell me long complicated stories about all her other host kids. I realized then that along with some irritating things I unconsciously did, most of the other kids were much worse.

Well, I've done everything I wanted to do, I thought, laying out the futons that night. *Had my last sushi, my last bowl of ramen, my last melon pan, my last excursion with my host mother.*

Somehow it didn't feel like the last time, as if I knew I would be back. I slept well that night.

Chapter 25 - Home Again, but Where is Home?
June 28 and 29

My body dragged more than usual as I lugged my suitcases through the airport. It was as if my spirit were resisting leaving. Boarding the plane seemed like entering a gateway to a different world. When the plane started lifting off the ground, I burst into tears.

During the long flight, I picked up a manga, a Japanese comic called *Basilisk Vol 2*. Much to my amazement, I was able to read the whole thing.

I last tried to read this in April, I thought. *That means by the end of June I've improved so much that I can just sit down and read it, only using my dictionary once in a while!*

Feeling much like an ant, I hauled my stuff into my dad's apartment in Boston's North End around 5:40pm. I let myself in with the spare key. No one was home. The familiar rooms felt strangely welcoming and lonely at the same time. Lingering sunshine still peeked in through the tall windows overlooking the main street.

I sure have missed good Italian food, though, I thought nostalgically.

My dad and Marion walked in just as I was starting to unpack.

"Well, well, look who's here!" he exclaimed in his deep booming voice. I ran into his arms. I didn't want to let go.

"Welcome back, Roxanne," Marion said as we embraced. It felt as though I never left.

He cooked stir-fry with shrimp, broccoli, water chestnuts, carrots, and brown rice. Brown rice? It was drier than soft Japanese rice, and chewy and...brown. Good, but different. I got a hankering for Japanese white rice something fierce.

"Do you have any chopsticks...?" I asked hesitatingly, after a few bites.

"Chopsticks?" my father repeated incredulously. "No, I don't. You can't use a fork?"

"Uh, sure, no problem." It felt so wrong to eat rice with a fork, but I didn't press the issue. If there was something I'd learned in Japan, it was how to conform. Or try to.

"Dad, I'm going for a walk," I announced.

"You are? Where?" he demanded, relaxing on the sofa. He picked up the TV remote, but waited for my answer.

"Um, to the supermarket."

"It's dark."

"I know." I suddenly felt a little unsure of myself. It wasn't too dangerous in Boston. Was it?

"I'll be back soon!" I said brightly, and headed out.

I took a 15-minute walk around the apartment. I considered how I'd get to Joal Amaral's BJJ if I wanted to train. If I calculated the distance correctly, walking there might only take one hour, if I were lucky. I had no car. And no Chuo line.

Reverse culture shocks hit me in rapid succession.

Three screaming ambulances zoomed by during my walk. In Japan, the entire year, I saw exactly two. Shortly after that, a burly-looking black fellow walked by, and I actually feared for my safety. Guilt immediately followed the fear.

"Are you afraid just because he's black?" my mind asked myself.

"No," my heart replied. "I was afraid because he looked menacing and scary!"

"Well, that's okay, then," my mind replied.

"Is it, now?" my heart retorted. "Walk faster."

In most places in Japan, it was perfectly safe to walk around at night outside.

Once inside the huge, familiar grocery store, I noticed the fruit and other produce was so cheap! Plums, cherries, strawberries all year round. Not just seasonal like in Japan. And so much meat! Huge mounds of thick juicy steaks, cutlets, ground beef. Not like I cooked for myself, but I noticed.

On the way home, I saw one, and only one person walking a dog. In Japan, if someone is walking, it seemed to me that nine out of ten people have a dog.

I loved the USA, but I'd left my heart in Japan. Both had become my home. I set my MP3 player to play only Japanese music that night.

June 30

After a pancake breakfast, I started walking to the town of Everett, the home of my jiu jitsu club. Joao Amaral's Brazilian Jiu Jitsu had since become a Brazilian Top-Team affiliate. I got there just in time for the Wednesday afternoon class. The large dojo with its spacious tatami mats was a site for sore eyes.

"Hey, Roxy's back!" they all cried out, seeing my grinning face.

I greeted my teammates one by one. I noticed that many of them sported slick new purple belts. Neither my elbow nor knees bothered me, and I sparred as hard as I could, to my heart's content.

"Nice guard, Roxy," instructor and black belt Mirel commented once, after sparring. In the back of my mind, I felt I hadn't improved as much as I would have liked. In reality, the level of technique at Joao's definitely surpassed that of Cross-Point Kichijoji. Sho ga nai. I'd wanted to come back purple belt level, but not by their standards, I feared. The broken elbow and injured knees halted my progress for a while.

"You're a professional fighter now!" the Brazilian guys congratulated me, hugging me and slapping me on the back. Joao Amaral himself took me aside.

"Hey, how you been?" the muscular black belt said in his strong Brazilian accent. As usual, he sported a shaved head, a contrast to his easy-going expression. "You look different," he added, warmly grasping my hand between two of his.

"Really? How? Besides gaining weight."

"Haha, I dunno. Happier, maybe?" he offered. I saw nothing but grinning faces everywhere I looked.

294

"Many people got purple belts, I see," I said.

"Yeah! Maybe it's your time soon?" he said, winking. "We'll see."

During the hour-long walk home, I really started to miss Japan.

That evening, over a meatloaf and spinach dinner, my father asked me what I did that day.

"I trained."

"You trained. In Everett?"

"Yes," I said. It was the next town over.

"How did you get there?" he asked.

I would have borrowed his car if it weren't for that incident. I had accidentally rear-ended someone on my spring vacation. It was a slight bump from a stopped position, and I'd inspected both bumpers for damage. There was none, and everyone was fine, so I had forgotten to tell him. Apparently, some damage magically appeared, and the insurance company called my father, asking him to pay hundreds of dollars. Therefore, I was forbidden to use the car for a set period of time. He was right, of course. It was stupid to have forgotten.

It wasn't going to keep me from training, though.

"I walked there," I said.

"You walked."

"That's right."

"How long did it take?"

"One hour."

"One hour."

"Yes."

"I see."

I felt the tension in the air. Marion was looking at her plate. We finished our dinner. About 15 minutes later, he told me he wanted to talk to me.

Uh, oh.

Sitting down at the table again, I watched him take out a pen and notepad. He drew a graph.

"Diagrams," I thought. "Fitting for a businessman who majored in mathematics. But he's always been good at explaining things clearly."

He labeled the Y axis as "parental care," and the X axis being "time." He then drew a curve going from the top left down to the bottom on the right.

"When you're a newborn," my father began in a patient voice, "parents provide 100% of the care. When you're like 60 years old, your parents provide 0% care. As you get older, your parents provide less financial and physical care, except for emergencies, etc. Right?"

"Right," I said. Somehow, I guessed the conversation would lead into me sucking up the costs for cell phone bills and gas expenses next year.

He continued. "I pretty much don't provide physical care, since you're 21 and you take care of yourself. But I think that walking to Everett is dangerous, and I object to it. Also, when you were talking before about riding your bike, it is too dangerous for you to be on the road with cars riding on Rutherford Avenue ....." He went on for another few minutes.

It was all I could do not to laugh at the fact he drew me a picture, but actually, it was quite a good one. I couldn't argue with that logic, and I could see his points quite clearly. I had told him several times there were sidewalks on the way to Everett, but he seemed to think I was sharing the road with crazy Bostonian drivers.

"Won't he be mad if he knew that I was planning on walking to Everett again to train," I thought. "Well, if he won't let me use the car, how else am I going to get there?"

It had become a personal challenge, and I would not back down. If I couldn't use the car or a bike, I would walk! Stupidity goes hand-in-hand with youth. I felt rebellious at the time, but I ended up not going the next day. The more I thought about it, the less brilliant the idea of walking seemed.

Later that night as I was unpacking, I pulled out a Japanese MMA magazine. Inside, there was a picture of Tiger-san posing for the camera after winning a fight.

"Hey Dad, look at this! This is my kickboxing sensei! Isn't he cool?"

He took one glance and then spoke animatedly about kickboxing being different from jiu jitsu because you can get kicked in the face and die.

"You also get Parkinson's disease like Muhammad Ali," he said.

"Well, I don't do kickboxing-only fights," I said. "MMA is different..." I'm definitely going to lose this conversation, I realized, wishing I hadn't started it. Unlike boxing with repetitive blows to the head, MMA involves a few hard clean hits, and then it's over. Actually, verbalizing the last part that sounded even worse, so I swallowed the words before they came out. "All over" means the guy was knocked out and the fight gets stopped.

"I've never gotten hurt in kickboxing," I told him flatly. "It's when I was doing jiu jitsu that I broke my elbow..." That didn't help the situation at all.

I decided that from then on, anything martial arts related was taboo.

Of course, if I were in his shoes, I would feel protective of my daughter, too. Actually, I wouldn't want my kids doing MMA at all. Isn't that ironic? I feel bad for my parents, but I'm grateful they support me to follow my dreams.

Disgruntled, I checked my email before going to bed. An e-mail from my mother popped up:

A word of advice. It's going to be a big adjustment for you coming from Japan back to the USA. So be kind to yourself, and try not to overreact to situations. Recognizing that this may be a difficult period for you may help reduce your frustration. Don't forget reverse culture shock!

You got that right, Mom, I thought, nodding to myself and smiling ruefully. *Thanks.*

Eight months later - March 4, 2005

"Man, I'm so thirsty," I said out loud, pushing open my heavy wooden dorm room door. A plastic bin tucked under my left arm held shower supplies. My shoulder-length wet hair was wrapped in a towel, tied into a cone on top of my head.

"Yeah?" mumbled my roommate Caitlin, her eyes glued to her computer screen. Ogres from *Diablo II* grunted as they did whatever it is they did.

"Oof. Oof. Alright then," they said.

Morning sunlight streamed through the windows.

"Yeah. I'm cutting weight," I said, as I hung my wet towel on a metal bar in my closet. "Gotta be 135 pounds. I didn't drink anything today since last night, when I trained in a sauna suit today...you know a plastic suit that makes you sweat?" I stepped all the way into the room and set the basket down on my bed. "I actually sparred in it to lose water weight!"

"That sounds rough," Caitlin said distractedly. Sounds of slashing and metal clanking emanated from her speakers.

"Yeah..." I turned and kicked the door shut with my right foot, and then screamed in pain as something sharp pierced the soft part of my foot.

"Are you okay?" Caitlin asked, finally turning around.

"Ow! Yeah...maybe." Standing on one foot, I inspected the damage. A large wooden splinter from the bottom of the door stuck into where my toe joined my foot. I pulled it out with my finger and slathered some disinfectant on the hole.

"But it hurts like hell."

Two hours later that Friday morning, I slung my gym bag over my shoulder and walked – or rather limped – out the door. Together with my coach Kirik Jenness, we boarded a plane to Utah. I was about to rematch Jennifer Howe for a title belt in a promotion called International Fighting Championship (IFC).

298

After returning home from Japan, I had fallen back into my usual schedule of studying and training. It was my senior year at the University of Massachusetts, and I was set to finish my major in Japanese Language and Literature, along with a minor in Linguistics. In November, I flew to Indiana and defeated the legendary Jennifer Howe in the all-women's promotion HOOKnSHOOT. I wasn't supposed to win. She had been undefeated 10-0, and I heard rumors that people ducked her left and right.

Suddenly, people knew my name. Although the HOOKnSHOOT audience consisted of less than 400 people, pictures spread across the internet like a chain reaction.

That December right after final exams but just before Christmas, I participated in a one-day Smackgirl tournament in Japan. The promotion flew me in, accompanied by my coach Kirik Jenness. I won my first round match against Ana Carolina via decision, but lost the second round match by decision to Megumi Yabushita, who went on to take the victory from Erin Toughill by disqualification due to Toughill's illegal elbow to the spine.

Before long, I received a fight offer to face Howe again in the larger IFC promotion. On March 4 we would be the main event on an otherwise all-male card. The event title: Eve of Destruction.

Due to unimaginable stupidity on my part, or so I believed, I hadn't dieted enough beforehand, thus resulting in me to cutting lots of water weight. One train of thought is that such a thing gives you an advantage the day of the fight when you drink back the weight and step into the cage heavier than your opponent. It was incredibly stressful, however. That explained my sauna suit ordeal the night before. The day of the weigh-ins, I nursed half a bagel all day, taking only a sip or two of water. When the flight attendant asked me if I'd like a beverage, I merely laughed. Inside, I really wanted to cry.

By the time we got to the hotel in the early afternoon, I was starving, thirsty, and exceedingly cranky. The promoter Paul Smith greeted me warmly. He was a shorter man, dressed in a smart business suit, and gave off an air of authority. After shaking my hand, he asked me if I needed anything. I told him I needed to weigh in, and then needed dinner. And my toe hurt, but I didn't say that.

"The weigh-ins are this evening," he explained. "Why don't you go to your room and relax?" he suggested.

We complied, and found a simple twin room waiting for us.

I sprawled out on the bed, trying to ignore my aching stomach. A few minutes later, the phone rang. Kirik picked it up.

"Hello? Roxy, it's the promoter," Kirik said, sitting on the edge of one of the twins.

"What's up?" I asked, groggily.

"He says he wants you to be on a town radio show to promote the show."

"Okay, cool. But what should I say?"

Kirik covered the mouthpiece as he spoke. "He wants you to talk smack."

"Huh? I don't know how to talk smack," I answered wearily, giving him an exasperated look.

"Oh, it's easy," Kirik shrugged. "Just say you're gonna beat her up, and she's nothing, and you'll wipe the floor with her or something," he suggested.

I rubbed my eyes. "No, I don't want to do that. It's disrespectful."

"Not really....everyone does it!"

"I'd rather not."

"She'd rather not," Kirik repeated into the phone. He was quiet for a minute while listening. Then to me, "But you'll do the radio show?"

"Sure. But no smack talk."

"Yes, she'll do it, but no smack talk," he repeated. Then he hung up. I closed my eyes. Glasses of water danced all around.

The phone rang again. Barely five minutes had passed. Kirik put down the magazine he'd been reading.

"Hello? Yes? Roxy, the promoter really wants you to talk smack..."

Something snapped.

300

"I don't WANT to talk smack! You can forget it! Tell him to forget it! No radio show! Leave me alone!" I practically screamed.

"Uh, she says she'd prefer not to," Kirik said calmly into the receiver. "Yep. Okay, yeah, I think the radio show is a no-go. Okay, bye."

Snapping at people was greatly out of character for me, but Kirik didn't seem disturbed in the slightest. I immediately apologized, blaming it on the lack of food and water. My coach only laughed at me.

"I've seen waaaaay worse," he said. "Everyone is miserable when they're cutting weight! How's your foot, by the way?"

I readjusted a bag of ice that I was pressing. "It hurts a lot. I don't get it."

Four months later, I noticed a lump on the top of my toe. I ended up picking at it and pulled out a large shard of wood that, unbeknownst to me, had remained lodged in my toe! It had worked its way through the entire thickness of my toe and out the other side. I had no idea for four months.

Weigh-ins went without issue. I chowed down a power bar, followed by some kind of pasta and salad afterward, provided by the promotion. Finally able to refuel, I sat watching tattooed, tough-looking burly men striding around.

"It's funny how alpha men act around each other," I thought. Fighters stripped off their clothes left and right, and then got in line to step on the scale. I averted my eyes, just in case someone got embarrassed, but nobody seemed to care. Jen and I were the only females in attendance.

I saw Jennifer Howe sitting in the corner with her boyfriend Jeremy Horn, the former UFC fighter. We did no more than say hello – I preferred not to get friendly with my opponent before the fights.

"I think she's drinking Pedialyte," Kirik said. "She must have cut hard."

Then I saw her and Jeremy downing McDonald's hamburgers and fries.

"How?" I wondered.

The cage door clanked shut.

I'm locked in a cage.

Focus, focus. There she is.

The ref called us to the center. He said some rules. I stared into her face, the image of composure and determination. As was mine. Confidence filled me, eagerness burned inside, spreading like a brush fire.

The ref sent us back to our corners.

The bell rang.

"Fight!" the ref called.

I inched into the center of the ring, my gloved fist extended. She met me in the center and touched gloves. A touch of respect.

Then it was on.

She's coming. Last time I couldn't take her standing. This time will be different.

I jabbed, trying to gauge the distance. Jab. Jab.

Punch!

We punched. Her one-two combinations landed, driving me back. No pain, only pressure. Being driven backwards. I covered my face with my arms, trying to slip my head to the side. Trying to avoid the barrage. Failing. Cold, unfeeling plastic slammed onto my forehead, on my cheek, on my chin.

Move! I slipped my head to the side and threw one-twos of my own. Any combinations I knew flew out the window. One-two, one-two.

I must go forward. Forward! Forward! Forward!

Driving her back.

Kick! It landed. Kick! It didn't land. Being driven back. Can't recover.

It's time to take her down. I ducked under her punches and snatched her legs out from under her. She fell on her backside with a thud. I doggedly kept my grip, hugging her legs together to my chest. She scooted backwards until her back was against the cage. I couldn't pin her. She pushed my head down, keeping pressure on it, and worked to stand back up.

I could feel it, and worked to pull her away from the cage, but she threatened me with a headlock and guillotine.

Finally scrambling back to her feet, she clamped on a head-tie and threw uppercut after uppercut. I felt them connect around my eyes. I tried to throw my own, but she had the advantageous inside grip.

Bam! Bam!

I pummeled in, shoving her back against the cage. I got underhooks. I threw a few knees, but they slid harmlessly off at the wrong angle. We jockeyed for position.

I managed to get one inside grip, and pulled her head down. I threw some knees. A few may have connected. I turned into a judo throw – a low uchi-mata – but she wasn't having it. Failing, I stood back up and resumed the knees.

They landed!

I lost my grip. My hands slid off, and before I knew it, her hook-hook combination landed on my face. I backpedaled a few steps, placing myself just outside her range.

Okay, okay, circle, circle, I can do it.

Punch!

A strand of hair fell in my face. It got in my eyes.

Damn girl at the hair salon! I knew she didn't do the French braid tight enough! It was coming out.

Punch! Another lock fell in my eyes. I raised my guard, at the same time trying to tuck the rebellious strand behind my ear. My eyesight was poor enough without hair getting in the way.

"What is she doing?" Jennifer thought (which she admitted to me later). "I hit her and she fixes her hair!"

NOW!

I closed the distance, lunging in with a jab and throwing a straight as hard as I could. It connected! Her counter tagged me back, though. Hair fell in my face again. I couldn't see!

I swung wildly, off balance. She didn't follow me.

My punches connected! Keep doing it!

I led with a sloppy kick, which she easily saw coming and countered, but at that point I didn't care. I swung and swung, closing enough to clinch. I reached for the back of her head to get the head-tie, but she drove me back with punches.

I dropped for a double-leg, but she sprawled, obviously having learned her lesson from our previous fight, where I'd successfully taken her down multiple times. It had been her undoing, and she had prepared for it this time. She stood back up, but I used an outside-leg trip to hook her leg, and took her back down. She fell on her butt again.

I tried to put her on her back, but like before, she scooted backwards until her back was against the metal cage. Same as the last time.

Her arms clamped down around my neck.

Damn! Gotta watch the guillotine!

I pushed and twisted and finally managed to get my head out. I postured up and tried to do ground-and-pound, letting go of my grips in the processes.

Howe stood back up. I grabbed her legs and tried to pull her down. She tripped and almost went down, but popped back up. I hooked my leg around hers and got her back down.

The crowd was screaming.

I finally got her on her back.

"Get up!" Howe's corner was screaming.

I gotta pass! I thought.

She kept me back, so I struck at her face. She hit me back.

"Pass!" my corner was screaming.

I passed. Howe immediately twisted to her knees, the turtle position with me on top. I threw some body shots.

The bell clanged, ending round number one.

I went back to my corner. Kirik shoved a water bottle into my hand. I took sips as he pressed a cold metal compress against a lump forming under my eye.

"How do you feel, champ?" he asked.

"Do you have a hair tie?" I gasped.

"What?"

"A hair tie. I can't see!"

"Um, nope…I have Vaseline, water, lots of stuff, but no hair bands…."

304

"Oh, okay." Damn.

ROUND TWO!

Two tornadoes, thundering into existence and spinning around the canvas. Raw power, destined to live a short life. A life in a cage.

We threw down. Clashed, exchanged punches, ate punches, circled out. Met again, threw down, circled out. My hair kept annoying me, impairing my already poor vision.

I shot for a takedown. She sprawled backwards beautifully, totally foiling my attempt. In getting back to our feet, she managed to land a knee to my face before I could release and make distance. She was landing much more than me, but I didn't care. I flurried. One, two, three connected, driving her backwards. I kept the pressure on, but she fired right back, landing hooks of her own. I switched gears and ducked under for yet another takedown attempt.

I got the single leg!

This time, I wouldn't let her scoot to the cage. I flowed from side control to north-south. She twisted to her knees again, but I slid myself into guard, yanking on her head to keep her down. I hooked my feet over her shoulders, getting a high guard.

Locked down!

I peppered her head with some annoying light punches, and as fast as I could, twisted my body perpendicular and attacked with a straight armbar. I tried to extend her arm.

Howe stood up. I felt myself lifting up off the ground. Rather than get slammed, I let go of the arm and hooked her leg, forcing her back to her knees. She tried to turn away from me and escape her arm. She drove her knee into my throat.

I tried to switch to an omoplata. Howe turned into me and prevented it. I faked threatening a triangle choke. At the same time, I aimed some shots at her face, causing her to turn away. It created the angle I wanted, and I tried for the omoplata again.

I got it! Here we go!

I twisted myself around and transitioned from being on the bottom, to being on top. Howe found herself on her knees, with her arm twisted behind her in a weird angle. I knelt next to her, her arm intertwined with my legs.

She wasn't tapping yet.

This is it!

The crowd screamed.

I sat upright next to her, pushing her arm the wrong way, up towards her head. It created a painful shoulder lock, and she should tap.

What? She's not tapping, I thought, pushing harder. Slowly. Slowly. I didn't want to hurt her. Smears of blood on the canvas nearby caught my eye.

Push harder! Of course she'll tap. She won't let her shoulder break.

She didn't tap.

Frantically looking up at the ref, involuntarily uttering an expletive. "Why is she not tapping?"

If her arm bent too far, it would break. I tried to readjust my position, and used my body weight to lean into the arm to push it harder. Push push push. The crowd went crazy. They thought it was the end. I thought it was the end, too.

She didn't tap.

"Try a wrist lock!" I heard some man holler from the audience, to my right.

Good idea, I thought, laying off the pressure. Instead, I pushed down on her hand, putting pressure on the wrist joint. I know this really hurts. Omoplata and wrist lock...she's gonna tap!

She didn't tap.

I put all my body weight forward, onto her gloved hand, onto her shoulder.

She squirmed around a little, but didn't tap.

How is she not tapping? My brain couldn't comprehend it.

The crowd was screaming. The ref hovered over us, ready to stop the fight in an instant.

The bell sounded. The second round had ended.

I released the hold. I hadn't won. We stood up. She hadn't tapped. As I headed back to my corner, I looked over my shoulder to see if she was holding her limp arm in pain. She wasn't.

306

What?

I couldn't believe my eyes.

Some of the audience was on their feet.

Kirik hustled into the cage, carrying a medical kit, towel slung over his shoulder.

"How ya doing, champ?" he asked, as he again pressed a cold metal block to the swelling developing under my left eye.

"She didn't tap!" I exclaimed breathlessly. The fight still filled my mind. I couldn't think clearly.

"Yeah! I know!" He started giving me fight tips, but it wasn't entering my brain.

"Do you have a hair tie?"

"I...uh yeah! I got it from a ring girl," he said, handing it over.

My hands shook from adrenaline and fatigue. Watching me try and tie back my messy hair, Kirik's face showed a mixture of concern and amusement.

"So this is what it's like to corner a female fighter," he said.

The minute between rounds felt like ten seconds, and before I knew it, the round-bell clanged.

ROUND THREE!

Dust rose. The wind picked up again. Airflows mixed, and the storms formed again, meeting in the center of the cage.

Punches flew, both of us banging away as hard as we could. Forward! Backward! I knew the punches were tagging me, but I barely noticed them.

That escape was ridiculous. It's time to end this! I thought.

Yes!

I finally got a solid head-tie with both arms inside this time. I muscled her off balance and she fell to the side. I fell along with her and pulled her into my guard, immediately locking my legs around her head and shoulders. When she tried to pull out, I pounded on her head until she gave me the arm. With a fully sunk triangle choke, I pulled down on her head with both hands, and squeezed. And squeezed.

She tapped. At last!

The referee waved his arms, and I let her go.

I jumped around, hands raised in elation. Kirik rushed into the cage. I threw my arms around him.

Returning to the center of the cage, the ring announcer called the result of the fight: "At 1 minutes 47 seconds of the third round, winner by triangle choke, and NEW middleweight champion: Roxanne Modafferi!"

He raised my hand. The overhead lights of stardom shown down on me as they wrapped a belt around my waist. Then the promoter wrapped another one over my shoulder.

I tried to ask why I was getting two belts, but he said something I didn't understand about a kickboxing title being part of the deal. Whatever. I had won!

The win solidified my place in women's mixed martial arts. I proved my legitimacy as a fighter. I proved that my previous win over her hadn't been a fluke.

"I just want to fight strong people," I told all the interviewers afterward.

I set my sites on the best women out there. In the years to follow, female fighters increased. Large promotions like Bodog, Strikeforce, and Bellator would give women a chance to fight on pay-per-view and on the '"big stage". I'm delighted to see more and more new fighters popping up, more and more challenges to test myself. To test my heart, test my mind, test my body, and test my spirit. Only in this way can I become stronger. Even if I beat the best out there, there is no end. Another fighter will appear to challenge me.

I couldn't wait!

About the author:

Roxanne Modafferi was born to two loving parents in Wilmington, Delaware, in 1982. She graduated from the University of Massachusetts, Amherst, with a Bachelor's Degree in Japanese Language and Literature, with a minor in Linguistics. Ever since middle school, she's been training in various forms of martial arts, finding her best fit in grappling arts such as judo, Brazilian jiu jitsu, and submission grappling. She turned to mixed martial arts, debuting in her junior year of college, and climbing to the top of the 135 lb weight division. After graduating, she moved to Japan, where she became an English teacher. She worked and trained full time. In September of 2013, after participating in *The Ultimate Fighter Season 18*, she moved from Japan to Las Vegas to pursue MMA full time.

Acknowledgements:

*Eternal love and gratitude to my wonderful
parents and family
Also, my sincere thanks to all my coaches,
teammates, friends, and fans who've supported
me on my unique journey*

CPSIA information can be obtained
at www.ICGtesting.com
Printed in the USA
LVHW020426161218
600641LV00048B/2619/P